Same Time Tomorrow?

Bob Cryer

BARRY CRYER

Same Time Tomorrow?

The Life and Laughs of a Comedy Legend

BLOOMSBURY PUBLISHING

LONDON · OXFORD · NEW YORK · NEW DELHI · SYDNEY

BLOOMSBURY PUBLISHING
Bloomsbury Publishing Plc
50 Bedford Square, London, WC1B 3DP, UK
29 Earlsfort Terrace, Dublin 2, Ireland

BLOOMSBURY, BLOOMSBURY PUBLISHING and the Diana logo are trademarks of
Bloomsbury Publishing Plc

First published in Great Britain 2023

All photographs are courtesy of the Cryer family unless otherwise stated: p.45: Popperfoto via
Getty Images/Getty Images; p.53: Popperfoto via Getty Images/Getty Images; p.57: Whittington/
Popperfoto via Getty Images; p.70: Popperfoto via Getty Images/Getty Images; p.99: Popperfoto
via Getty Images/Getty Images; p.100: Photo by © Hulton-Deutsch Collection/CORBIS/Corbis
via Getty Images; p.113: Shutterstock; p.117: Stan Meagher/Express/Getty Images; p.135: ITV/
Shutterstock; p.136: Terence Spencer/Popperfoto via Getty Images; p.143: Jeremy Grayson/Radio
Times via Getty Images; p.151: ANL/Shutterstock; p.158: Trinity Mirror/Mirrorpix/Alamy Stock
Photo; p.175: ITV/Shutterstock; p.187: ITV/Shutterstock; p.197: TV Times via Getty Images;
p.220: Fremantle; p.233: Don Smith/Radio Times via Getty Images; p.245: Piers
Allardyce/Shutterstock; p.248: Alastair Muir/Shutterstock; p.257: Shutterstock.

A catalogue record for this book is available from the British Library

ISBN: HB: 978-1-5266-6531-7; EBOOK: 978-1-5266-6535-5; EPDF: 978-1-5266-6536-2

2 4 6 8 10 9 7 5 3 1

Typeset by Newgen KnowledgeWorks Pvt. Ltd., Chennai, India
Printed and bound in Great Britain by CPI Group (UK) Ltd, Croydon CR0 4YY

To find out more about our authors and books visit www.bloomsbury.com
and sign up for our newsletters.

To Mum
For Dad

Author's note

I began writing this book six months after Dad died, but I don't think I could have mustered the strength to do so had it not been for the tremendous outpouring of love and goodwill that filled that period. We will go on to discuss my dad's ability to connect with people, but I owe a debt to those of his fans, especially those who knew him through *I'm Sorry I Haven't A Clue*, who got in touch and connected with me and my family when he died. Thank you also for supporting him throughout his career. While he entertained, many of you shared cigarettes at bus stops, chatted with him at stage doors, and asked for photographs. It was an energy that fuelled him, and while he is commended for making the time, he did so because you were kind, considerate and polite. I used much of this positive energy to inform my approach to the book. This is how we keep people alive – by telling stories about them.

To all of Dad's writing partners and collaborators. Every single one of you. You provided the inspiration, companionship and imagination that informed the work detailed in many of these pages. By making Dad laugh, you also ensured the entertainment created by both of you was passed on to thousands across many different media and decades. Writing the book was inspired by the example you set, and I would mention you all by name, but our readers are busy people, and besides, if I listed you in a particular order, it would appear to give a preference that Dad never implied.

My research was mostly drawn from Mum and Dad's archive, newspaper articles and many of the usual film, television and theatre catalogues and databases that are freely available. Still, informal stories from friends, family and colleagues were always the most fruitful additions to any chapter. Thank you to Lucy and Keith Buckroyd for sending me photos and memories of Dad's time at school, as Brenda Bear did some years back to remember his university adventures. Thank you to the team at the City Varieties archive in Leeds and Simon Donald for giving facts to a family myth and even retracing my father's tiny footsteps in Newcastle.

I interviewed several people representing different aspects of Dad's life. My appreciation goes to Graeme and Helen Garden, Michael Palin, Eric Idle, David Sherlock, Denis King, David Mallet, Colin Sell, Tony De Meur, Karen Koren and Steve Ullathorne. Whether you found time to welcome me to your home or made time to travel to meet me, I am in your debt.

To Sandi Toksvig, I am grateful for saying more succinctly in a foreword what I've laid out in several chapters. To Jack Dee, Harry Hill and Lawrence Miller for supporting me either in the memorial evening that preceded this book or the festivals that followed it. These experiences gave me the confidence to take on my father's story. My dad's ability to make people feel welcome and stay loyal to that feeling was reciprocated by you, for which I am truly grateful.

To my friends Josh Levine, Piers Torday and Neil Forsyth, writers who inspired and challenged me at various points in the process, you gave me timely, considered and thought-provoking advice when needed.

To Val Walsh, Karen Hall and Alex Lowe for your archive material and interview audio that gave me some tremendous extra insight into my father's thoughts and opinions.

To people who supported my dad in many ways over many years: Paddy O'Connell, Ben Preston, Harry Mount, the Great Ron Pember (IYKYK), Sarah Chanin, Emma Darrell and Dr Chris Jenner. You know how and why, and the book is richer for it.

To Marc Haynes and Dave Cribb for helping Dad and me create the podcasts that laid the foundation for how I approached the material for this book and, perhaps more importantly, found the tone for my effecting it. We didn't know how timely and important that project was. Thank you.

To Ian Marshall and the team at Bloomsbury for giving Dad's story a home and guiding me through the process of delivering it with patience and balance. I hope I've rewarded your investment in me. To my literary agent Annabel Merullo for championing the story in the first place and making sure I had the resources I needed. Your knowledge, support and belief made all the difference. To my acting agents Tara Lynch and Michele Milburn, thank you for understanding and protecting the time I needed to complete this hiatus. You always understood what my dad means to me, and I hope this process makes me a better performer because of it. One he would be proud of.

And to Humphrey Lyttelton for constantly reminding Dad to 'never lose touch with silly'.

Special Thanks

Dad would be the first to point out that 'this year's drama will be next year's anecdote'. So, to my siblings, Tony, David and Jack, I offer that thought. We didn't know at the turn of 2021 quite how deep an impact that year would have on all our lives, and the strength, resilience and compassion we'd all need to make sure the end was dignified, considered and respectful. It was a beginning for us, and I thank and value your humanity daily. Much love to you all. Thank you for staying strong and lifting each other up during that time; I remained intact and could write this book because of it. Thank you for being so supportive throughout – may we continue to be so.

Finally, to my own family. My wife Suzannah and my daughters, Hope, Martha and Connie. Thank you for understanding quite how much time I needed to give to Grandpa and his story and for encouraging, sustaining, and helping me get over the line, even when it meant sacrificing my time with you. It's reassuring to see his joy of life in all of you, and I hope this book will keep that memory in our generations to come.

Foreword
by Sandi Toksvig

Here's a quick question: what's analysing comedy like? I mention this because if we're going to talk about Barry Cryer then we must sit down and examine comedy of more than six decades. Barry would have been eighty-nine as I write this and the only reason he's not ringing me to tell me about his latest gig is that calls from the hereafter are the devil to place. If over the years you have laughed at comedians like Dave Allen, Stanley Baxter, Jack Benny, George Burns, Tommy Cooper, Ronnie Corbett, Les Dawson, Dick Emery, Kenny Everett, Bob Hope, the Two Ronnies or Morecambe and Wise (to name but a few), then the chances are that Barry's genius was often at the core of it.

Working with Barry was one of the great pleasures of my life. He was a one-off. There are now, and I think this is a mistake, no comedians who would turn up in a natty navy blazer to deliver the words of Little Richard's *Tutti Frutti* to the tune of *Greensleeves*. He would do so with aplomb, as if this were the way both the lyricist and composer would have wanted it. Being kissed soundly by Barry between sips of a bottle of beer backstage was one of the nicest preparations for an evening of comedy I can think of. Travelling with him by train meant I could sit back and relax as I, and everyone else in the carriage, enjoyed a non-stop parade of anecdotes and jokes. It was the surreal ones which will stay with me:

> *Two goldfish in a tank.*
> *One says to the other, 'How do you drive this thing?'*

I first worked with Barry in 1997 when I was one of the few women permitted to join the illustrious panel of the legendary radio show *I'm Sorry I Haven't A Clue*. The fact that the programme had mainly been a boys' club and they were all considerably older than me never showed in any of their attitudes. I was welcomed and encouraged. Knowing what I do now, I suspect the lack of female involvement was everything to do with the management at the BBC and not my lovely boys. They charmed me – even though when I toured with them as temporary host I used to joke that I was there more in my capacity as a nurse than a comedian. Barry would step out onto the stage with his silver mane of hair glistening in the light and the audience would roar. After every show more beer would be consumed, and I don't think there was a single evening where Barry would not say something fond about his wife Terry, whom he had been married to since 1962.

He came from a different era. How I should have loved to have seen him back in the late 1950s when he performed at London's Windmill Theatre doing his comedy act in-between nude tableau shows. His work was often surreal, and no wonder. We could sit and analyse his genius but in answer to the question – what's analysing comedy like? Barry would tell you – it's like dissecting a frog. Nobody laughs and the frog dies.

I miss Barry. I miss him ringing me and announcing himself as my 'celebrity stalker'. If there is an afterlife, then that is one bloody lucky audience.

A man is weaving along the street at two o'clock in the morning, holding a drink and a cigarette.

He is stopped by the police, who say: 'Excuse me, sir, what are you doing?'

'What am I doing? I'm going to a lecture.'

'It's two o'clock in the morning, sir. Exactly what kind of lecture are you going to at this hour?'

'It's a lecture on drinking and smoking.'

'And who is giving a lecture on smoking and drinking at two o'clock in the morning?'

'My wife.'

Introduction

It seems appropriate to start with a joke. You won't be surprised to learn that there will be many more of those during our journey. However, I will try to avoid describing a joke as *belonging* to Dad. He never claimed to have written any of the jokes he told and was usually diligent in naming the source as well. Instead, he saw himself as a custodian of a joke, fixing it, polishing it and giving it a good run out before handing it over to an audience to do with as they saw fit. He was a true devotee of the oral tradition. A folk comedian, if you will (or even if you won't). As Vaughan Williams was to English folk song, Dad was to three men in a pub. Instead of summoning *Beowulf*, *The Iliad* or *Greensleeves*, we got chronicles of married life, errant clergy or parrots. And who's to say we're not the richer for it?

A joke is one of those elements of folklore that seems to arrive in the cultural consciousness fully formed, yet is still stored with generations' worth of evolutionary psychological conditioning. It imbues each teller with as many different possibilities and variations as the joke will allow. You'll soon find out where this limit ends. Somebody somewhere had the original idea, made the construction and birthed the poor beast into existence. Still, the handing over of the original gift is often lost to the ages, and those brave pioneers went to their reward unheralded. The joke, now an impish orphan, reappears in a pub, at a family dinner table or in a WhatsApp group ready to be fostered. I suppose we'd call it a *meme* now, but I'll refrain from doing so here, less our conversation becomes drowned out by the sound of my father spinning in his grave (he was cremated, but this is neither the time nor the place to split hairs). Dad didn't like deconstructing humour, declaring: 'Analysing comedy is like dissecting a frog. Nobody laughs, and the frog dies.'

While he didn't write the jokes he told, he did become synonymous with some of them, and you'll be pleased to know that many of his old friends are joining us for the ride (some of them are too old and frail to stand on their own, but please do join in when we get to the punchline, it makes them feel at home). Each joke comes with a warning: it is only as good as its teller. From an early age, Dad taught me not to copy the way someone else told a joke (which was difficult because he was usually the person who'd told it). 'Find your voice and stick to it,' he advised, but acknowledged that when starting out, being influenced by or parodying people you admire is essential to finding that voice. However, if you develop a good ear alongside that, you'll sooner be able to tell the difference between yours and others and leave that imitation game behind. That's where true authenticity lies. When it came to telling a joke, Dad was one of the best and the main reasons he was so good is that he could hear a joke and almost instantly translate it into his way of telling it. This was the same 'ear' that made him so good at writing material for others too.

A good example of his translation skills is the line about a dead frog quoted above. It's not his, or at least, the original thought isn't his. Dad didn't invent that notion, E. B. White did (yes, *that* E. B. White – the author of *Charlotte's Web* and *Stuart Little*). Writing about humour, White coined his thoughts thus: 'Analysts have had their go at humour, and I have read some of this interpretative literature, but without being greatly instructed. Humour can be dissected, as a frog can, but the thing dies in the process, and the innards are discouraging to any but the purely scientific mind.'

You see? Not exactly a zinger. It's the same sentiment, but Dad's version is more concise, punchier and designed to be spoken. To be fair to White, he was writing to be read in a 1941 collection entitled *A Subtreasury of American Humor* (available at all good bookshops and some terrible ones too).

If any of you are surprised that Dad didn't write the jokes he told, I should point out that *material* is very different from a joke. Strictly speaking, material is the generation of a comic idea fused with an original creator's persona and point of view. In that sense, it can be considered watermarked with someone's character or personality. Think of doctor jokes and Tommy Cooper, or mother-in-law jokes and Les Dawson. This material obviously contains jokes but it is the telling that is primarily driving the laugh. That's why it can sometimes be a grey area. Dad didn't always recognise that dividing line (not many people do) and he'd be the first to admit that he didn't always get it right. I will take this opportunity to grasp the nettle and mention a story that illustrates this, mainly because it has a happy ending, much to the credit of everyone involved.

Dad, famously, had very few run-ins with people in the business and laboured to be on good terms with most people, most of the time. He hated confrontation. But, it is sometimes inevitable in an industry dominated by strong characters. Your job is to be heard and not everyone will like the sound you make. Jimmy Tarbuck once took exception to what he thought was Dad's appropriation of some of his material. Dad maintained that he told a few similar jokes to Jimmy and claimed that jokes should be fair game in the comedy world. Legend has it that Jimmy called Dad out at a charity lunch in the mid-1980s, announcing: 'I'm speaking slowly so Cryer can write this down. Last time I had dinner with him, a week later, he was doing my act.' Dad was as crestfallen as Jimmy was irritated, and the two didn't speak for many years.

Then, in 2021, Dad heard that Jimmy had been unwell and had an overwhelming pang of regret. He called and left a message mentioning hatchets and olive branches and wondered if that might be the end of the story. A couple of days later, Jimmy called back and the two talked for quite a while about the industry, friends they missed and getting old. However, as far as I know, they didn't tell each other any jokes. Perhaps thirty years was too soon, who can say? When Dad died, I sent a message to Liza, Jimmy's daughter, to say how glad I was that the two had made up before Dad left us. She put things into perspective, wisely observing that men of their generation often didn't know how to process rejection. It was regularly left to their wives and families to protect them from each other and themselves. A lot of love greeted Dad's death and this was perhaps the most welcome expression of them all.

Thank you, Jim. Thank you, Liza.

It wasn't the only time this kind of thing happened – look out for an interesting exchange with Spike Milligan later in this book – but as I say, it was rare. It was also something that Dad was occasionally the victim of, as he related in one of his books. It seems Jeffrey Archer was not quite so ambiguous in his definition of jokes and their relationship to material. Dad was once at a charity lunch (what is it about the free-flowing wine that encourages such incidents?) at a hotel near Hyde Park and Archer was one of the guest speakers. Dad sat there, stunned, as Archer seamlessly delivered five minutes of what he thought was word-perfect Barry Cryer. He didn't know where Archer had heard him speak. Dad decided to let it go, instead choosing to go for a walk after lunch. The weather was pleasant enough and it didn't seem like the kind of day to remonstrate with one of Britain's best-selling authors. As Dad wandered down Park Lane, he heard footsteps behind him followed by a familiar voice: 'What did you think?' It was Archer.

'I think I'll settle for lunch,' Dad replied, playfully.

Three weeks later, Dad received an invitation to one of *Punch* magazine's infamous Friday lunches. Alan Coren, the editor at the time and a friend of Dad's, welcomed him, and shortly afterwards introduced him to none other than Jeffrey Archer: 'Jeffrey, have you met Barry Cryer?'

'No,' Archer replied, a twinkle in his eye.

Why is this book called *Same Time Tomorrow?* Unfortunately *Gone With the Wind* and *A Brief History of Time* were taken, so instead I thought using one of Dad's catchphrases would be a better way to honour him. If one of his shows had gone well, a charity event had been successful, or a night out with friends had been fun (and when *weren't* they fun?), Dad would often turn to a theatre audience, a table of pub regulars, a marquee crowd or even a couple at a bus stop and announce, 'same time tomorrow?' I saw it happen countless times, and the effect was always the same. It invariably got a laugh, comforted people and sent them off into the night (or the chemists) reassured that all was right with the world. Baz had promised them that more fun was on its way. He'd usually time it (perfectly) just as the collective out-breath of the room had signalled that the time had come to say goodbye. A smile and a wave followed. And he was gone.

When he left us for the final time on 25 January 2022, our family assembled at Northwick Park Hospital in north-west London to say our farewells. We all wanted him to say 'Same time tomorrow?' one last time but of course, it never came. Hopefully, by writing this book, filled with his adventures and tales of his wit and wisdom, I can go some way to delivering the tomorrow he was always promising.

I also wanted this book to celebrate him in a way that he was never comfortable embracing in his lifetime. Like a lot of his generation, Dad didn't take compliments well. He felt so undeserving of them. 'I feel like a complete fraud,' he once claimed. 'I never intended to be a writer. I wanted to perform but I just didn't have enough sparkle.'

I think it's time to bang the drum and blow the trumpet. My approach won't be too inflated, I'll spare him that much, but I will shine a light on aspects of his character and his career that you may not have been aware of or that he may not have spoken about publicly. The most common element of the praise that Dad received (and one that he actually acknowledged) was that he always held his hand out to younger comedians and writers. He didn't believe in a golden age of comedy, but rather that every age had some good comics and a lot of average ones (you can read about Arthur Askey's less polite version of that observation later). When Dad saw Ronnie Barker, he also saw Peter Sellers. When he saw Rik Mayall, Spike Milligan came to mind. To him Jimmy Carr was a latter-day Bob Monkhouse or Joe Lycett a more nuanced Kenneth Williams. To him, comedy was a continuum and a much longer conversation that no one person could ever own, so there was no point in planting your flag or marking your territory. The sands would shift soon enough, so just enjoy the ride.

If the British comedy world can sometimes seem like an endless game of snakes and ladders, then Dad managed to maintain a consistent presence in the middle of the board. He had a knack for cropping up in every era, simultaneously adapting to his surroundings, while resolutely remaining completely the same. He was a Leonard Zelig of light entertainment, re-emerging through each decade, never being the star but usually finding himself close to the room where it happened. As Ronnie Corbett once said to him: 'I don't know what rung of the ladder you're on, Barry, but you've got it right. Stay there.'

As we'll see, much of his success was down to his affability but it's worth acknowledging at this early stage that he also benefited from the kindness of people like Vivian Van Damm, David Nixon, Ray Galton, Alan Simpson, Frank Muir, Denis Norden, Danny La Rue and David Frost on the way up. He became quick to mirror that behaviour when the opportunity arose and his reputation for 'paying it forward' to the younger generation no doubt resulted from the benevolence he himself received.

Before we begin in earnest (it was nice of him to join us), I have a confession. I felt it best to get it out of the way at the top of the show, so we can march forward into his life with full transparency. Any trepidation on my part concerns a secret that my family and I have known about and held on to for a very long time. It is so explosive that I was concerned its impact might affect how this book is received. A biography of a much-loved comedian comes with a certain amount of goodwill and support, but how much goodwill and support could withstand the full force of revelation?

Close the book. Not because I want you to stop reading, far from it, but you'll need this moment to gird you for the journey ahead. The revelation is staring you in the face. Hiding in plain sight, if you will. Off you go. I'll be here when you get back.

Music plays (probably Herb Alpert).

Welcome back. Shocking, isn't it? There, as plain as the nose on his face is the problem. It's ON the nose on his face.

His glasses.

The confession? His glasses are not real. Well, they're real in the sense that they are glasses, but as essential to his visual health? Not for one second. The truth is he didn't need them. There. Deep breath. It feels so good to share that with you all. Thank you for your patience.

If there has been one factor that has underscored my thinking while writing this book, it has been the development of Dad's persona. It's an important aspect of any performer's arsenal, and in Dad's case, his premature hair whitening needed something to offset it. The glasses were a key part of that persona for as long as we can remember. Once his hair had turned white (around the age of twelve, we believe), Dad was seemingly fixed for all eternity with a certain look. He became the uncontested holder of second place in a perpetual Barry Took lookalike contest. First place, of course, always belonged to late-period Ronnie Barker. Barry Took came third.

Incidentally, one of Dad's most unfortunate mistaken identities was during the sombre period that followed the death of much-loved film critic Barry Norman in 2017. The *Mail Online* (that bastion of forensic journalism) ran the requisite story when he died, detailing his career and completed the tribute with a picture of Dad. Beaming with pride, he said: 'I hope they return the favour when I go,' before adding, 'Barry was a mate, he'd have loved this.' I'm sorry to report that when Dad did eventually leave us, the picture they used was that of Barry Cryer.

That wasn't the first time Dad had been mistaken for Barry Norman, so perhaps there was more to that attribution error than meets the eye. The other occurred sometime in the mid-eighties when a man greeted Dad very warmly in the street. The man seemed to know a lot about my father, but Dad struggled to work out where they'd met. The opportunity to establish formalities never presented itself and before long, farewells were being expressed.

Despite the confusion, Dad thanked the man for his kind words and, just as they were about to go their separate ways, the man said, 'Goodbye Mr Took, please do give my best to Diana.'

Barry Took mistakes were run of the mill, so this was something Dad was able to take in his stride. In fact, so many people confused the two of them that they used to share jokes about it. Took once met Princess Anne at a Royal gala and she said to him, 'Can we have an event with both of you buggers present? That way I can at last sort out who is who.' Back in the street, Dad nodded to the man as he left and imagined the phone call to 'Tookie' later. One thing puzzled Dad. Who was Diana, though? A friend in common? An acquaintance of Took's? Diana? Of course, he meant Diana *Norman*. Barry Norman's wife. This was a first. He'd never been mistaken for two people at the same time.

To return to his persona. I've realised, upon closer inspection, that it was something Dad crafted quite carefully. Some things you can't control but how you present yourself is not one of them. Show business is famously a fickle beast and maintaining an image can be crucial to your survival. Dad possessed the kind of fame that meant he was often stopped in the street, even if the person didn't know why (unlike the scenario above). I'd often wonder whether some comedy fans who approached Dad knew what their favourite Barry Cryer sketch was, or what line they liked best from the many different comedians he had written for. In some ways, that was the point. He was sometimes guilty of being famous by association and the warmth that he elicited was as much to do with his naturally open demeanour, as it was his connection to a time in people's lives that they felt sentimental towards. He was often a friendly face from their childhood. Being a non-threatening presence in people's lives suited Dad down to the ground. He enjoyed being a benign presence in a cut-throat business.

He told the story of how, once, when his face had become a regular sight on TV, someone came up to him in the street and asked: 'Can I have your autograph, Bal?'

'Of course,' he said.

'Leave it out,' said the man. 'You didn't think I was serious?'

Dad then got into a taxi and recounted the story to the driver.

'Oh dear,' the driver chuckled. 'Imagine that happening to someone well known!'

Dad loved telling stories like this and used the following line quite a bit: 'I'm arrogant in my humility.' He saw it as cathartic. Like most comedians, he loved telling stories about when he 'died' on stage, revelling in the twilight world between anonymity and the spotlight. As we'll see, for a while he was literally in the wings, battling a skin condition that forced him to pause his performing and concentrate on writing instead.

As Eric Idle remembers: 'It was really nice that he became famous because everybody loved him. More and more he became liked on radio and then became a star. That was not necessarily a given when we were all together writing. I think he was quite comfortable being in the back room.' As with Ronnie Corbett, with this last comment, Eric seems to be hinting at a dynamic most people in the public eye reflect on at some time or another. Be careful what you wish for.

In my other job, as an actor, I recently worked with a well-known name on a movie. As we sat in the make-up chair, readying ourselves for the day's shooting, we discussed a Sunday night drama series we'd seen on TV. It was a classic terrestrial water-cooler event, with lots of publicity, and was generally well received. The star of that drama was an actor we both knew, who seemed to be cropping up in a lot of these types of shows. 'Wouldn't you like one of those quite soon?' I asked.

'One a year, maybe,' he said. 'But not back-to-back. All the time. Who needs that kind of pressure?'

While Dad was busily working away mastering one-liners and generally revelling in silliness, I'd sometimes wonder if he was subconsciously offering guidance by dropping hints about who he was and what he stood for. At first glance, it wasn't immediately obvious and that was frustrating. It's common for children to lament that their parents didn't give them a route map through life. The impression that they are just making it up as they go along isn't very helpful when you're seventeen and looking for your own way through the crowd. Then you have children of your own, and the penny drops. They were just making it up. However, the clues were there if you looked hard enough but some of them have only just occurred to me as I write this book.

I've been trying to think of the right word for two weeks. And then it hit me. It's fortnight.

Barry Cryer

One thing I have taken from Dad's example, particularly as I chose to work in the same industry, is that it's often not how you act but how you react. He had plenty of obstacles to overcome and situations to respond to and we'll look at a fair few as we go along. Invariably he'd answer them with dignity, grace and patience. For that, I am proud of his legacy and if there is any lesson to pass on to aspiring comedians and comedy writers out there (and even those no longer aspiring) it's that. This too shall pass and so long as you don't let it spoil your lunch, you'll be okay. Take in the room, relax the shoulders, put on a smile and on the count of three: 'Same time tomorrow?'

I've greatly enjoyed piecing together these clues and look forward to sharing material from the Cryer family archives in the coming pages, alongside interviews with friends and colleagues, and my reflections on living and working with a comedy legend. He'd have hated me saying that last bit.

You've been a wonderful audience. If you've enjoyed this half as much as I have, then I've enjoyed this twice as much as you.

Barry Cryer

There's a man driving down a country lane and he runs over a cockerel. He goes to the farmhouse and knocks on the door. The farmer's wife answers, and the man says: 'I appear to have run over your cockerel. Is there anything I can do to replace him?'

She says: 'Well, please yourself, the hens are round the back.'

I

There was a constant hum in Dad's life that he never really silenced. His father, John Carl Cryer, died from meningococcal meningitis just a week before Christmas Day in 1940 (when Dad was only five years old). It left him with a lifelong hole in his consciousness that this book will inevitably return to at various points. I'll try not to be too mawkish on the subject (despite using phrases like 'a lifelong hole in his consciousness'), because Dad was rarely mawkish about anything. However, I think it is significant and the single most important dynamic in Dad's life. It shaped the way he interacted with the world and explains his desire to fill his house with noise, connect with people, entertain audiences and write in a partnership.

The loss was keenly felt, but Dad spent most of his life cautious about finding out too much about it. Maybe he feared he wouldn't like what he found or would discover that he wasn't emotionally ready to relive the trauma. His mother, Jenny, had told him that Carl (like many of that generation, he went by his middle name) was ill in hospital, presumably to save her son from shock, when he'd already been dead for a couple of days. But the school playground rumour mill had already ground into action. Dad had the misfortune of having the news rather unceremoniously broken to him by another boy in his class. 'Your dad's dead,' the boy is said to have exclaimed. Apparently, Dad hit him. This is a detail that we, as a family, have always found hard to believe as it seems to be so at odds with the soft reflexive character we knew and loved. However, none of us can imagine how stark a jibe that must have felt at his tender age, let alone how we would have reacted. I'm just grateful I never had to experience a similar situation, instead enjoying the love and company of a father who lived to be nearly eighty-seven years old.

Despite his reticence to find out details of his father's life, Dad did grow up with some vague memories but always maintained that if he was played a recording of his own father's voice, he probably wouldn't be able to recognise it. There are pictures at home of the family walking along the seafront and Dad claims to have remembered those trips. There's also a very distinguished photograph of Carl that now sits in Mum's living room (see page 25). However, it's the only individual photo that we own of him. One memory that Dad remembered keenly was when Carl bought him a balsawood aeroplane kit. They built it together in the front room and when the time came to fly it, the plane looped sideways before landing in the fire. Of all the memories, this is the one he clung to and with its heart-breaking combination of intimacy and tragedy, provides the perfect analogy for their brief relationship.

However, sometimes the subject found him. One evening, before Dad was about to give an after-dinner speech to the Waddington games company in Leeds, he was tapped on the elbow in the bar by a man who asked if he was 'Carl Cryer's son'. Dad was understandably taken aback but welcomed the man's approach. What followed was something of a balm to Dad. This man told Dad that Carl was the life and soul of his local social circle in suburban Leeds. He was an accountant in the Council Education Department, a Mason at the Aurora Lodge and a golfer at I know not where (I also don't know if that was the order of importance for Carl). Dad maintained that this (in any combination) was about as far away from a description of himself as you could get.

Young Barry at the seaside (tongue firmly in cheek from an early age).

The Masonic connection is largely responsible for the family's solvency after Carl's death. School dinners, uniforms and kits all had to be paid for (during a time of rationing) and as Jenny wasn't earning a wage, the family savings would have been depleted quickly. My dad remembers men (obviously from the Lodge) visiting the house to check in with the family and Mum says that Jenny was still being sent flowers by the Masons on the anniversary of her husband's death well into her seventies.

The fact that a friend of Carl's confirmed to my dad that he was sociable, affable and well-liked proves that while Dad's professional apple might have fallen far from his father's tree, his character may not. It's a thought that I know he took some comfort from and there's a lot to suggest that Carl and Barry would have made a happy father-and-son odd couple.

On his *Desert Island Discs* appearance in 1987, Dad said his luxury would be a collection of recordings of the hubbub made by his family. One of his favourite sounds was a busy house, full of children, laughter and noise. It's effectively what he and my mum, Terry, created and nurtured for nearly fifty-nine of their sixty years together. There were four of us children, my brothers Tony (born in 1963) and Dave (1965), my sister Jack (1968) and me (1973). Although we were loud enough, the addition of the veritable menagerie of dogs, cats, mice, rabbits and assorted reptiles turned our house in north-west London from a mere cacophony into an actual din. But when you consider the stark contrast between our upbringing and Dad's own, it's not hard to see why he craved such a regular shot of organised chaos. Once his brother John had left for the Merchant Navy soon after their father's death, it was just Dad and his mum.

Leeds Grammar School Prefects photo, 1952 (cross country shortcut map possibly in blazer pocket).

Dad didn't have anyone to teach him how to be a father, meaning he was never comfortable in his own role as a patriarch. He was always happier trying to be your friend, which in many ways is a very modern form of parenting. He'd sometimes ask his adult children, 'Did I do okay back then?' That was always quite a difficult question to answer, not because we necessarily thought he'd done badly, but because it was such an odd question to ask in the first place. It's hard to narrow such a complicated dynamic as fatherhood down to a pithy soundbite and Dad would've preferred it if we gave the kind of glib riposte he would have offered himself. He rarely got that. However, if I was feeling indulgent, I might reply, 'A bit cold in the mornings, with disappointing views, but overall, a pleasant stay. Would recommend.'

He later claimed that this lack of a father figure meant he was looking for someone else's approval and it was rarely my grandmother's, not because she was unsupportive (quite the opposite), but because she didn't seem to seek his attention for herself. Jenny was a woman of few words and her approval instead came across as silently unconditional.

So where else was this approval lurking? With life at home largely underscored by the ticking of a clock rather than the din of the busy family he craved, like many only children, he escaped into his own imagination, which he shared with a small circle of friends. In the immediate post-war period, the agent of inspiration was 'modern' technology, which meant the wireless. His main obsession with his new companion became the shows he heard making an audience laugh like *Hancock's Half Hour* or *The Goon Show*. It's unlikely at this age that he'd imagine going on to work with not only all four members of the Goons, but also having Tony Hancock's brother as his agent. Radio would obviously go on to play such a big role in his career, and such was his love of the medium that he confessed to dragging the family wooden Marconi wireless cabinet upstairs, so he could listen to music and comedy in his bedroom.

My grandmother never remarried and she hardly ever spoke about Carl after his death, which resulted in Dad talking relatively little about his Yorkshire family in general. At various points in life, not to mention in this book, I have described Jenny as a classic Yorkshire housewife. Aside from being patronising (even the 1939 Register chooses its words more carefully, describing her contribution to national life as 'unpaid domestic duties'), it's also factually incorrect.

Jean (or 'Jenny') Harrison Yarker, as she was originally known, was born on 19 September 1896 in Carlisle, which was then in the historic county of Cumberland, now Cumbria. There must have been some pull towards Yorkshire, though, as I discovered that while her mother Agnes's family largely came from Cumberland, John Yarker was an engine fitter from Ingleton, on the western edge of the Yorkshire Dales. Maybe this was the vital piece of Nana's DNA that lured her back to God's Own County. One other discovery that only came to light during research for this book is that Jenny worked as a designer in a Carlisle carpet factory for a while when she was a teenager. Dad loved drawing, especially cartoons, and I had always wondered where his love of drawing came from.

Even though my grandmother had a reputation for being reserved, I'm cautious not to label her as too 'dour' (mainly because it's another Yorkshire cliché), as I think it mispresents her. Occasionally she would give away a side to her personality that Dad referred to as a 'twinkle'. My sister remembers it on one occasion when, as an elderly woman, Nana came round for dinner, but she didn't realise that she'd got her dress on the wrong way round. My sister Jack, who was a teenager at the time, had to take her into our playroom to adjust it for her. The two of them giggled away before the dress was righted and order restored. The 'twinkle' had been unleashed.

My dad saw it when she took him to see Max Miller, on one of Max's rare forays north, at the Leeds Empire Palace Theatre (a venue that would be about to play a big role in Dad's life). There used to be a reluctance for southern comedians to venture north (and vice versa). When asked about a tour in Scotland, Max once told his agent that he was 'a comedian, not a missionary'. The rarity of this performance must have added to an extra feeling of exclusivity between mother and son. The twinkle in my grandmother's eye that Max Miller unleashed seems to have been the thing in people that Dad chased for most of the rest of his life, both personally and professionally. She'd let the mask slip and Dad had found it compelling. Jenny was clearly charmed by Miller and Dad said the change in her during those couple of hours went a long way to convincing him that a career on the stage might not be met with complete resistance.

Even I saw a glimmer of it when I was a young boy. Late in life, when she came to live with us in London, I would sometimes go next door to her flat in the morning, and sit at her breakfast table. She would give me cereal and a plate of plum jam toast before setting me down to watch some children's television. I remember one afternoon she left me in front of *Blue Peter* while she went shopping. The craft activity that week involved the obligatory loo roll tube or two, which I had to fashion into a palm tree or submarine (I can't remember which, it was a long time ago). I didn't realise that you had to wait for the roll to finish before using the cardboard roll. I gleefully set about unwinding paper sheets from several rolls, meaning Nana returned from the shops to a living room that resembled the away end at a seventies European Cup game. She darkened her brow, tutted and sighed, which I expected. I thought I was in real trouble at first but it didn't last long. Realising that my intentions were at best 'creative', she smiled and winked at me. There was that 'twinkle' again.

Carl Cryer was born in Keighley, Yorkshire to Charles and Harriet (née Bloomfield) and was eventually the eldest of seven children. He came from a very long line of Airedale Cryer men, with most of those generations being born in and around Kildwick in North Yorkshire. Leeds only really came into the picture for this branch of the Cryers when Charles, an Education Department officer, moved the family to Potternewton when Carl was eight. For Dad to swap Leeds for London, aged twenty-one, and for his brother John to join the Merchant Navy would have been a big deal for any Yorkshire Cryer. No one in several generations on Dad's father's side of the family had even left the county, let alone the country.

Carl was twenty-four when the First World War broke out and he became a Gunner (the artillery equivalent of a Private) in the volunteer Royal Field Artillery, before rising through the rank of Bombardier to become a Battery Quartermaster Sergeant and then a Second Lieutenant. His service at the Somme (where it's most likely he would have been responsible for loading and transporting medium-range guns) earned him the 1914–1915 Star and a Victory medal at the end of the war. He eventually received his officer's commission in September 1918, just two months before the war ended. This status was part of a trend during the First World War known as 'Temporary Gentlemen'. Once the war was over, you were expected to revert to your preceding status. In short, you needed to 'know your place'. Thankfully my grandfather doesn't seem to have suffered from the demotion. If anything, his social standing seems to have risen, rather than declined. His experience of being an officer, albeit only for a few months, inspired him to focus on more achievable forms of mobility. Like being a golfing Masonic accountant, for instance.

It was a distinction of Dad's position in his professional life that he never seemed to belong to any class or tribe. He was never intrinsically part of the older variety school, nor perceived as one of the younger satirists. He was neither specifically a writer or a performer, nor a storyteller or a joker. He was all these things and also prided himself on being all things to all men. He was also seemingly neither liberal nor conservative, neither alternative nor mainstream. Rather than being criticised for being non-committal, Dad was celebrated for being an everyman. It turns out that Carl's similarly mercurial status as a gentleman and a player may have had an unconscious influence on Dad's persona after all.

Another fact about Carl only came to light when Dad was in his seventies. My brother David started researching our family tree and discovered something quite remarkable. Jenny was not Carl's first wife; more surprisingly, Dad had never been told this. In 1921, when Carl was thirty-one years old, he married twenty-six-year-old Florence Facer, originally from Durham but living in Hunslet, South Leeds. The ultimate tragedy at the heart of this hidden detail of family history is that Florence died only a year later. How she died has so far eluded me. I've searched every record I can find but can still find no trace of a cause of death. The only mention I've found relating to her death is the description 'dearly loved' in a copy of the *Yorkshire Post*. A resurgence of deadly influenza in Leeds during 1921 and 1922 seems to be the most plausible explanation, but regardless, the loss, just one year on from marriage, must have been unbearable.

Thankfully, Carl married Jenny two years later, when he was thirty-three and she was twenty-eight. I don't know if he told my grandmother of his previous union (or even if that was 'the form'), nor if the two women knew each other. Intriguingly, one thing they shared (apart from their ages) is that their fathers were engine fitters. A peculiar sidenote perhaps, but startling that they had the same profession. It may also be a tantalising glimpse into my unknown grandfather's interests. Perhaps he had a penchant for visiting bus factories and courting the workers' daughters. The subject for another book.

We are now a little better acquainted with Carl Cryer, which is one statement my father would have loved to have made himself. It's a source of regret for me that it has taken writing a book about my own father to gain more knowledge of Carl. It is information that I would have loved to have discussed with Dad, but as I alluded to before, his own curiosity was limited. Directing it towards his own lineage, even more so.

Carl and Jenny found themselves in the mid-1920s living with his parents in Potternewton, with a baby on the way. Following the arrival of a boy in 1925, John Charles Cryer, the family moved to Mount Pleasant Avenue, with Carl now ready to put the trauma of Florence's death behind him.

I never did ask my grandmother about my father as a baby. Not generally the kind of question a six-year-old asks their nana. Maybe it is in some families, but emphatically not ours. Lady H (her middle name was Harrison) would not have indulged me. Knowing Dad, however, when he did arrive, his timing was probably spot on. He obviously made an impression at a young age as media fame greeted him early. The days have gone when local newspapers had 'Children's Corners', or similarly named columns. These were hosted by so-called 'uncles' or 'aunties' and featured topics and competitions, especially for youngsters. Often the column was based on the activities of their membership club, which the kids were encouraged to join in order to receive benefits such as cards and badges. Ostensibly, they continued a Victorian tradition of didactic moral instruction dispensed to younger readers by an older, benevolent relative. The *Leeds Mercury* at this time had an 'Auntie Joan' and on Wednesday 31 May 1939, she reported:

Now I want to thank Pauline, Barry, John and Michael for the silver shilling they sent to swell our fund and the S.P. [silver paper] that went to swell old Sammy Sack. And talking of one Barry reminds me of another little friend, Barry Cryer, whom I met in the Store last Friday week. I do hope to see him NEXT Friday at the Party, Mother.

Dad was clearly working the room from a young age. The following week's Children's Corner didn't relate whether Jenny did take Dad to the party, but I like the idea of a four-year-old Barry Cryer being referred to as a 'little friend'. I often think of him that way myself. Childlike, rather than childish, and giddy with enthusiasm for the next bout of silliness. By all accounts, he was an impish, ebullient and popular boy who used to tear around with a gang of local kids (usually John Andrews, Dean Tasker, Dave Milligan and Alan Brown) pretending to be cowboys, speedway riders or Buck Rogers.

Bracken Edge football ground was just around the back of his house and Dad used to go and watch Yorkshire Amateurs play with his gang. His favourite player was slick-haired outside right Eddie Joyce, who'd casually walk over to the crowd and take a drag on a supporter's Woodbine during the match. He'd then hand it back when he'd received the ball, jink past three players and rocket a shot into the top corner. Dad's gang also provided him with an early glimpse of what it might take to be a comedy sketch writer when they put on regular 'Bracken Edge Concert Parties'. One programme (sadly undated) details their 'Easter Follies', which was a mixture of songs and sketches, all topped off with a quiz and community singing. Dad appeared in bits entitled 'The Snake Charmer', 'Barry Cryer & Tommy', 'Human Marionette' and 'Mysterio'. I regret not asking him many things before he died, but 'What were the gags in your snake charming sketch?', 'Talk me through your process in the "Human Marionette" sketch' and 'Who the hell was "Mysterio?"' might now be quite high up the list.

If Dad wasn't at Bracken Edge, he was cycling to Otley or Ilkley, playing on a piece of waste ground near his house called the Dell, or running around Pithills, where he'd watch the motorbikes scrambling. He said he used to attempt to copy their trademark foot drags on his own bike on the way home. To go to see professionally organised speedway meets, he and his mates would have to get on a bus to Bradford. League speedway finished in Leeds just before the war and didn't return while Dad was living there, so Bradford was the nearest stadium to go and watch. They always made sure they packed their homemade cardboard masks, complete with small eyeholes, as the riders used to spray gravel at the front row as they went round. Dad used to get quite excited when he recalled the thrill of being shrapnelled at high speed. He never took drugs, so I'm guessing this was the next best thing.

Mum describes him as being 'pretty wild' during those formative years, filling the silence and the hole in his life with stories and noise (I did promise I wouldn't be too mawkish). The most incredible part of his childhood testimony is that he told me his mother would often cook him five meals a day (he even went home for lunch when he was at school) no matter where he was and expected him to be home for each one. The Dad I knew didn't have a huge appetite and sometimes even used to pick at things without finishing a meal. Perhaps he had to account for the fact that there's a finite amount of food a person is allotted in their lifetime and Dad's mother oversubscribed him early in his life.

I went to visit his house in Leeds once. The street, Mount Pleasant, as the name suggests, is up on a hill, and the most noticeable aspect of the Cryer house's position is that there is a gap between the houses opposite revealing Leeds city centre in all its glory beyond. I imagined him in his top-floor room, with that huge radio crammed next to his bed, listening to Bill Haley, Chuck Berry, Tony Hancock and Tommy Handley while looking out of the window at the grammar school, the university and the City Varieties, dreaming of what was to come.

From the age of five to eight, Dad went to an infant school on Easterly Road. It was a little private school in a house run by sisters – two actual sisters, not nuns (unlike my mother, who went to a convent) and he recalls being very happy there. From eight to eleven he went to a school on Talbot Road, also run by two people, but this time, a married couple called the Gannons in what was their semi-detached house. Dad remembered the man's 'florid complexion and slightly slurred speech' which he thought hinted at some of the 'extra-curricular activities' he might have been practising after the school bell rang. Dad hated the school, describing Mrs Gannon's discipline as like something from *The Seventh Veil* (the James Mason melodrama about a young concert pianist who is rapped on the knuckles by her teacher when she makes a mistake). There were only about twenty-five pupils at the school, meaning singular attention (often of the wrong kind) was almost impossible to escape. Dad says they 'huddled together for warmth'.

However, once Dad had moved to Leeds Grammar School on a scholarship, in 1947, and despite being run over on his first day ('I landed on my feet,' he said, partly in recollection and partly in metaphor), he began to flourish. He clearly enjoyed two things: studying English (he was often top of both language and literature percentiles) and entertaining people, so naturally he began favouring activities where he could write and perform. It helped that the headmaster had a name that seemed to resonate with Dad's aspirations: Terry Thomas. His namesake the comic actor Terry-Thomas (at that point a theatre star) added the hyphen to his name in 1947, although it's unlikely it was to avoid being mistaken for the head of a Yorkshire grammar school.

Dad was remembered by his classmate Keith Buckroyd as a 'great creator of mirth for his classmates' and was 'usually amusing and often hilarious'. Even the *Yorkshire Post* recognised his promise, carrying a story about his scene-stealing turn as Falstaff in *Henry IV Part I* in front of the Princess Royal (the older 'Princess Mary' version, not current incumbent Princess Anne, with whom Dad would go on to have many later meetings). 'I had a bolster up my shirt and it fell out,' he said, 'which got a laugh.' The Princess awarded the Acting Cup jointly to Dad and his friend John Gledhill, who was playing Prince Hal. My dad managed to elicit another laugh when they received the award, by keeping the cup for himself and giving the plinth to John.

John Carl Cryer, the Masonic golfing accountant father my Dad never knew.

Dad described himself at Leeds Grammar as being something of a 'Bilko' (the wheeler-dealing army sergeant from *The Phil Silvers Show* on US TV) although I suppose the British term 'spiv' might be more apt. In his words, he was 'ducking, diving and working out all the angles'. One such scam came after a cross-country run. Not a huge lover of school sports, Dad decided to take a shortcut. When he finished the race, a master was waiting around the corner, and he asked Dad what the advert was for at the halfway point. Rather than become embarrassed by his inability to answer, he doubled down and decided to sell shortcuts to the cross-country in sealed envelopes, for tuppence. He was soon undercut by a boy who bought one of Dad's maps, copied it and sold it for a penny. It was an early lesson for him in market economics and left him wondering whether his gullibility might prevent a future career as a conman. However, just as I've discovered time and time again in reinvestigating my father's life, it did not deter him. He got back up, dusted himself down and started all over again. To paraphrase a popular song of the time.

His last school report, which we still keep at home, stated: '[Barry] must learn that glibness is no substitute for knowledge.' I cannot think of a more appropriate send-off from school for Dad. It's one that he meticulously ignored as a criticism and instead took it up as a challenge. I'm glad he did as not only did glibness lay a foundation for Dad's worldview, but it also put a roof over my head.

A woman sees this beautiful blue and gold parrot in the shop and she says to the man: 'He's gorgeous! How much?'

He replies: 'Twenty pounds.'

'Really? He's beautiful.'

'Yeah, I know. I'm sorry, but he's got form. He's got a history. He was in a brothel, you see. And to put it delicately, he's got quite a colourful vocabulary.'

'Oh, I don't mind. I'll take him now if that's okay?'

So, she takes the parrot back to the flat, takes the cover off, and the parrot looks around and says: 'New place. Very nice.'

And the woman's two daughters walk in and the parrot says: 'New place, new girls. Very nice.'

And her husband walks in and the parrot says: 'Hello, Keith.'

2

In 1954, following a year of working in various menial jobs around Harehills and Roundhay, Barry won an exhibition scholarship to Leeds University to study English, based on his excellent A-level English results. I think he must have felt he could do no wrong. His intention at this stage in his life was to become a journalist. This meant being a 'serious' writer and he even managed to engineer an interview with the famous *Yorkshire Post* for work during the holidays. He was told to come back after his degree, as he was too old to work as a post-room delivery boy and too young to have enough experience of life to write about. His enthusiasm for the *Yorkshire Post* remained undimmed however, as evidenced by this absurd letter he wrote to the newspaper in 1955:

ROPE THOSE PASSENGERS IN! B. C. CRYER (Leeds 8): When will the Leeds public realise that the only practical system of transport in this city is the one I pioneered in St Albans in 1908? Our 37 trams were each powered by treadmill, pedalled by the passengers in turn. Between spells of duty, they could buy refreshments from a buffet towed behind – on proving, of course, that their journey was really necessary. This was stated on a chit signed by the conductor.

The then transport manager of St Albans, E. Letts Milkum-Drye (L.C.T. and tow bar), said at a meeting of the Transport Department and Sewage Development Committee: 'Gas trams are the thing of the future. Recruitment must be whipped up!' Shortly afterwards all conductors were given whips.

The present economic structure wherein the passenger pays the conductor is totally illogical. Passengers must be enticed on to the tram by the conductor with bribes (e.g., reduced rates, say 6d. for 200 yards).

Other devices for persuading the public to board the tram include:

A lasso manipulated by the conductor.

A large net suspended on each side of the vehicle.

A large suction vent to inhale the public, ejecting them at specified termini.

As Sir Frinstone Lurchill has so truly said: 'We shall fight them on the platforms, we shall fight them on the staircase: I offer you nothing but blood, sweat and increased fares.'

A happy New Year to you all and pass right down the car, please!

Much of Dad's spare time was now taken up with comedy writing, and this letter provides an insight into the way his style was evolving. It was no surprise that the transition to university with its new sights, sounds and people had sharpened the hunger to develop further. Dad soon found himself tempted inside the Empire Theatre again (as a writer/performer this time) as part of the Leeds University Rag Revue. It was basically a sketch show with songs that raised money for local charities. When he wasn't writing sketches for that, he was singing outside the town hall with the university jazz band. His father Carl had been an accountant and an officer in the same building. It's funny to think of Carl climbing those same front steps to go to work in the 1920s and 1930s.

The Rag Revue started in the 1920s at the old Hippodrome Theatre before switching to the Empire in 1949. It was often a means for agents and producers to spot young, fresh writing and performing talent. An introduction to the programme for the 1955 revue rather prophetically states: 'Patrons may remember that in the 1949 show, Frankie Vaughan made his first public appearance and was spotted by talent scouts. Perhaps it is someone else's turn this year.'

From the moment he started raising laughs in school theatre productions and performing in his own sketches at local concert parties, Dad had decided that he was comfortable entertaining people. Could he continue this at university? Could he be the new Frankie Vaughan? The fact that the original Frankie Vaughan would soon go on to play an important part in his career makes the reference in the programme even more intriguing. Despite being only a first year, Dad wrote and appeared in four sketches (also co-authoring a radio parody with David Robinson called 'Have A Crack'), and even had a solo spot in the middle of the second half. This was described variously by reviewers as 'blatant patter' and 'restless … with some pungent points to make', which I assume was a good thing in 1955.

The *Bradford Observer* was far more encouraging: 'Where else could one find a more natural comedian than in 20-year-old Barry Cryer … His versatile performances, ranging from superb compèring to off-the-cuff patter, are a delight.' It seems that Dad was off and running.

Alongside his revue appearances, Dad's singing on the town hall steps was also beginning to get noticed, according to an unidentified newspaper clipping from the family scrapbook: 'A first-year English student at Leeds University, who wants to be a journalist, is rapidly earning his place as entertainer-in-chief of the Leeds Students' Charity Rag. He is 20-year-old Barry Cryer, of Leeds, who gained a quick success in "Rag Revue 1955" and carries a large part of the show. Yesterday he was carrying another show: the first of the lunchtime entertainments from Leeds Town Hall steps. This time he was the jazz singer of the Black Prince Stompers' Band from the University Rhythm Club.'

In order to gain some experience as a journalist (which, let's not forget, was the reason why he was at university in the first place),

Dad began writing for the student union newspaper. His love of comedy was never far from his thoughts, even then, and he used to leave notes at various Leeds theatre stage doors requesting interviews with the comedy star who happened to be performing there at the time. These even included people he would go on to work with, like Terry-Thomas and Max Wall. While they were happy to give interviews, evidently Frankie Howerd (another Yorkshireman) was keen to go a little further. Frankie was a big radio star back then, but as Dad told our podcast 'Now, Where Were We?' in 2021, he got a swift reply:

Frank says, 'Come and see me between the shows twice nightly on a Friday night.' So, I go to the stage door. Frankie greets me personally with a dog, which has nothing to do with the story. We go to his dressing room, I think it's Frankie Howerd! Fantastic. And I'm talking to him and he suddenly turned it round, going 'what are you doing with your life?' And I said, 'oh, I'm supposed to be interviewing you.' He then produces this bottle of embrocation. He said, 'Oh dear. I get these terrible pains. And it's not the same when I rub it in.' So, I thought, game on. I sidestepped and managed to get out of the dressing room. And he took the rejection. And that was the end of that.

Years later, I'm in the Captain's Cabin pub off Lower Regent Street, where we all went after radio shows at the Paris Studios. I'm with the young Rory McGrath and Jimmy Mulville, who'd become Frankie Howerd writers. So, I'm telling them the embrocation story. And Griff Rhys Jones walked in. And he's listening. And he said, 'I don't believe it.' I said, 'It's true.' He said, 'No, I don't mean that. I mean he did it with *me*.' And we all started laughing and saying, is it the same bottle of embrocation? Is this a prop? Turns out he did the same thing with Bob Monkhouse.

With journalism, singing and performing all part of his varied university cultural diet, it seems like things could not have been going any better for Dad at this point. He was popular, busy and revelling in all the silliness and fun that university had to offer. What could possibly go wrong?

Dad's memory of Leeds University geography at that time was that the undergraduate social and academic worlds were divided down the middle by the imaginatively titled University Road. He said that he rarely crossed it. The one part of undergraduate life that he'd forgotten to factor in was his actual degree. As a result (or lack of one) he failed his first-year exams and felt the disappointment keenly. He could have stayed to re-sit the exams, but his experiences of performing seem to have convinced him that his energies lay elsewhere. He decided to leave.

He often described himself as his mother's 'blue-eyed boy' and it's not hard to see why. Losing a husband to meningitis and an elder son to the Merchant Navy, both within a couple of years of each other, had left Jenny with little option but to coddle young Barry. Up until this moment, he'd barely put a foot wrong. I can't speak for his teenage nights at the Astoria Hall on Roundhay Road so we'll perhaps leave that to the discretion of others. But, given his mother's indulgence and the amount of money invested by his father's Masonic brethren, Dad was beginning to feel his first real sense of failure. He thought he was a disappointment. As far as I know, Nana never made her feelings overt (not an unusual trait, admittedly) but an uneasy period followed, during which Dad admitted later to feeling depressed.

Not for the first time in his life, though, Dad decided to double down on an uncertain situation. The signs were there at Leeds Grammar School and Leeds University that he had an aptitude for performance, quick wit and mischief, but could this form a career? One thing was certain, anything that happened from this moment on would be down to his own graft. He often claimed that he was a very lucky man and that his own career was a series of happy accidents. I always disputed this with him, saying that you needed to be talented to make use of the opportunities given to you. It can't just be luck, especially when you're involved in making people laugh, as the results of your endeavours are immediately obvious. He'd usually change the subject or tell a joke to fend off the potential compliment. Over time, he'd even make a joke about his first-year failure at university: 'I'm a BA (Eng. Lit) failed. I failed on account of the outbreak of the Second World War. Which was sixteen years before but upset me very deeply.'

Following his academic hiccup, he decided to get a 'proper job'. However, he'd only really had the experience of working in shops during his year out, including a disastrous spell in Lewis's department store in town, where he had a knack for disappearing to smoke a cigarette every time a customer appeared. Now, a job as a clerk in the Leeds Highways Department emerged. It was a position that held particular significance for him and the family, because as we've already seen, not just his father but his grandfather before him had been local government officers. It probably felt as if fate had finally caught up with him. Dad had decided that it was all over regarding a university career, and now show business too was to be put very far from his mind. Surely a respectable life as a local official now lay ahead and family tradition would be preserved. A second act was waiting close at hand and Leeds Town Hall's loss was to be comedy's gain.

The 1955 University Rag Revue had been co-produced by a man called Cyril Livingstone. A true Renaissance man, Cyril would go on to become something of a Leeds cultural legend. After the war, and as part of a family that owned a clothing salon on North Street, Cyril's haute couture inspirations helped define a nascent Leeds fashion industry. Yet it was as the founder of the Jewish theatre company, the Proscenium Players, that he was to have the most profound influence on Dad. Cyril wrote and directed pieces for the company and performed in them at the (now defunct) Leeds Theatre Royal and Opera House.

If there was one assumption the odd casual historian of my father's life nearly always leapt to, it's that he was Jewish. I know that this was an accolade Dad would like to have been awarded and, while Chapeltown, Potternewton and Harehills were all Jewish areas of Leeds and he had many Jewish friends, we can't claim any heritage. He'd often say: 'We were never lucky enough.' After Dad died, and like many other comedians, David Baddiel tweeted his thoughts on his passing: 'He told me a story – this was only about three months ago – about how he was described as Jewish in his local paper. He told them he wasn't. They said: "Do you want us to print an apology?" That really made me laugh.'

The *Jewish Chronicle* also described him as Britain's 'most Jewish non-Jewish' star. In the early sixties, Dad was on a show called *Stars and Garters*, which featured the unique Jewish comedian Ray Martine (who was so unique that he left the business to return to his first love, antiques). Also on the show was his friend, music-hall icon and fellow Jewish comic Bud Flanagan, famous for the songs 'Underneath the Arches' and 'Strolling'. Dad asked Bud if he ever got tired of singing them. 'No,' he said, 'and I'll tell you why. I run a shop and I know what things customers want to buy. So I stock that. I might feel like singing a bit of opera or Noel Coward some nights, but as long as they want "Arches" and "Strolling" that's what they'll get.' A lesson Dad never forgot – especially when telling moths jokes. Bud then said to Dad, 'Are you Jewish, son?' 'No,' said Dad. 'Don't worry,' said Bud, 'it doesn't show.'

Dad often worked Jewish humour into his own act. This part always began with him obtaining permission from any audience to culturally appropriate by saying 'My local Rabbi calls me an honorary Jew' and he would then talk about his friend and classmate, Louis Lipman. Louis was once answered by the maths teacher, 'Lipman, what's seven per cent of £58?' He came back with 'Exactly, sir, what's seven per cent?' I was always uneasy about that one because it perpetuated a stereotype, but I suppose if you've told an audience that you're not Jewish but you'd like to be and you're a big fan of Jewish humour, there's an assumption that the targets are going to be benevolent.

There was a kindness to Dad's treatment of the subject that hinted at stereotype, but always from the mouth of the joke's

Rag Revue 1956: Roger Dickinson, Tony Harrison and Dad as the Three Wise Monkeys.

protagonist. It's certainly not punching down, but maybe if you're not Jewish, it could be perceived as the comic equivalent of shadow boxing. Dad preferred to call it a celebration of Jewish humour. He'd continue: 'Jewish scientists are reported to have discovered five new ways of disappointing their mothers.' I was quite proud of one that I brought him later in his life. I'd heard a cultural historian talking about Yiddish on Radio London and referenced this classic of the genre: 'Four Jewish women are in a restaurant and at the end of the meal, the waiter approaches and says: "Was *anything* okay?" '

Cyril Livingstone offered Dad a lifeline by accepting some sketches he'd written (for the Rag Revue) to be performed there. Furthermore, because he recognised Dad's talent in that revue, he suggested to the rag committee that they use him for their 1956 show. To Dad's great surprise (and no doubt delight) they offered him the opportunity to also produce the following year's show. It wasn't uncommon for outside professionals to do this and, by virtue of his Proscenium Players work, Dad was now technically qualified in that regard. It also made practical sense for the committee, as Dad still knew half the company, had their support and based on the previous year's show, clearly had the talent. He didn't hesitate in accepting. In many ways, it was the best of both worlds. He got to carry on in an environment he loved, without the minor inconvenience of having to do a degree. Every now and again, though, he'd admit that as a result of not completing his studies, he sometimes felt intellectually inferior to some of his peers who'd attained their degrees. It was a sensitivity that he wore lightly, admittedly, but it nonetheless perpetuated a narrative (usually his own) that he was now an artisan rather than an artist.

Among the 1956 Rag Revue cast (in addition to the previous year's Brenda Bear, Eric Mountain and John Wood) were two new talents. Future Nobel Prize literature laureate and Nigerian civil war hero Wole Soyinka was a keen singer back then and made two solo spot appearances in the show. His biography in the programme (most likely written by Dad) reads: 'Genial Nigerian "Wally" is studying English Literature and indulges in the singing of merry folk songs in his spare time. If you'd like to join in the jolly choruses, we wish you luck – we've never mastered them.'

Wole was joined on stage by future Whitbread Poetry Prize winner and National Theatre playwright Tony Harrison. He appeared in an impressive six sketches, including one with Dad and Roger Dickinson called 'Three Little Bears'.

Tony's introduction in the programme ran thus: 'He was seen at rehearsals, and as he turns up every night at the Theatre, we assume he must be something to do with the Show. You'll recognise him tonight – he's the one who appears on the stage reading from a script. Rumoured to be a misogynist but insists he's a Conservative.'

There was a fashion for greased hair and smart costume on stage in those days, which Tony fiercely resisted. Dad said that they used to have to hold him down, force him into a dinner jacket and slick his hair back with Brylcreem. It seems that despite his part in such roughhousing, Tony was rather charmed by Dad. In an edition of BBC Radio 4's *Front Row* Harrison was asked about Dad by Mark

Lawson. Tony even remembered a poem Dad had contributed to the university poetry magazine, *Poetry and Audience* (which Tony edited):

> Lot became naturally rather peeved
> When his sex life came to a halt
> Well wouldn't you, when you had to make do
> With occasional pinches of salt?

These three careers obviously took very different paths (in poetry terms at least) from 1956, but at the Rag Revue, there was only one name that seemed destined to shine as a comedian. Although given his self-styled and self-effacing introduction in the programme, you wouldn't know it:

> He is probably the youngest producer of the Revue so
> far – local, born and bred in Leeds. He previously confined
> his activities to performing (last year's Revue) and what he
> laughingly calls singing, with local jazz bands. He is known
> as the 'Headingley Hobo', because of his valiant but largely
> unsuccessful attempt to grow a beard. Hobbies include
> breathing, sleeping and bison hunting ('I've been waiting
> twenty years for it to catch on in Leeds'). He was engaged in
> tattooing the Bayeux tapestry on the top of his head for want
> of something better to do, but now he has little time to spare as
> producing this show is a full-time job.

Dad did manage to get noticed at the Empire that summer and the reviews ranged from the sublime: 'Leeds-born Barry Cryer, an actor of character, a singer with appeal, who also produced the show. His timing and placing of the many contrasted items proved well considered and perfectly prepared.' Via the surprising: 'Producer Barry Cryer is an aggressive comic whose solo spot (incorporating a priceless crack about liver salts) is a highlight.' And finally, to the ridiculous: 'Barry Cryer in a Davy Crockett burlesque.'

While I let that image settle in your head, let's recall the 1955 programme prediction that 'a new Frankie Vaughan was just waiting to be discovered'. Perhaps in Dad, this had just come true, only a year late. Had his gamble paid off? And more importantly, what was the liver salts gag? Surely not this old favourite?

'My grandfather took liver salts every day of his life. With the result that when he died, we had to beat his liver to death with a stick.'

Like the start of any career, Dad needed the right person at the right time to give him the confidence to make the leap from a casual interest to a profession. No different from anybody else, of course, but how did this young man, who'd lost his father so early, and later struggled with eczema, decide that an extroverted career in the public eye was the answer to battling those early perils? The description of him as an 'aggressive comic' might contain the answer. He clearly had a hunger, but the truth of most 'big breaks' is that they're usually years in the making, so did he have the patience?

When he was producing the revue at the Empire, Dad became friends with the stage manager, a Glaswegian with the impossibly rock'n'roll name of Johnny Gunn. He gave Dad a job as a stagehand and taught him all the ropes (literally, as the letter below confirms). In a somewhat ironic twist, Dad became known backstage at the Empire as 'the toff', simply because he had been to university. The fact that he hadn't completed his degree, didn't seem to matter.

The theatre introduced Dad to big stars who he would go on to work with, such as Arthur Askey, Des O'Connor and Max Miller. Dad remembered how generous these three were with their time. This example of behaving in a nurturing, kind and compassionate way backstage seemingly set the example early on for Dad. Johnny's advice to 'keep at a distance and be objective – because it's all unreal' provided Dad with a more practical angle on fame. Johnny was all too aware that the industry could be a harsh environment for a young performer.

Dad once witnessed a very young Petula Clark sound-checking at the theatre. She'd had a big hit with 'Suddenly There's a Valley' and the vogue in those days was to put pop singers on at the top of the bill. There were a few old variety comics who didn't like that trend and could be disruptive as a result. Also on the bill was Jimmy James, who decided to get to the theatre early to run through his music cues. Clark was therefore kept waiting in her dressing room while James took his time rehearsing. He then told the musical director to get the band to play 'Suddenly There's a Valley' when Clark got to the side of the stage. Understandably, she became a bit unsettled and eventually stepped forward to protest and was told that not only had James been singing it for years, but he was also going to close the show with it. He kept the ruse going for quite a while before eventually putting her out of her misery. Dad never forgot that, thinking it was unnecessarily cruel.

It appears that this experience behind the curtain made Dad even more impatient to get his shot in front of it. Thankfully, he didn't have to wait long. Leo Lion (yes, the Leeds Empire 1950s staff list really is the gift that keeps on giving), who was the theatre manager, gave Dad a chance to appear as a comic in their regular charity show. It wasn't long before he was 'showing off' (his words) again to a Leeds audience.

Among that audience were famed theatre impresarios Stanley and Michael Joseph (of the City Varieties Music Hall down the road). Their father Harry produced shows with titles like *Nudes of the World* and *We've Got Nothing on Tonight*. Punters tended to greet stand-ups not with a heckle, but with indifference. In short, no respectable middle-class Leeds boy would have been seen within a hundred yards of the place. In fact, Dad had already been to the Varieties a few times and seen Phyllis Dixey, known at the Whitehall Theatre in London as the wartime 'Queen of Striptease' in the flesh. Although, as it turned out, not quite as much flesh or sauciness as her moniker might suggest. He described her legendary 'Peek-a-boo' revue act as 'quite decorous and all rather prim'.

To Dad's amazement, the Joseph brothers had liked his spot at the Empire so much that they offered him a week's work at the Varieties. The following letter, a personal one, gives us an insight into his thoughts on that impending professional debut:

12, Mount Pleasant Avenue
Leeds 8
Yorks.

Dear Faith,

Just a few lines (modesty) to bring you a little news from
the Cryer, as if you cared … It is now Saturday evening, I've
nowhere to go and nothing to do, and no one to do it with.
Pathetic, isn't it? Actually, I'm bewildered, as these last few weeks
I've been praying for nothing to do – and now I've got it, I don't
want it!

'Nothing' is a word I use loosely, as mornings and most
nights I'm working at the Empire. Mornings – carrying crates
of beer from the CELLAR to the GALLERY bar (a rest cure)
and at nights, practically everything backstage from props (guns,
telephones, alabaster what-nots etc) to hauling on ropes, and
moving over 35 feet high flats (scenery, not dwellings). This
afternoon I've been hard at work on my script for the City
Varieties (AUGUST 6-11th prices reasonable – book now)
you knew about it, I suppose – I hardly think I DIDN'T tell
anyone!

The week before (was that me?) I'm giving a 'press
conference', sort of 'local boy makes good' to the local press.
My act runs 12 minutes, and on timing it (solo performance in
front of bedroom mirror) I found to my amazement it ran for –
12 minutes. Something must be afoot (12 inches?).

I am writing to an agent in Manchester after this, by the
way, as I'm aiming to do some cabaret work your way, at the
Cromford and Stork Clubs – do you know them? Anyway,
I'll let you know if I'm coming over anytime as I would like
to see you and your parents – but I've just remembered –
you're coming over to Leeds – help! Will this letter miss you?
If you've not read this letter by the time you've got it, burn
it and send it back to me, and I'll write it again. Love to Ian
(I'll send him the dog food with the new flavour 'Postman's
Leg'). Regards to your wonderful ma and pa, all my love
to you.

Barry

I must confess, I don't know who Faith or Ian are (let alone Faith's parents) but if any of you are reading this in Cromford (or otherwise), please do get in touch. That way I can find out what kind of reception Dad got at the Cromford and Stork Clubs and whether he tried the liver gag there. It's just possible they would have been treated to a slightly different Barry Cryer routine back in those days. If you can believe it, Dad tried to model himself on Terry-Thomas (the actor, not his old Leeds Grammar School headmaster). Apparently, he wore a dressing gown, smoked a cigarette in a holder and sat in an armchair. An older northern comic said he thought he must be from London, which Dad cringed at because he was still using his Leeds accent.

How bold he must have been to step out onto that City Varieties stage in 1956 (perhaps in a dressing gown and pipe), no longer 'showing off' for charity, but suddenly a professional comedian. It was a real induction too, for someone with only a handful of student performances under his belt. Eight shows in a week, in front of 'commercial travellers' in raincoats, who were only there to see the strippers. Dad described the experience as walking 'on and off to the sound of my own feet'. He later claimed that he learned as much about the business at that venue in that one week, as he did at any other time in his career.

A favourite story of his was how his mother came to see him at the City Varieties but nearly didn't tell him. This prim, quiet suburban Leeds housewife, not your average demographic for a strip show, went to the box office and asked when 'Barry Cryer' was on. To their credit, the management worked out who she was, and offered her a free ticket. Rather than sit and watch, my grandmother stood at the back of the stalls and once Dad had finished his set, she left the theatre and fled into the night. She didn't mention it that evening and a couple of days passed. Still nothing. Eventually, after dinner later in the week, once they'd both settled down in the front room, she said: 'The suit looked nice.'

Unfortunately, no regular work as 'a turn' immediately followed that stint at the City Varieties, despite a couple of one-off appearances on the cabaret circuit in places like Cromford (thanks Faith!) and Batley. However, it was too late. Dad had the bug. Returning to the Empire to work backstage, he started work on the pantomime, *Cinderella*, starring David Nixon, the magician. Nixon's introduction to Leeds coincided with a shocking personal tragedy. He and his wife had driven up from London in separate cars, but she had a heart attack in hers, crashed the car and died. Nixon was told of this upon his arrival in Leeds and promptly collapsed. Dad recalls that the doctor who came to see him suggested that Nixon rest up for a while, but Nixon insisted he go on regardless. Leo Lion called him to his office and said, 'You are now going to look after Mr Nixon.'

Dad became his assistant and dresser, with the two men quickly developing a bond. During his time at the Empire, Nixon sensed that Dad had some potential as a comic. When *Cinderella* came to an end, Nixon gave Dad his number and urged him to go down to London to give comedy a real shot. Dad bought a seventeen-day return and jumped on an overnight train to London. Things were starting to happen.

When he arrived in London, he met Nixon in the West End. The entertainer, who by this point in his career had become something of a celebrity as a panellist on the game show *What's My Line?*, was also a party magician at some well-heeled gatherings in Mayfair and Piccadilly. He showed Dad around, mainly visiting theatre managers and seeing the odd show. Nixon introduced him to some important agents, producers and performers, and it seemed Dad's happy knack for finding the right person at the right time was continuing. Where Stanley and Michael Joseph might have given young Barry his big professional break, David Nixon had now nurtured it. The bond between dresser and performer is often described as like that of patient and nurse. This was no better exemplified than in Dad's kindness during Nixon's bereavement and the support he was shown in return.

It's worth acknowledging the bravery Dad displayed during this period but he also had a natural talent for connecting with people

Homemade publicity poster for Dad's debut show at the City Varieties in Leeds.
August 1956.

and his friendly disposition endeared him to others. This gift stayed
with him until the very end and he became inured to the cynicism
that sometimes greeted his bonhomie. When they were touring,
Willie Rushton was often bemused when Dad would go to great

David Nixon, the magician who took Dad under his wing
at the Leeds Empire in 1956.

lengths to get to know the names of people at each venue they visited. In Willie's mind, they were just there for one performance, and it was likely they would never see them again. He would always much rather get on with the sound check.

Dad's take? 'I'm a people-a-holic. I enjoy getting to know them. Besides, you'd also know whose name to shout if the lights went out.'

A woman is lying in bed with a gentleman she should not be with. Her husband is in Hong Kong. A classic start to any joke — the sound of the key in the lock. The woman says to the man: 'Get out of here! It's my husband, get into the bathroom!'

The man does as he's told just before the husband comes into the room. The husband sees his wife, as you might say, 'en déshabillé'. She says: 'Oh darling, I have missed you. Welcome home, you must have jet lag, come to bed…'

He says: 'That's a lovely thought but I'll just go to the bathroom to freshen up.' And before she can say anything, the husband is in the bathroom, confronted by a man, who is barefoot to the neck, clapping in the air above his head.

The husband says: 'What are you doing here?'

The man replies: 'Council. Your wife phoned and said the flat was infested with moths.' The man continues clapping.

The husband then says: 'But you're naked!'

And the man looks at himself and says: 'The bastards!'

3

In January 1957, Elvis Presley attended Kennedy Veterans Hospital in Memphis, Tennessee, for his army medical. He was subsequently declared physically fit and ready for active service (spoiler alert). Elvis would become a fully fledged soldier at some point during the following year, and the cultural story of rock 'n' roll would take another epochal turn in its history. Fans around the world would go into mourning while sneering critics would cheer the successful shackling of this 'menace to society'. More importantly, a young comedian would scribble down his thoughts on the subject in a small bedroom in the Harehills area of Leeds.

Dear Diary: 'What if Elvis was only dressed in a towel for the medical but was forced to wait outside for it in a freezing corridor?' 'Could these conditions have given rise to his convulsing pelvic thrusting and hip-shaking stage persona?' No, obviously. Elvis had been a global superstar for several months and his midriff gyrations were already the stuff of music legend. Not that this deterred young Barry, of course. There were laughs to be had.

Two months later, he's performing this bit on stage in front of the celebrated theatrical impresario Vivian Van Damm at London's famous Windmill Theatre. It's 10.30 in the morning and he's on day sixteen of his seventeen-day return ticket. It's all or nothing as this is the only audition in London he has left.

'Next!'

A clown is packing up his stuff on stage in silence. It's gone disastrously. He's wearing a sticky-up wig, heavy make-up and clutching a large box that's rattling with props and instruments. He's also carrying a collapsible music stand, a bent trombone that fell apart when he played it, and a rubber clarinet under his chin. People were meant to laugh.

Dad is next. Dressed simply in a business suit and carrying a single songsheet, he said he felt lazy in comparison to the clown with all his props. He sings his song, gets through his act (Elvis impression included) and is about to trudge off back to his digs. Instead, a voice from the back of the stalls asks him if he knows any more jokes. It is Van Damm. Dad tells some more jokes. Van Damm then asks if he has another song. Dad says that he has, but not the music. Ronnie Bridges, the evergreen Windmill pianist, offers to busk the tune and Dad sings a second song. He waits nervously for the next instruction. After what seems like an age, Van Damm says: 'Dressing room 12A. You're on at midday.'

Dad calls my grandmother to tell her that he is now a Windmill comedian. She has no idea what that means but wonders if he's coming home for tea. It's clear he might not be home for many teas to come. As he returns to his dressing room, the manager tells Dad that someone is at the stage door for him. How could that be the case? Nobody knows that he is at the Windmill. Could it be his brother John? Or David Nixon? Van Damm? Intrigued, Dad goes downstairs to find out. Dad doesn't recognise the man but notices he is carrying a wig and a pair of baggy trousers. There's a smudge of white make-up on his temple. It's the clown. He's now a smartly dressed, average-looking man who could pass for an office worker. He heard Dad got the job and wanted to congratulate him. Dad doesn't even know his stage name, and the clown walks away before he can ask. That remarkable gesture of professional camaraderie haunted Dad for a long time.

When Dad stepped onto that stage to audition, he was doing so in the knowledge that comedians were very far down the list of priorities for the average Windmill patron. In fact, when they inched onto the stage, they were often greeted by the sound of newspapers being opened. A Geordie comic called Jimmy Edmondson went on one afternoon and a man in the front row opened his newspaper. Jimmy said: 'I see you've brought your own comic.' You won't be surprised to learn that the opposite was true when the nudes came back onto the stage. The comic would finish, and these same patrons would then leap over the seats to get to the front. There was even a loudspeaker announcement: 'Patrons are requested not to climb over the seats…' which was inevitably drowned out by the noise of patrons climbing over the seats. The comics called this the Grand National.

What wasn't tolerated was 'ogling'. One day, a man came wearing a pair of 'binocular glasses', the kind you might see worn at horse racing or sported by evil professors in cartoons. Evidently, he wasn't there to admire the cornicing and Big Peter, the house manager who was noted for (you guessed it) his size, decided to remove him. Big Peter whispered in the man's ear and very gently picked him up by the coat collar. He then took the man over to the stairs at the back of the theatre and nudged him towards the exit. As the man was still wearing the glasses, he missed the first step and fell down the stairs, breaking his leg. None of this exactly helped the reputation of the theatre and I wouldn't be surprised if a few acts had second thoughts about treading the boards after these stories began to circulate. However, the feeling in the industry was that if it was good enough for Jimmy Edwards, Tony Hancock, Spike Milligan, Harry Secombe, Peter Sellers, Harry Worth, Tommy Cooper and Bruce Forsyth, then it was good enough for anyone.

Vivian Van Damm erected an 'honours board' outside the theatre to celebrate comedians who went on to make an impact on the industry after they'd left the Windmill. Bruce Forsyth was the first comic to be added to the honours board while he was still performing at the venue. He was top of the bill when Dad joined and Dad remembers how dynamic he was compared to the other acts. He did everything: comedy, impressions, singing, playing piano and dancing. Dad said it was intimidating sometimes because, in his words, he was 'brilliant six times a day'. This was

Licensed by the Lord Chamberlain to
VIVIAN VAN DAMM

WINDMILL

288th EDITION *Revua*

A VAN DAMM PRODUCTION presen

This Programme is subject

1 **"SIMON'S NOT SO SIMPLE !"** (*Bridges and Rose*)
   JACK DENNING or ROY SONE or ANTHONY ADAMS
   and THE WINDMILL GIRLS

2 **RON ROWLANDS**

3 **"NAPOLI"** (*Arranged by Keith Lester*)
   SYLVIA BARBER or IRENE KING and LESLIE WARNE
   or TONY DALLMAN and THE WINDMILL GIRLS

4 **"IN LOVE FOR THE VERY FIRST TIME"** (*Arranged by Tony Dallman*)
   The Girl .. .. .. JILL TURNER or JACKIE JOY
   or MAUREEN O'DEA
   The Boy .. .. .. TONY DALLMAN or KEN ROLAND
   or ROY SONE

5 **"MY LADY'S FAN"**
   ADRIENNE DURAND or MYRA COWEN or SHERRIE LAN
   and THE WINDMILL GIRLS
   The Vocalist .. .. KEITH WARWICK or KEN ROLAND
   or NUGENT MARSHALL

6 **CLIVE ALLEN & BOBBY JOY**

7 **"GIVE ME THAT OLD ROUTINE"**
   JILL TURNER or JOAN HODGINS or JULIE WHITEHEAD,
   TONY DALLMAN or JACK DENNING or ROY SONE
   and THE WINDMILL GIRLS

8 **"THE COUNTRY COUSIN"** (*Roberts & Rose*)
   JOAN HODGINS or JACKIE JOY or ADRIENNE DURAND

9 **BARRY CRYER**

10 **"THE PERSIAN ROSE"** (*Arranged by Keith Lester*)
   Girl at the Window SANDRA PENDERS or LORNA WAYNE
   or JANET LEACH
   The Letter-Writer SYLVIA BARBER or FRANCES HAMILL
   The Lover .. KEITH WARWICK or KEN ROLAND
   The Scarf Boy .. LESLIE WARNE or TONY DALLMAN
   The Lord & Master NUGENT MARSHALL or JACK DENNING
   or ANTHONY ADAMS
   The Slave Girls .. .. THE WINDMILL GIRLS

REVUDEVILLE No. 289 with complete change of Prog

FOR SI

---

*Dad's London debut: Revudeville at the Windmill Theatre, May 1957. A young Bruce
Forsyth regularly stole the show in the second half. Whatever happened to him?*

THEATRE

eville "A" COMPANY

d in collaboration with ANNE MITELLE

o *alteration without notice*

11 **"FIRE, FIRE, FIRE !"** (*Bridges and Rose*)
The Fire-Girls .. JILL TURNER or ADRIENNE DURAND or FRANCES HAMILL, JOAN HODGINS or SANDRA PENDERS or MAUREEN O'DEA and JACKIE JOY or CHRISTINE FRASER or VALERIE HILL

12 **"TEMPTATION BOLERO"** (*Arranged by John Law*)
The Girls .. SYLVIA BARBER or SANDRA PENDERS or JULIE WHITEHEAD and IRENE KING or JILL TURNER or JOAN HODGINS
The Boys .. .. JACK DENNING or TONY DALLMAN or ANTHONY ADAMS and KEN ROLAND or ROY SONE or NUGENT MARSHALL
The Vocalist .. KEITH WARWICK or KEN ROLAND

13 **BRUCE FORSYTH**

14 **"CRISIS AT THE CAFE"** (*Bridges and Rose*)
Maitre Raymond NUGENT MARSHALL or KEITH WARWICK
Claudette .. .. JACKIE JOY or JOAN HODGINS
The Waitresses ADRIENNE DURAND or SANDRA PENDERS and CHRISTINE FRASER or JILL TURNER or MAUREEN O'DEA
The Gendarme .. TONY DALLMAN or KEN ROLAND
Fluffy Fifi .. JILL TURNER or ELAINE RIVERS
The Prefect of Police JACK DENNING or LESLIE WARNE
The Can-Can Girls SYLVIA BARBER or JANET LEACH or VALERIE HILL and FRANCES HAMILL or SHERRIE LAN or JULIE WHITEHEAD
The Customers .. .. THE WINDMILL GIRLS

WINDMILL GIRLS

SYLVIA BARBER, MYRA COWEN, ADRIENNE DURAND, CHRISTINE FRASER, FRANCES HAMILL, VALERIE HILL, JOAN HODGINS, JACKIE JOY, IRENE KING, MEGAN LAN, SHERRIE LAN, JANET LEACH, MAUREEN O'DEA, SANDRA PENDERS, ELAINE RIVERS, JILL TURNER, LORNA WAYNE, JULIE WHITEHEAD

amme will commence here **MONDAY, MAY 6th, 1957**
WEEKS

mainly because he was never settled with his act, and certainly never relaxed.

Dad would go on to write for Bruce at regular intervals over the next five decades and the two became friends. For a brief period, they were both part of Windmill's 'B Company' (Van Damm would alternate casts weekly) and they would often sit and chat in the canteen together. Dad recalled Bruce becoming disillusioned one day. 'I'm packing it in, Barry,' he said. 'I've got as far as I can go. I'm opening a tobacconist's instead.' A year later he landed his career-defining stint as compère on *Sunday Night at the London Palladium*. Dad met him in the street around this time and asked him: 'Bruce, what happened to the tobacconist's?'

'Postponed.'

The Windmill, like the City Varieties, gave Dad the closest thing he could get to an apprenticeship in the comedy world. Van Damm would often call young comics into his office ('between the desk and the fish tank') and dissect their material. Not just rearranging the order of gags and 'bits' but offering a different choice of words and advice on their delivery. It was a masterclass, no doubt helping Dad develop a bullet-proof exterior in front of a tough crowd, as it's fair to say that the Windmill regulars were unique. You learned to die with dignity and sometimes without (mainly without). All this for six shows a day, six days a week, which given he was there for seven months, worked out at over a thousand performances.

Each individual 'Revudeville' show ran for three weeks and then Van Damm would refresh the line-up. In what Dad thought was a particularly sadistic exercise, he'd make everyone audition all over again. In civvy street, this was the equivalent of interviewing for your own job. A job you'd fought hard for. Van Damm would also want new material, which must've been punishing. Dad said that for one show, he got auditioned on a Monday, got turned down, auditioned again on a Wednesday, and was turned down again. He auditioned three times and after that third attempt, was told to report for duty at Sunday's dress rehearsal. He'd been strung out all week deliberately because Van Damm wanted to see how much new material he could generate at speed.

No wonder Dad would grow into a sketch writer with a reputation for fast turnarounds and an impeccable ear. He'd been made to work this muscle several times at the Windmill. Dad was now battle-hardened. The *Stage* newspaper could see the potential at the Windmill, but it was evident that there was still much room for improvement. Ironically, it's his material that draws the most comment: 'Comedian Barry Cryer displays some original ideas in humour but lacks the necessary material to make them as effective as they might very well be.'

Vivian Van Damm, with his daughter Sheila watching dancers rehearse at the Windmill Theatre in 1957, the year Dad took to the stage. The comedians at the Windmill had to fight for the audience's attention.

He returned to Leeds as a Windmill comedian when his seven months were up, and because of this credit on his CV, was now able to book a few variety dates around the country, including the Royalty Theatre in Chester and the Regent in Rotherham. If the *Stage* review wasn't enough to warn him of the distance he still had to go in the business, then the sign backstage at the Regent would have left him in no doubt: 'Jokes about the size of the audience are not appreciated at this theatre.'

The Chester venue was no picnic either. As a theatrical history listing describes it: 'The Chester Royalty Theatre in City Road first opened its doors in 1882. The Royalty was built on the site of a primitive theatre, known as The Prince of Wales, "where music hall acts of poor quality were mainly presented to the railway workers for years".'

The saying goes that the road to success is paved with sweat and if Dad wasn't cutting his teeth on harsh crowds at the likes of the Windmill and the City Varieties, it sounds like he was cutting his feet leaving gigs on the harsher floors of Rotherham and Chester. However, these experiences only increased his desire to get his act on television, or even his first love, radio. He'd had a taste of broadcast experience just prior to the Windmill (and just after the University Rag Revue) on the BBC North Region radio talent show *What Makes A Star?* The TV version of the show would introduce Dad to a name he'd become very familiar with later in his career. It was produced by a man called Barney Colehan, who would go on to create *The Good Old Days*.

One of the great joys (and occasionally one of the great headaches) of this project has been to sift through Mum and Dad's archive of ephemera collected into various shoeboxes and crates over the years. As I have already mentioned, although there is a paucity of Dad's writing material in that collection, there is no shortage of reviews, listings, programmes, posters, flyers and even the odd poem. However, every now and again a rare gem pops up. In between a pantomime programme from the nineties (the Hackney Empire, in case you were wondering), and a corporate after-dinner brochure (for ICI – no, I'm aware you weren't asking),

I found a rather Orwellian-looking document, covered in official stamps and serial numbers. It's Dad's 1957 application for a BBC Variety Department audition.

I don't know how he got hold of it from the BBC archives, but if they want it back, they'll have to prise it from my cold, dead hands. The audition application is much the same as the ones that, by turns, yielded false starts and early beginnings for such diverse luminaries as Bob Monkhouse, David Bowie and the Beatles. Potential acts, like Dad, filled in an application to the Variety Department, in the hope of gaining an audition. These auditions were usually recorded and listened to by the wonderfully named 'Talent Selection Group', who would then submit a report. If approved, a contract would be issued. He'd applied to the BBC once before, exactly a year earlier, when he wrote to them at Manchester Piccadilly on 6 September 1956 (while he was still working at the Empire). As far as I know, he didn't succeed in getting an audition either time. This 6 September 1957 application paints a picture of Dad that is not too dissimilar to the 'Baz' persona we'd come to know and love much later in his life. However, there are some crucial differences that I will leave to the twenty-two-year-old Barry Cryer to explain:

Professional debut at City Varieties Music Hall, Leeds (Aug '56)

(Oldest in the country) after being 'spotted' in students'
annual show at Leeds Empire. Followed by Variety dates, and
a BBC North Region Broadcast in *What Makes A Star?* Won
Round on Listeners' Vote, but unable to take part, due to
having commenced season at Windmill (started same day as
I auditioned). Spent six months at Windmill, being retained for
three shows. Write all own material. Gained real training here (six
shows a day, six days a week) to audience who hate comedians!

The only thing missing is the self-deprecating tone that he'd come to adopt later. That last line about the Windmill audience really struck me as refreshingly honest about his experience. Perhaps because it was still so raw.

He was represented at that time by Lorenzo Medea, a pianist and singing teacher who'd originally wanted to become an orchestra conductor. He'd already led quite a colourful life, including a brief marriage to an eminent Italian opera singer, before he became a theatrical agent. His fluent Italian meant he worked for the British Intelligence Service during the Second World War, where he was tasked with looking after prisoners of war. Along with his second wife Mary and Jack Billings, they formed the LM Agency and had their offices in Wigmore Street. To a young lad from Leeds, he must have seemed impossibly exotic. For an ambitious young comic, though, it seems an odd fit for Dad, but it does perhaps explain why singing and not comedy was about to be come a focus for Dad in his early years. In the BBC application, he sums up his routine at the time thus:

> Patter comedy. Conversational, not 'gags'. Song burlesques. Origin of songs ('Garden of Eden' written by pneumatic drill operator; Presley's style evolved at army medical etc). Off-stage voice acts (man at audition, comedian's nightmare, requests from audience etc). Straight 'pop' singing. Jazz singing (sung with Pro Jazz Bands). Impressions (singers, comedians, actors).

Dad's description of himself in his BBC application as a 'patter comedian', with its echoes of the *Bradford Observer*'s early review of him as 'a natural comedian … (with) off-the-cuff patter' is interesting. Meriam Webster gives 'patter' to mean 'a quick succession of light sounds', whereas Collins goes for 'a series of things that [people] say quickly and easily, usually in order to entertain'. I quite like a combination of both to describe Dad's energy as a performer in those early days. It's just possible that he'd read the review and inserted this description for want of proper self-analysis. It's a very seductive dynamic in the business and no doubt Dad succumbed to it. He was searching for an identity and a persona and he hadn't quite hit on the thing that would define him yet. His assertion that he is of the 'conversational' style is obviously also resonant, but it's the qualifier that he doesn't do 'gags' that most people will find surprising.

The application lists his references as Vivian Van Damm, David Nixon and Frankie Vaughan. Nixon we've covered and Vaughan we'll come on to, but Van Damm's name here acknowledges that even though he was a tough taskmaster, he was also a nurturing presence for many young comedians at this time. When Dad left the Windmill after seven months, Van Damm apparently said: 'It's time you tried somewhere else. I still think you're funny.' Dad eventually made his BBC TV debut at 7.30 p.m. on Tuesday 18 February 1958 (just a month before his twenty-third birthday). The show was *Robinson's Roundabout*, a fortnightly programme in which 'artists new to television are presented by Eric Robinson'.

Eric Robinson, who gave Dad his TV debut, on the set of the television series I've Met the Lot, *with Bob Monkhouse in 1955.*

Eric Robinson was a conductor by trade (clearly Dad had an affinity with them given his agent at the time) and also the musical director for the 1960s London stagings of the Eurovision Song Contest (somebody had to be, I suppose). Crucially for Dad, Eric was also from Leeds. Now, I'm not for a second suggesting that any Northern favouritism was at play here (okay, maybe I am) but the more 'organic' side of show business networking was now presenting itself to Dad. It's here that the David Nixon connection continues, as Eric Robinson's daughter Vivienne married David just a few years later, in 1961. Dad was learning that these kinds of networks and connections were invaluable and would remain so for the rest of his career.

Dad was alongside the telepathy act the Bewildering Zodias, comedians Dailey & Wayne, animal impersonator Gerry Lee (not just sounds, he dressed up as them too), and Australian singer Helen Lorain completed the line-up. If it wasn't already obvious, *Robinson's Roundabout* was a variety show with eclecticism the name of the game, but trying to stand out alongside this cavalcade of eccentricity must have been difficult for young Barry. I suppose after the Windmill it was just nice to be on stage with some people wearing clothes.

While his first TV appearance may have been underwhelming and things in general may have been moving at a snail's pace, all was about to change.

An old man is sitting on a park bench, crying. Another man walks past and stops to ask him what the matter is. He says: 'I have a young wife at home. She's incredible. She wakes me up every morning and rubs my back before getting up and making me the most incredible breakfast with everything I love.'

The man is confused: 'Why are you crying, then?'

The old man says: 'She then makes me a packed lunch for when I go for a walk and cleans the house while I am away. We watch old movies together in the afternoon.'

'Seriously, why are you crying?' the man asks again.

'For dinner she makes me a gourmet meal with wine and then makes love with me until the early hours of the morning.'

The man is impatient now: 'Well, why on earth would you be crying?'

The old man says: 'I can't remember where I live!'

4

I learned at a young age to treat any story my father told me with a certain amount of caution. He wasn't an overt liar or a fantasist, just someone more interested in what made a better story rather than strict adherence to the facts. He was a Walter Mitty with a flair for a ditty or a Billy Liar hidden in a Barry Cryer. Dad often said that 'life is badly written' or, as Eric Idle remembers it, 'well written' and it appears that his answer to this conundrum was to make sure he was in charge of the edit. If the facts didn't fit, or the information was clumsily arranged, he wouldn't hesitate to trim, cut or reshape a line, even if it was to do with events in his own life.

Comedians are notorious for being unreliable narrators. Sometimes making up spouses, siblings or events that never happened in order to neaten the rhythm or add power to the punchline. Unsurprisingly, he gained a reputation as a brilliant editor who had a good ear for the rhythms, sounds and nuances of other performers too. One of his great skills was being able to subordinate his personality in order to write for other people. He described this art of writing for other comedians as akin to a tailor making suits, cutting the cloth to fit the person, and because Dad was so used to writing for others, he could sometimes see his own public persona as an 'other' too. However, every now and again, my siblings and I would speculate as to whether the adjusted memory was a deliberate fabrication, a misremembering or even a false memory.

I'm not sure how familiar Dad was with the Platonic concept of memory as a physical alteration of the brain, or the challenge presented to that concept in the twentieth century by not only Richard Semon's 'engram theory' but also Donald Hebb's 'synaptic plasticity theory'. The likelihood is that because he considered himself a Luddite, he never searched Wikipedia as furiously as I have just done. Dad also had very little curiosity about his own mind or body and, as such, wouldn't have thought twice about why he thought twice. For most of his life, he suffered with various ailments: eczema blighted much of his twenties, a heart operation caused some midlife concern and, towards the end of his life, lung cancer caught up with (but didn't kill) him. His treatment of them was largely the same. Ignore them.

I can't decide whether this was the best or the worst strategy to employ at any time of his life, but he had a pretty good hit rate when it came to overcoming health issues. This relationship with his conscious mind and his active body also goes a long way to explaining why he was so vague with the recall of events – it was partly because he was very often not fully taking in what was happening around him. Instead, his focus was usually on scanning for the opportunity to tell a joke or pick up inspiration for future anecdotes. I'm highlighting this as an example of his talent, by the way, not complaining of a lack of empathy. That'll come later.

Dad liked to tell stories and it's my belief that the constant repetition of certain tropes (particularly about his own life) meant that, as the pebble smooths at the bottom of a river, a few rough edges were knocked off along the way. Namely, key facts. Originally, Dad wanted to be a journalist, as evidenced by his frequent correspondence with, and application to work for, the *Yorkshire Post*. This is significant in our assessment of him in a number of ways. Firstly, it led to the economy of language being at the heart of his comedy and the brevity of expression as key to his treatment of it. Secondly, when it came to writing for others, it meant he was comfortable being invisible. By that, I mean he never wanted his own voice to get in the way of someone else's. Like a good journalist, he wasn't the story. Lastly, when he reported on his own life, as we've seen, he never let the facts get in the way of a good story.

If false memory syndrome exists (I believe it does – I just can't remember where I read that) then here is a good example of how it can have a twist in the tale. It concerns one of Dad's great heroes: Humphrey Lyttelton. According to Humph, the story goes that he was playing his trumpet outside Buckingham Palace during the VE Day celebrations of 1945 while being pushed along in a handcart. Not something you think you'd forget in a hurry. Except that he did. In his anecdotage (Dad's phrase), Humph admitted he'd told the story so many times that he no longer knew if it was true or not. I'm sure most of us can relate to that. With no evidence to corroborate his tale, he was lost in a fog of his own making.

Well, it turns out that there was some evidence. He was listening to the VE Day anniversary celebrations on the radio, when during a rerun of an old BBC broadcast from the time, he heard the unmistakable sound of his own trumpet playing 'Roll Out The Barrel'. Humph was vindicated and continued to tell the story in his trademark measured authority, but now with the facts to back him up. Would it have made any difference if it wasn't true? Perhaps not. This brings me to the most persistent of all the claims made by Dad throughout his life.

On 27 January 2022, two days after Dad died, I received an email from a newspaper editor, who was fact-checking his obituary. Fairly straightforward, I thought. Although I couldn't imagine what elements of Dad's career needed checking. A sequence of high-profile writing and performing engagements was surely part of longstanding public record. The thought then crossed my mind that this wasn't in relation to his professional life at all, maybe it was about his *private* life. Maybe someone with white hair and impeccable timing had come forward claiming to be his long-lost son? Maybe he had some greyhound racing debts we weren't aware of? Maybe Sharon Stone had finally grown weary of living in denial. Dealing with the sins of the father was all part of the grieving process, but surely two days in was a little early.

I dialled the number nervously. I was ready for whatever he had to divulge. The man, who was charming but obviously nameless for these purposes, had only one specific query. He wanted to know if Dad really had a number-one hit in Finland with 'The Purple People Eater' in 1958. Silence. I bristled. *This* was the bone of contention? Everybody knew this fact, so it's hardly worth checking. Besides, who in their right mind would brag about being number one in FINLAND? Unless they were Finnish, of course. I asked if they'd discovered Dad was Finnish too (he wasn't). Dad had told everyone that 'they gave away a free car with every record' and this was all part of a spectacularly TRUE story. These were the cold, hard facts.

He continued: 'It's just that we've spoken to a Finnish music historian and he's confirmed that Barry Cryer has *never* been number one in his country. Or any other, for that matter.'

Was I hallucinating? Did he just say that one of Dad's foundation myths was now a *lie*? Maybe it was just a little more information than I was able to process at this point, but I resolved to face the sorry truth. Hold on. What's 'The Purple People Eater', you say? Time then, I think, to revisit the (now disputed) story of Barry Cryer and the Finnish Number One.

It all begins in 1928 when a little boy is born in Liverpool. Frank Abelson, an upholsterer's son, shows artisan credentials from a young age and by his late teens is on his way to winning a scholarship to the Lancaster College of Art and a place at Leeds University before the Second World War intervened. Demobbed in 1949, young Frank then went on to study at the Leeds College of Art before becoming a student teacher. It was at the college that he got his first taste of performing at Leeds Empire during the student rag revues. Sound familiar? When it came to deciding on a stage name Frank – now Frankie – already knew what surname to choose instead. As a little boy, back in Liverpool, he was the apple of his Russian-Jewish grandmother's eye. She was unable to pronounce the phrase 'special one', and as a result, Frankie became known to the family as her 'special *vorn*' instead. 'Frankie Vaughan' had arrived. The play on words at the origin of Frankie's new surname was not lost on Dad further down the line. He recorded a song with trumpeter Murray Campbell called 'A Star Is Vaughan' for Frankie's thirty-first birthday, therefore making the whole childhood pun worthwhile.

Frankie Vaughan is one of those names synonymous with an era. His look was pure composite fifties. The Tony Curtis wonky smile, the Denis Compton Brylcreemed quiff and, when singing, the Tony Bennett phrasing. He oozed charisma and class but did so in a humble and authentic manner. It's no coincidence that he became famous during the transitionary period between Frank Sinatra and Elvis Presley, as he had a hint of both: the old-school charm of Old Blue Eyes coupled with the regal swagger of the King. He was in his pomp in the late fifties, with a recording contract and a movie career, yet somehow decided to use this power to give a leg up to a young twenty-three-year-old comic, fresh from the same Leeds University stomping ground as himself. Dad had been in the audience when Frankie began singing in Leeds, little knowing how much he would influence his destiny. Frankie then returned the favour when he saw Dad performing comedy in London, courtesy of the agent Paul Cave, who they shared (Dad had now moved on from Lorenzo Medea). Given what happened next, it's likely he also saw Dad singing, probably in the West End musical, *Expresso Bongo*, in 1958. Frankie must have been impressed, as he invited Dad to dinner at the Vaughan home.

Afterwards, he asked Dad if he would sing along with him at the piano. Frankie liked his voice so much he suggested he record something. Dad was not so sure. He'd only really thought of himself as a comedian up until that point. Frankie insisted and a meeting was arranged at Fontana Records, a subsidiary of Phillips, where Vaughan was a big star. The label's A&R manager, Jack Baverstock (who had worked for the *New Musical Express* and assisted in introducing the Top Twenty chart to the UK), agreed about Dad's talents as a singer. Frankie accompanied Dad to the audition, which Dad claims swung the recording deal in his favour. Bandleader Johnny Gregory and his orchestra were lined up and Dad embarked on yet another baptism of fire. He'd come a long way in just two years and the confidence, determination and energy he displayed boded well for the future. The fact that he emerged as a singer at this point was a tribute to his innate ability to grasp an opportunity regardless of which direction it sent him.

As a side note, it's strange to think that Miles Davis was also recording material for Fontana Records at the same time as Dad. However, Miles was in Paris scoring the Louis Malle film *Ascenseur pour l'Échafaud* and Dad was in London belting out 'Nothin' Shakin''. A small stretch of water separated us from getting the collaboration we never knew we needed. *Kind of Blue Parrot* was to be but a dream.

'The Purple People Eater' was made in a session that included five other tracks (the above-mentioned 'Nothin' Shakin'', 'Hey! Eula', 'Kissin'', 'Seven Daughters' and 'Angelina'). 'The Purple People Eater' is a gimmicky song about an encounter with a 'one-eyed, one-horned, flying' alien who descends to Earth because it wants to be in a rock 'n' roll band. We used to joke that was really a metaphor for Dad's first years living in London as a Yorkshireman. The song was written by the country singer and actor Sheb Wooley (one of the baddies in *High Noon*) as a response to a joke told by the son of a friend of his. History doesn't record the joke but no doubt if Dad had heard it, he would have been telling it for many years afterwards. It only took Sheb an hour to write the song and, as a wag noted at the time, 'it shows'. Although the original American recording was a hit throughout Europe, apparently Wooley's contract didn't include the Nordic territories. One of Fontana Records' functions, when it was launched in 1958, was to market recordings licensed from labels outside of the US. A Barry Cryer-sized loophole had been created and Dad's knack for seizing opportunities continued.

Is it a bird? Is it a plane? Is it a Purple People-Eater? Or is it Number One in Finland? Dad jumps for joy at the launch of his pop career.

Among the first batch of singles released in 1958 by Fontana (incredibly, still on 78s) were ones from Jimmy Jaques, Al Saxon, a then unknown Matt Monro, and several US Columbia recordings that included Frank Sinatra, Johnny Mathis, Marty Robbins and Screamin' Jay Hawkins. Dad's was the only 'The Purple People Eater' at Fontana, but not the only cover available on the market. Even Scotland's '15-year-old Elvis', Jackie Dennis, was rolling his Rs around it on Decca in the same year. I don't know how that version fared in Finland. The early signs for Dad's version, although encouraging, were hardly ecstatic: 'Keep an eye on Barry Cryer, new discovery of Fontana, whose debut disc has caused quite a lot of appreciative comment,' said *Disc Weekly* on 21 June 1958.

Nothing quite says rock 'n' roll juggernaut like 'appreciative comment'. This brings us back to the obituaries editor and the now contested fact of Dad's recording success. Further digging provoked some more devastating news. Apparently, Fontana didn't start releasing records in Finland until 1962. Up until this point, only a small batch of Dutch imports of 'The Purple People Eater' was available to the beat-hungry denizens of the Land of a Thousand Lakes. Not content with ruining my cornflakes, the discovery was then presented that Finland didn't get weekly charts until the 1990s. The claim that Sheb Wooley's original was not released in Nordic countries for contractual reasons is apparently incorrect as well. Wooley did have vinyl releases in Finland and Norway, as well as an EP in Denmark. I was crestfallen but took solace in the fact that it wouldn't have meant much to Dad. I can guarantee that his response to this explosive revelation would not have elicited any expression of shame or remorse. Instead, he would've said, 'I must remember to bring these things up at the next meeting of my local get a life club.'

What really happened? Well, in Dad's usual telling of the story, he receives a phone call from Baverstock to say that the disc was selling well in Finland and Fontana was happy. I can only surmise that from 'selling well' and 'really happy', Dad gleaned that the record might have a favourable showing in the Finnish charts. It's only a short leap from here to letting proud relatives know he'd scored a number one, surely? Perhaps, like Humphrey Lyttelton, Dad had told the story so many times that even he'd forgotten himself whether it was true or not.

The main heart of the Finland story is not really the factual inaccuracies, but the presence of another mentor in Dad's life: Frankie Vaughan. Just like David Nixon, Frankie seemed to respond to Dad's affability and his enthusiasm encouraged their affection. People came along time and again in Dad's life to offer him a break, and he took these opportunities with grace, gratitude and authentic ease.

In *The Heart of A Man* (1959), Frankie played an out-of-work sailor, who meets Bud, a tramp who claims he is a millionaire. Bud gives Frankie a shilling and promises him that if he can make £100 from it, he will be given £1,000. Armed with this, Frankie goes off to pursue a singing career and win the heart of Julie, the girlfriend of upper-class criminal Tony. One of his other money-making ventures sees Frankie trying his luck as a boxer, and in a changing-room scene there's Dad, busy with the towel as Frankie's second. His movie career was up and running: 'I only had one line but was then asked to reshoot the scene the day I was due to do stand-up in Dublin,' Dad recalled. 'The studio flew me to Pinewood then back to Dublin, just in time for the second half of the show. What a day!'

That's quite a commitment from the studio for just one line but the gig in Dublin in March 1959 led to another significant connection. It was here that Dad first met Roy Castle and Denis King, two men who would go on to become great friends and future collaborators.

However, it's after this that the Frankie Vaughan chapter of my Dad's life comes to an end, due to Frankie's move to the US. Although they shared an agent, it was a while before they saw each other again. As for Dad's recording career, he wasn't asked to make any more singles by Fontana. Losing Frankie and a recording deal could have been a crippling setback for most but as Dad often said (quoting Kingsley Amis): 'A bad review may spoil your breakfast, but you shouldn't allow it to spoil your lunch.'

Carole Lesley, Jackie Lane and Dad's mentor and fellow Leeds Uni grad Frankie Vaughan rehearse a scene from These Dangerous Years *as Anna Neagle watches on.*

Dad was not seeking a singing career, much as he enjoyed singing, but rather taking an opportunity and running with it. Had he been more ambitious, the legacy of his misfiring years as a crooner might have been ushered to the cutting-room floor. However, as a comedian, what do you think is the better story? A lukewarm reaction to a handful of singles or number one in Finland? It's a perfectly innocuous place to be number one and it makes for a better line. A better story. Barry the comedy writer won that battle once again and it was starting to become clearer what the direction of travel might be for Dad.

As for Frankie, as I mentioned above, he swapped Totteridge for Las Vegas (where he was the first British performer to top the bill at Dunes Hotel) and then Hollywood when he was cast opposite Marilyn Monroe in *Let's Make Love* in 1960. Staying true to his family man credentials, Frankie behaved himself while abroad although that is not to say he wasn't tested. Once, Marilyn wanted

Dad with Denis King and Roy Castle, a lifelong friendship with both men that began in Dublin in 1959.

to ensure their dialogue was perfect and asked Frankie to come over to her bungalow, so they could build up a 'rapport'. Frankie had brought his wife Stella with him to Hollywood and when he mentioned Marilyn's idea, she asserted that if anyone was going to assist Frankie with his lines, it would be her.

At the time of *Let's Make Love*, Dad was in Paul Cave's office one day answering his mail when the phone rang and as there was no one around to answer, Dad picked up. A voice said, 'It's

Miss Monroe for you.' Marilyn then came on and said: 'Hello, who are you?' Now, at this point, the young Barry Cryer must have had a thousand different answers scrolling through his head. From 'Frankie speaking' to 'Never mind that, who are you?', not to mention 'Look, I'm having these calls traced, you know'. However, this was 1960 and a twenty-four-year-old Dad instead chose the following, devastating response: 'Hello, I'm Barry Cryer.'

He expected to be hurried off the call, but she continued: 'What do you do, Barry?'

'I'm an out-of-work comic,' he parried.

He told me that they then talked for a further three minutes until Paul Cave walked back in. I asked him what they talked about during those three minutes and all he could say was that although he couldn't remember, it was wonderful. He was just so shocked that it was her on the end of the line. I was disappointed. He's quite happy to make up a Finnish success story but *not* details of a chat with Marilyn Monroe?

One of the many reassuring aspects of grieving in public is that in the days and weeks following Dad's death, people sent me and the family many memories and pictures of their time with Dad. However, following 'the Finnish incident' (as we now call it), every now and again a story would come up that needed me and my siblings to consider whether it was another example of his false memory. A case of a Cryer Crying Wolf. One such came in the form of a story about Newcastle, from none other than Simon Donald, one of the founders of *Viz* magazine and Geordie royalty par excellence, who told me about one of Dad's stories:

'It was a lovely story. He said that his parents would be working over the summer and he'd be sent to stay in Newcastle with an aunt and uncle. As was common at the time, he would share a bed with them. The address was in Newcastle, on Cartington Terrace, about half a mile from where I live now. He told me the house number, but sadly I've forgotten it, though I do know whereabouts to within three or four houses. He said he would go to bed and later in the evening his aunt and uncle would come to bed. As the uncle climbed in with him, he would deliver the same line, every night, in a Geordie accent that your dad would deliver perfectly: "Aaaah! The bloke who invented bed should've got a medal!" It was a little piece of history.'

'The bloke who invented bed should've got a medal!' is a lovely line but, incredibly, it was one that had completely escaped the notice of our family. Why hadn't Dad mentioned it before? I asked Mum and my siblings. We all doubted it had come from Newcastle, as we knew of no family in the north-east. If you look along Dad's uncles and aunts on his father's side, all of them spent their lives either in Leeds or West Yorkshire. Dad's mum, Jenny, hailed from Cumberland and had no brothers or sisters move out of that county either. However, while looking into Dad's genealogy for this book, I came across Beatrice Townson, who was a *great*-aunt. It turns out she did leave Cumberland when she married a man called Thomas Midgley, which would've made the author of the bed comment my father's great-uncle. Sure enough, a further census search gave me the detail I was looking for. Beatrice and Thomas lived on Cartington Terrace in Heaton, Newcastle. At number 76, to be precise, which is exactly where Simon had been describing the events.

Thomas would have been in his sixties when Dad came to stay and it made perfect sense for a recently widowed Jenny to seek out this kind of help from her side of the family. Especially if she was looking to give her young son a holiday. I'm therefore grateful to Simon for three things. Firstly, restoring my faith in Dad's memory. Secondly, the story of sharing a bed with a great-uncle brings an unexpected *Charlie and the Chocolate Factory* dynamic to thoughts of Dad's childhood. Lastly, 'Aaaah! The bloke who invented bed should've got a medal!' has now given the family back a fantastic catchphrase.

It was also on this stage that I first saw Delmonte and his Dancing Duck. A true story. It was a wholly feathered act. An ornithological act. And the climax of this act was: the birds would do tricks and run up and down steps and onto perches and all sorts of things. Whistle away, that kind of thing and the end of the act was a duck standing on a biscuit tin that would tap dance. Wonderful climax to the act. Music builds. The spotlight. And the duck would tap dance on the biscuit tin. And I loved this act. I used to watch it every night.

And one night the act came to its climax and the spotlight came on this duck and he just stood there and looked at the audience. Complete anti-climax. Nothing happened at all. It was an awful moment. So, in the bar after the show, I was with the great Delmonte, or Reg as we called him, and I said: 'What happened with the duck tonight?'

And he said: 'Oh, the candle went out.'

5

Dad thought his career was a series of 'happy accidents'. You won't be surprised to learn that I disagreed with him vehemently every time he said that. I believe you still need to be talented to make use of the opportunities given to you in life, no matter how fortunate you think those opportunities might be. Even spotting an opportunity requires skill. Dad was no exception and I told him so. My protest was usually met with a wave of the hand. Being 'fortunate' was a much more comfortable place to be for Dad. Anything else was sticking your head above the parapet or, God forbid, 'getting too big for your boots', as his mother preferred to style it.

Dad had an instinct for knowing what the right joke for the right audience was. He was quite proud of his ability to 'read a room' and he'd invariably get it right, but it was a skill that took years and years of practice to perfect. By the time I was able to come with him to shows, it was a joy to see the craft of gradually working up a crowd to a point where they were ready for the belly laugh. He'd then know which joke would finish them off. Sometimes after a performance, I'd ask him why he didn't tell a certain joke. 'Not this audience,' he said. 'It didn't feel right.' But let's not get ahead of ourselves. This is still the early part of Dad's career and he's still learning his trade.

As we know, he often had hundreds to choose from, and I was tickled to think that as his act was developing, he was scrolling through options in his head. There were ones I knew he really enjoyed telling, yet he'd often employ restraint as he decided to save them. Most people would just be happy to have a handful of favourites, try them all out and then hope to win an audience over on points. We used to call Dad the 'comedy jukebox' or the 'anecdote jukebox' because of his seemingly endless supply of jokes all teed up ready to go. The mood would then determine which buttons to press. He always seemed to know the difference between a pros' joke and a public joke, or a clean room and a blue room. If you've ever seen the documentary *The Aristocrats*, you'll know what I mean and if you haven't, *why* haven't you? Dad's equivalent of the joke featured in that movie was the following, much cleaner, classic:

A man walks into a pub and the landlord is astonished. Half of the man's head is an orange. 'So sorry to be nosy,' says the landlord. 'But why is half of your head an orange?'

'Well,' says the man. 'I was cleaning up the loft, and I found an old lamp. I polished it up, and a genie came out, saying: "Master, I must now grant you three wishes. Ask for anything."'

So, the man said: 'I'd like to have a million pounds – and every time I take the million pounds out of my pocket, another million appears there.'

The genie said: 'Your wish is granted. And your second wish?'

The man says: 'I'd like to have a big house filled with a hundred beautiful women who all find me devastatingly attractive.'

'Your wish is granted,' says the genie. 'And your third wish?'

'I'd like half of my head to be an orange.'

Although the surreal style of the joke is not perhaps what you'd associate with Barry Cryer, the classic rule of three, the subverted punchline and the brevity of the structure all point to the kind of traditional gem he might tell. Yet he rarely told it outside of his professional mates. The joy, for him, was in the conversation he'd have with them after telling it. How did you picture the man? Which half of his head was an orange? If it was the bottom half, how did he speak? David Renwick even sent him a sketch (complete with orange colouring-in) of how he saw the man talking to the landlord.

Like the comics in *The Aristocrats*, the real pleasure comes in the idea that you would dare tell 'The Man With Half His Head An Orange' to an audience. Unlike *The Aristocrats*, the dare is in the obscurity of the joke, not the obscenity of it. The thrill of it *not* landing is what comedians sometimes get a kick out of. It's essentially an un-joke, like 'The Old Lady on the Train' or 'The Chicken Crossing the Road', and telling it to other comics acts like a palate cleanser after spending time tailoring jokes to fit the audience. It's like a sommelier opening a can of Coke or a head chef coming home to beans on toast.

If Dad could judge a room impeccably, could he extend this intuition to judging trends in British comedy and navigating them? The answer here is a little less clear cut. He did seem to move on from certain art forms, like variety and music hall, just before they went to seed, but only because the money was elsewhere. Some people have credited Dad's longevity in the industry to a prescience when it came to fashions in humour, saying that he was able to predict which way the wind was blowing and alter his course accordingly. It could be suggested that it was because he didn't change his style at all, meaning he was neither in nor out of fashion.

Dad talked about being between generations. As he started as a professional in the late fifties, he was neither a 'traditional variety comic' nor a 'satire wunderkind'. He began his Leeds career at that bastion of old-school variety, the City Varieties, and had student forays at the equally populist Empire, where Charlie Chaplin had once performed. London was introduced to him via the notoriously bawdy Windmill. All three of these venues marked him out as a bone fide music-hall turn. However, when he began life as a David Frost writer, he was also there with proto-Pythons, nascent Goodies, mature Angry Young Men and the already famous giddy high-jinkers Marty Feldman and Barry Took. The leap from one to the other appears to have been a seamless one, yet that might be because he resolutely refused to change his approach to either tribe. The common denominator here, in terms of his developed style, was not his experience of telling jokes, but in his writing and performing of what was known at that time as revue.

For younger readers (and there must be some), revue is defined by the Oxford English Dictionary as 'a light theatrical entertainment consisting of a series of short sketches, songs, and dances, typically dealing satirically with topical issues'. If you break down this definition into its core elements, you'll find the words 'light', 'sketch', 'song', 'dance' and 'satire'. To a young Barry Cryer, at the start of his career, at least four out of those five must've felt like an easy fit. I'll leave you to guess which one he was less comfortable with, but to my knowledge *Strictly Come Dancing* never called.

The history of revue in the UK, despite having its roots in music hall, sees it develop initially as a much gentler and less abrasive style of performance. In the fifties, when 'pre-joke' Dad was finding his comedic feet, part 'patter' comedian and part visual surrealist, it provided the perfect forum for his talents. Fast-paced, multi-skilled and topical, revue relied on one aspect that he was very comfortable with and you could say it defined him to the end of his days. It is the deceptively noble art of 'professional amateurism'. Danny La Rue, Kenny Everett, *Hello Cheeky* (the seventies radio and TV show he starred in with John Junkin, Tim Brooke-Taylor and Denis King) and, of course, *I'm Sorry I Haven't A Clue* all practised this most British form of performance style. 'We're taking this work seriously,' it would say, 'but not TOO seriously.' The professional amateur shows you their workings out in the margin.

Dad always said that he was happiest when the 'wheels were coming off' a show. He felt that the audience got a thrill watching high-wire acts that look unsure of what they're doing, but have fun doing it anyway. You can hear it in the glee the camera crew gets when Kenny Everett can't get the cigarette in his mouth as Sid Snot, or the joy an audience gets when Humphrey Lyttelton sounds bewildered during a round on *I'm Sorry I Haven't A Clue*, or the off-camera laughter during EVERY episode of *Hello Cheeky*.

When Dad and I were recording *Mrs Hudson's Radio Show* (the two-part adaptation of our book *Mrs Hudson's Diaries*), Dad's eyes lit up every time there was a missed cue or a sound malfunction. He'd turn to the audience and deadpan, 'Is this getting too slick for you?' It would always get a big laugh. It relaxes people to know that the performer is not so uptight and earnest that a mistake is likely to sour his or her mood. Dad never wanted an audience to feel awkward, but neither did he want things to come across as too polished. We'd call it 'authentic' now. He'd call it 'mucking about'. Revue, with its tiny budgets, quick-change limitations and fast pace, was the perfect playground to discover his love of this approach.

His versatility as a performer was apparent from the start and revue's reliance on sketch material obviously served him well as a writer for the rest of his days. The sketch was the writing that he was most in demand for in the 1970s, 1980s and 1990s and effectively made his career. Yet it was revue's budgetary need for the performers to double up as hosts, singers, musicians or novelty acts that really gave Dad the tools he needed to survive show business's vagaries and quieter moments later in life. When I was growing up, if he wasn't working full time as a writer on a radio or TV show, he was speaking after dinner at a charity function, providing warm-up for other shows, playing chairman at old-time music hall or appearing on panel games such as *Blankety Blank* or *Punchlines*. A lot of this diversity was fostered during the time he worked on revue shows. However, he wouldn't allow himself to be classed as a Renaissance man or a polymath, as that would again be seen as too pretentious. His line when tackling his adaptability would be 'I'm not versatile, just confused'.

It reminds me of a story he told me of a gig he did in the nineties called *Keillor & Company*. Dad was guesting alongside Elisabeth Welch, the American singer who made Britain her home. Eponymously headlining the show was US radio stalwart, Garrison Keillor, most famous as the author of *Lake Wobegon Days* and the creator of American Public Radio's *A Prairie Home Companion*, where he used to sing, deliver monologues and appear in sketches.

In those respects, he was a man after my father's heart and cut from similar cloth. During the evening, just as Keillor was coming to the end of a song and demonstrated his versatility by launching straight into a monologue to a loving audience, Dad purred to Welch about Keillor's talent. Welch leaned in and said, 'If he starts dancing, I'm going home.'

Before I started writing this book, I'm not sure I'd appreciated just how ubiquitous the tradition of revue was in the London of the late fifties and early sixties. The bar was set in 1959 by Peter Cook, then just twenty-one and barely out of short trousers with the Cambridge Footlights. His revue, *Pieces of Eight*, came to the Apollo Theatre in September of that year. A measure of the show's credentials, and Cook's standing, sees additional material for *Pieces of Eight* come from none other than Harold Pinter. Music was provided by Sandy Wilson, already a West End success due to his musical *The Boyfriend*. The cast were no slouches either, with Kenneth Williams and Fenella Fielding among the company.

The *Evening News* said that *One Over The Eight* was 'Scandalously funny', while the *Evening Standard* said it was 'Snappy and gay'. Yet, one thing was for certain, because of the precociously prodigious impact of Peter Cook (and others) revue had now drawn blood and the theatre-going public seemed to like the taste. As Dad sharpened his pencil, ready to deliver his own satiric barbs, he was to discover that the vogue for iconoclasm was difficult to keep up with. It was a daunting arena he was stepping into.

The West End revue that kicked things off for him was *And Another Thing...*, written by Ted Dicks and Myles Rudge, at the Fortune Theatre in the West End. They'd had a modest success there with a previous revue called *Look Who's Here* in 1959 (with some sketches written by future friends of Dad's, Barry Took and Dick Vosburgh) and assembled much of the same cast, including long-time collaborators Donald Hewlett and Dennis Wood. Dennis and his partner Ronnie Barnes remained friends with Mum and Dad for many years, with Ronnie eventually taking up residence in the flat next door to our house in the suburbs of north-west London. I saw a lot of them growing up. Dennis was a tremendously energetic and charismatically fun presence, with Ronnie his witty, urbane and droll foil. I remember them both fondly, mainly because they kept Mum and Dad laughing, singing and reminiscing. The song 'If' ('in B Flat' Dad would always add immediately afterwards) was a particular favourite. The last line 'You're not sick… you're just IN LURVE!' was belted out at many a sun-kissed garden barbecue.

Dad finishing dinner in style with great friends Dennis Wood (l) and Ronnie Barnes (r) in the late 60s. The brandy and Coke years didn't last long.

A pre-*Forsyte Saga* Nyree Dawn Porter was also in *Look Who's Here*, as was another young actress called Anna Quayle, who's perhaps best remembered now for her role in *Chitty Chitty Bang Bang*. Dad and Anna had become acquainted through mutual friends, and it was she who suggested Ted look at some of Dad's material for *And Another Thing...* The show ran from 6 October 1960 to 6 May 1961, and Anna was now joined by Bernard Cribbins, Sandra Caron (Alma Cogan's sister), Joyce Blair (Lionel's sister) Anton Rodgers (nobody's sister), Lionel Blair (Joyce's brother) and Penny Newington. Some of the material had to be altered when Cribbins was forced to play the early performances from a wheelchair due to a foot injury. Bernard Cribbins was clearly no stranger to this kind of mishap as he also managed to fall over leaving Dad's funeral in 2022. There was an audible gasp of concern from friends and family gathered in the Crematorium Rose Garden afterwards as the ninety-three-year-old Bernard took a tumble. This was followed by an equally audible gasp of amazement when the veteran actor simply rolled over and got back up again. His friend, John Radford, who had kindly escorted him that day, said that Bernard merely dusted himself down, straightened up and proudly boasted: 'National Service paratrooper training. Never leaves you.'

Although *And Another Thing...* wasn't a hit for Dicks and Rudge, it did spark a culturally significant and unexpected spin-off for Bernard. Future Beatles producer Sir George Martin liked him in the show and invited him to record 'Folk Song', one of Dicks and Rudges's songs from the second act. Martin also commissioned them to write two more comic songs for Cribbins. They were 'The Hole in the Ground' and 'Right Said Fred'. A new bowstring created for Bernard and, rather surprisingly, a new band name beckoned for a baldy pair of nineties pop brothers. This branching out into life as a recording artist is one of the many things that Dad and Bernard had in common and one of the reasons they felt such a kinship.

I'd only ever been told (usually by Dad himself) that his contribution to that revue had been a couple of sketches tucked away in the 'additional material' credits. However, when I eventually managed to get hold of a Fortune Theatre programme, it became clear that it was a little more than that. Of the twenty or so sketches and songs, eight are written by Dad. A solid contribution from a twenty-five-year-old comic turned singer in his first proper outing as a writer. Anna Quayle's intervention and recommendation had given Dad quite a harvest. He'd also acquired a useful ally in Ted Dicks.

According to Bernard Cribbins, one of the sketches Dad wrote for the show involved Anton, Sandra and himself sitting watching tennis. Imaginatively entitled 'Wimbledon', the sketch opened with the familiar scene of spectators moving their heads from side to side, engrossed in a rally. Only Bernard is slightly out of time. With each shot, he's looking in the opposite direction to the other two. The sketch develops when Anton spots Bernard doing this halfway through and becomes increasingly irritated. The three all carry on watching the tennis, but Anton's anger is now visibly rising. Eventually, he gives in and demands to know what Bernard is up to. Bernard slackens his jaw and with those big doleful eyes stares innocently back: 'I came in late.' It always got a big laugh, but according to Bernard, the laugh was always a beat or two after the blackout.

It's a good, solid visual gag with a nice conceptual twist. I can also see how this joke would work well at the Fortune Theatre, as these subtler actions could be seen by a small theatre audience, but on TV and in close-up, they'd land even more strongly. Perhaps it's no surprise that the material Dad supplied for *And Another Thing...* was written at the same time as he was submitting visual-gag-heavy TV material for *The Jimmy Logan Show*. In many ways, this sketch is like one Dad and Bernard used to do on *The Good Old Days* around a decade and a half later. Dad would come on in a brightly coloured shirt with ruffled sleeves, carrying hoops and clubs, and jump around excitedly to up-tempo Spanish music from the band. He'd throw a hoop and then a club and so on until they'd all been thrown and the music finishes. Bernard walks on. 'You're late,' says Dad with a face like thunder. They called themselves *Los Brillos*, as they both had similar grey/black curly hair like a Brillo pad.

Dad was concerned for Bernard Cribbins in the year following the death of his wife, Gillian, in 2021. He was particularly worried about his friend being on his own in his flat in Surrey: the old soldier left to soldier on alone. Dad made quite a few phone calls during that time, to agents, friends and then to Bernard himself, keen to make a difference. 'Just checking in,' he'd say, before launching into a joke. Ultimately, he was just making sure he was being looked after, even if the looking after was done by Bernard himself.

The two adored each other. Their partnership on *The Good Old Days* in the seventies and eighties was as close as either man got to forming a conventional double act. Their understanding of each other's rhythms was innate and it's only sad that they didn't get to perform together more. Bernie Clifton said that there was a running joke between the three of them that they should pitch a show called 'BC' to the BBC. As a running joke, they would add names to the cast-list like Brian Conley, Bob Carolgees, Billy Connolly and Brian Cant each time they met up. Bobby Crush on piano. Dad eventually said he knew the show was dead in the water when Barbara Cartland said she couldn't do it. It is a great regret of mine that we never got Bernard to guest on the podcast *Now Where Were We?*, which Dad and I started in 2021. What that conversation yielded would've been one for the ages. Bernard was lined up, ready to do it, but sadly ill health intervened. Of course, what we didn't know then, for all Dad's concern about Bernard, was that my father would die first. Bernard left us six months later, in July 2022.

Dad followed on from *And Another Thing...* in 1960, with a single sketch contribution to another revue called *On the Brighter Side* which debuted at the Phoenix. Firstly, it marks the first time he wrote for Ronnie Barker. That would have been reason enough to celebrate for the twenty-five-year-old novice writer, as Ronnie was making a name for himself on *The Navy Lark*. However, little did Dad know how pivotal that relationship would become, both professionally and personally. Secondly, the sketch, called 'Clubs', featured Stanley Baxter (effectively the star of the revue) and a pre-*Summer Holiday* Una Stubbs. Given the quality of performers, this was a big test of the strength of Dad's material and while, sadly, I haven't been able to find a copy of the sketch, *On the Brighter Side* was generally well received.

Perhaps the most pivotal connection to come from this show was that it was devised and directed by Jimmy Gilbert. It wasn't long after this revue that Gilbert started producing shows for the BBC, including several of the now infamous Comedy Playhouse anthology series of pilot sitcoms that gave us *Steptoe and Son, Till Death Us Do Part, The Liver Birds, Up Pompeii!, Are You Being Served?* and *Last of the Summer Wine.* As BBC Head of Comedy in the seventies, Gilbert oversaw the introduction of *Whatever Happened to the Likely Lads?, Fawlty Towers, The Fall and Rise of Reginald Perrin* and *The Good Life.*

Most significantly for Dad, though, he would go on to co-create *The Frost Report* in 1966. Dad was to be one of that show's remarkable intake of comedy writers. Jimmy's producing style allowed for experimentation, which Dad loved, and Jimmy rewarded this by placing great trust in the writers that he nurtured. Getting a script in front of him in 1961 for *On The Brighter Side* was a smart move, even if Dad didn't know it yet. He was in good company too, as other writers included people like Brad Ashton, Kenneth Williams, Johnny Speight and Spike Milligan. There was additional music from Vivian Ellis, whose musical *Bless The Bride* ten years earlier had included a young Terry Donovan (soon to be Mrs Cryer) in its touring cast.

And Another Thing… and *On The Brighter Side* were as traditional as British revues could get at that time, in the sense that their satirical targets were rather playfully dealt with. As I mentioned earlier, by 1961, the zeitgeist demanded that you skewer your targets, not just ruffle their hair. In *And Another Thing…*, for instance, the quarry that came in for gentle scrutiny were drama critics, the West End, Soho strip clubs, TV dance contests and *Lolita.* Not exactly subjects to rattle cages. Once those revues had finished their run, God was still in his heaven, the government remained in place, and national institutions were resolutely uncrumbled. There was honey still for tea.

It's rather unfortunate for the legacy of *And Another Thing…* that it was staged at the Fortune Theatre, as by the time it finished its run, the theatre was readying itself to welcome a new satirical show. One that had a little more bite to it and combined the burgeoning comic talents of Oxford and Cambridge Universities. It had taken the Edinburgh Festival by storm the previous year and was called *Beyond The Fringe*. The cast was Dudley Moore, Jonathan Miller, Alan Bennett and, perhaps inevitably, Peter Cook. The establishment now had a little more cause to look over its shoulder at the West End, while other revues were judged in comparison, including Dad's contribution to *And Another Thing...* *Beyond The Fringe* began a period for Dad of anticipating the storm and attempting to find anything to cling to for safety. This was an existential threat.

When Peter Cook opened London's first satirical nightclub in 1961, he ironically called it the Establishment. Cook said its inspiration was to honour 'those wonderful Berlin cabarets which did so much to stop the rise of Hitler and prevent the outbreak of the Second World War'. Cook was even satirical when defining satire. He clearly loved the genre but felt it had no lasting power and ultimately, made no difference. Maybe there was some truth in that, but it didn't diminish Cook's impact on national life, especially on those writers and performers who sought to emulate his example.

So it was perhaps with trepidation that Dad took the chance in 1963 to write his own revue. Having become friends with Ted Dicks and with his encouragement, Dad came up with *See You Inside*. With director Charles Ross, he assembled a cast that included Jon Pertwee, Hugh Paddick, Moira Lister and Amanda Barrie. Ted was on hand to provide the music.

Somewhat tellingly, the show began with a rather meta-theatrical speech by a compère, about revues in general and what *See You Inside* might be striving to be. For someone who hated analysing comedy, this foray into self-consciousness might be as much about Dad's fear of stepping onto the ice, as it is about his desire to be like Peter Cook. Dad was never controversial by nature but a sketch he wrote about Jackie Kennedy discussing her husband's job did make it seem as if he was prepared to be a little edgier. It got cut on the orders of the Lord Chamberlain. Apparently, foreign heads of state could not be mentioned in British theatre shows for fear they might be embarrassed. It's incredible to think that the Lord

Chambelain was still in control of licensing and censoring stage performances until as late as 1968. However, the publicity for the show was welcome:

> Actress Moira Lister has been banned by the Lord Chamberlain from playing Jackie Kennedy in a new Revue. She was to take-off America's First Lady in *See You Inside*, by 28-year-old Barry Cryer. The Revue opens in Liverpool on October 22 and is due in the West End next month. In a sketch called 'House Warming', Miss Lister was to have played Mrs Kennedy showing the White House to millions of visitors with the help of Telstar. But yesterday a terse note arrived from the Lord Chamberlain's office telling producer Charles Ross: 'This is to be omitted.' Said Miss Lister, flashing a Jackie-type smile: 'I have been practising my expressions so hard. This was going to be a big chance for me. This is my first proper Revue, and this particular sketch was my favourite. I'd worked hard at it. And all for nothing. I don't see why it should be banned. There's nothing defamatory about it. It's a bit sharp but it's all good, clean, fun.'

I managed to find some lines from the sketch:

> 'Caroline, darling, go and play with your ICBM. You know, the toy your daddy bought you. I know pressing buttons is a drag, but you've got to learn sometime.'

> 'Jack's father once asked him what he wanted to do, and he said: "I want to be President, Pop," and his dad said: "No, I mean when you grow up."'

> 'Jack couldn't be here tonight. He's gone to a reception at the Cuban Embassy. He's sure to get quite a reception. Twenty-two guns, they told me.'

> 'To the watching millions out there, just stick your noses into every little old nook and cranny – that's democracy!'

That's a lovely blend of straightforwardly satirical (that's democracy!), old jokes (when you grow up), daringly political (intercontinental ballistic missiles!) and bizarrely prophetic (twenty-two guns). It shows a real maturing of Dad's ability to cover more than one satirical base. Perhaps two years of writing for Danny La Rue's cabarets (which we'll come on to) had honed his instinct for the political jugular. It was only a shame that this material never made it to the final show, although knowing Dad, he'd have squirrelled some of those lines for a later date (I use the 'when you grow up' one myself, about being an actor). Had this sketch made the final show, the reviews might have been kinder to the show in general. But, as he shows in this interview, also from the *Daily Mail* (where he's described as 'former Windmill comic and pop-singer') Dad was sanguine about things: 'I can't say I'm really surprised at the ban. This was a bit of a test case in its way. Now there's a new man in the chair [Lord Cobbold had recently been made Lord Chamberlain] we're trying to find out exactly what the policy is.'

High praise did come for a running sketch that made the cut, in which Moira Lister tries unsuccessfully to launch a ship with a champagne bottle. Each time we return to her, the bottle bounces back off the ship and into her hand. Later, she begins drinking from the bottle and by the end she's become so drunk that she just gives up and says: 'Well, if I can't launch the ship, then at least it can launch me!'

Overall, the whole revue was considered a little old-fashioned. Between *And Another Thing…* closing and *See You Inside* opening, *Beyond The Fringe* and *That Was The Week That Was* had moved the goalposts in terms of what people demanded from political sketch writing. A further dip into the review archives does confirm the adverse reactions but they also reveal some sizeable crumbs of comfort:

See You Inside, the new Revue at the Duchess … The show is extremely uneven. An idea begins to blossom, then fails; the wit

flickers, rarely shines; novelty turns out to be familiar stuff. The
mixture of straight Revue material, of the sort that has made
this type of production often so successful in the West End,
is mixed with the current form of political satire and macabre
humour. Neither hits the mark firmly or often enough… Barry
Cryer, who wrote much of the material, obviously thinks that
to drop a famous name is enough: you must laugh at that,
without rhyme or reason. His vision is limited, rather stuck
in the nightclub category, where, of course, almost anything
goes, and the patrons are among the most unsophisticated in
the world.

Stage

See You Inside is a first effort at Revue by Barry Cryer, who
has given us some amusing things to laugh at but who plainly
needs more experience at this type of work before he can make
a perfect product.

Birmingham Daily Post

Spotting new talent in the theatre is always fascinating, and
there are two good reasons for seeing the Revue *See You Inside*
at the Duchess, disappointing though it is as a show. First,
there is twenty seven year-old Barry Cryer, from Leeds, who
wrote most of it. He has an undoubted talent and is full of
ideas; we shall be hearing more of him. His weakness on
this showing is that he is not sharp enough; some of his best
sketches drag on. He badly needs directing, but his is the most
inventive new mind in the realm of Revue since the astonishing
Peter Cook, or anyway Ted Dicks.

Unknown

This collection of reviews was kept stapled together in Mum and
Dad's clippings book. The quantity of them easily outweighs any
other show that he'd been involved in. Dad was by no means
meticulous in his archiving, so this might be an anomaly but
I think it's significant. His name was above the title, and perhaps

this humbling event convinced him he couldn't write alone. I think he may also have kept these reviews as a reminder of his mother's warning to 'not get too big for your boots'. In short, it seems like a pivotal moment for Dad. He's at a crossroads as a writer, searching for his 'voice' while trying to keep up with fashion. As the final review above states: 'His is the most inventive new mind in the realm of Revue since the astonishing Peter Cook, or anyway Ted Dicks.' Clearly, all was not lost but the next two years would be very turbulent for Dad. Does young Barry double down with traditional nightclub humour or attempt to pursue a more contemporary relevance? Tune in next week to find out!

A man goes into a pub and says to the landlord: 'If you give me free drinks, I will entertain your customers so much they will stay all night.'

The man gets a hamster out of his pocket and puts it on the piano. The hamster runs up and down the keyboard playing the greatest piano music anyone has ever heard. 'That's incredible!' says the landlord. 'Have you got anything else?'

The man gets a parrot out of his other pocket and puts it on the bar. The hamster begins to play the piano again and the parrot sings along – sounding just like Pavarotti. Everyone in the bar is amazed and they stay all night drinking, listening to the hamster and parrot.

The landlord is obviously delighted. 'I must have these animals. Will you sell them to me?' he asks. The man shakes his head.

'Will you sell just one then?' asks the landlord.

'OK, I'll sell you the parrot for a hundred pounds,' the man says. The landlord is delighted and hands over the money.

Another man comes up to him outside and says: 'You're a bit stupid selling that singing parrot for only a hundred pounds.'

'No, I'm not,' the man replies. 'The hamster's a ventriloquist.'

6

If I had to choose one moment that I felt distilled Dad's creative spirit and perfectly explains why he was going to be a success, then it must be his audition for the musical *Expresso Bongo* in 1958. Based on a story by Wolf Mankowitz, it was a pop music industry satire that was turned into a film, starring Laurence Harvey and Cliff Richard. It was Dad's first musical theatre audition and as he didn't really know what to do, he decided to write a song in his bedsit the night before. The next morning, he hired some bongos (by the hour) from a shop in Denmark Street, went up on stage and sang his song while bashing away on an instrument he'd never played before. 'Kid from the back street with the crazy beat' was its main lyric, apparently. This naive twenty-three-year-old with no previous experience of musical theatre also chose to call his song 'Expresso Bongo'. Composer Monty Norman (the man who was about to write the 'Bond' theme) rushed up on stage to stop Dad before he left.

'Where did you get that song?' said Monty.

'I wrote it,' said Dad.

'Thank goodness for that,' said Monty. 'I thought we might get sued.'

He got the part, but he looked back on that act of bravado with both bewilderment and no small amount of embarrassment. He thought it was blind panic. However, I think it is a great tactic for an audition. He made a bold choice, risked failure and it paid off. The previous year saw Dad become a comedian, a sketch writer, a singer and now... a dancer?

Julie Musgrove was a very tall woman who was partnered with Dad in a group dance scene. Dad had to pick Julie up at one point in a routine and couldn't quite manage it. The mirth that greeted his attempts didn't spare the blushes of either Dad or Julie and director William Chappell decided to alter the blocking. Dad was playing 'Beast', the leader of a skiffle group, and it didn't really work to have him struggling at the side of the stage wincing if his back gave out. Chappell had him posturing and glowering instead.

The lead, Paul Scofield, found it very amusing. The renowned film and theatre actor had never done a musical before and treated the whole experience as a surreal interlude in an otherwise traditional career. Dad and he got on well. It became an important friendship at a time when Dad started to see a return of his eczema. In celebrity columnist Peter Jones's *The Star and The Up-Comers* section, the headlines had become personal, rather than professional.

BAD LUCK FOR BARRY AGAIN...

YET another bad stroke of luck has hit the promising young singer-comedian Barry Cryer. And, as before, it has hit him bang in the middle of a most important part of his career. It started with the West End version of *Expresso Bongo*. Barry was playing 'Beast' at the Saville Theatre when he was taken ill and forced to spend several weeks in hospital at his hometown, Leeds ...

Then, during the week at Glasgow, Barry was again taken ill. He went to the Western Infirmary (Ward D.1) at Glasgow and was there for a couple of weeks. Particularly hard to take was the fact that the show went on last week, to Leeds, his hometown, and he was looking forward very much to this date with his family. In addition, Frankie Vaughan and his wife Stella were going to be there for part of the week ...

Welcome back – and good health, Barry.

As a child, I remember seeing some of the old stage make-up he kept in a round biscuit tin in his chest of drawers. Being the frugal man that he was, much of it probably dated from *Expresso Bongo* but he still used it from time to time. I remember thinking that the heavy waxy layers could not have been much of a balm during the episodes detailed above. All very different from the light, hypoallergenic stuff we use today. Dad didn't talk to me much about his eczema and I never really knew how he felt about the times it interrupted his career, even when I had my own outbreak, aged twenty. Imagine my surprise when I pulled out the following clipping from Mum and Dad's archive. It's a letter Dad wrote to the *Yorkshire Post* written in 1955 during a stay in a hospital. Dad was also twenty.

> Barry Cryer (St James's Hospital, Leeds): I was delighted to hear the question of skin trouble, allergy and the consequent effect of strains and stresses on the body discussed on the radio. For too long such complaints as dermatitis, eczema and psoriasis have remained taboo as topics of public discussion. At long last they have been brought into the limelight, and the thousands of sufferers who know the pain, inconvenience and embarrassment of such diseases can gain hope from such progress and the advent, for instance, of cortisone. Our modern world, with its nervous tension, inevitably produces physical reaction of which the skin is often the most prominent indicator. Total cure is impossible at present but further research particularly in psychiatric fields may ease this much under-estimated burden.

It is a measured response to a subject that was clearly not just on his mind, but also on his body and a long way from the older man I described in Chapter 4 as being disconnected from his body. I then found another letter, this time from April 1954 (he'd only just turned nineteen). It has a quite surprising target:

> B.C. (Leeds 8): In the last edition of *The Goon Show* I was shocked and disgusted to hear a joke about eczema, of all

subjects, greeted with a gale of laughter. As a confirmed
admirer of the inspired lunacy of these brilliant radio
comedians, I was amazed that such a distasteful jibe was passed
by the BBC. What next? Hilarious sketches about the blind
and cancer sufferers? If the Goons have run out of material let
them give their show a well-earned rest instead of scraping the
bottom of the barrel by sneering at those ill-fitted to retaliate.
The 'bad language' which offended an earlier correspondent is
debatable – bad taste is unforgivable.

It's hard to disagree and it points to an attitude to comedy that he
retained to the end, particularly the line about 'sneering at those
ill-fitted to retaliate'. Although he was famous for welcoming all
genres and types of comedy, Dad often drew the line when he saw
mean-spirited comedians 'punching down' on their subjects. In a
later interview, while talking about differences between radio and
TV, you can read between the lines to see his suffering from eczema
as influencing his opinion: 'In a way I prefer radio. There is no
make-up, no cameras, and you don't even have to learn anything –
you are either reading your script or ad-libbing (if it is a game
show). I hate watching myself on television. I usually do, but it
is a painful experience. You're more critical of yourself than other
people would be. Everything seems wrong, and whenever you see
yourself, you want to do it again.'

When Dad returned to the *Expresso Bongo* tour, Paul Scofield
was key in helping him settle again. The star's dressing-room
door was always open and his catchphrase, if you passed by, was
'Don't say hello, then'. Dad learnt a lot from the humility, quiet
authority and leadership Paul communicated to the company.
After all, this was an ensemble that also contained some strong
characters in Millicent Martin (replaced on tour by a very young
Jill Gascoine), Susan Hampshire, Trevor Griffiths and Victor
Spinetti, yet no one was ever in doubt whose name was selling
tickets. Scofield used to walk about with his script all the way
through rehearsals and the younger actors were worried that he
hadn't learnt his lines. Scofield told Dad that the reason he kept

it with him, was that you should never put a script away, even once you've learnt it, as there were always new discoveries to make. He kept the script open in the dressing room during the run for this purpose.

When *Expresso Bongo* opened in Newcastle, Scofield was obviously word-perfect, but there was still room for a little improvisation. There was a scene where he went into Millicent Martin's house and on tour, the door was built into a flat (that bit of scenery that creates a wall and uses weights to hold it still). On the opening night, Paul came through the door, kicked it shut behind him and the whole flat fell over with a crash, Scofield just managing to pull Millicent to safety and dust rose in front of the audience in the style of a Road Runner cartoon. Everyone could now see the back wall of the theatre. A terrible silence. Paul Scofield looked around at the damage and said 'Mice'. This perfectly illustrates his mischievous sense of humour and I think that's probably why he and Dad bonded. There's a theatre legend that claims that, during a tour of *Hamlet* in Moscow, he got so bored with the sound of all the earnest students in the audience turning the pages of their textbooks during one of his soliloquies, that he listed all the stations of the Northern Line instead. From Kennington to Edgware.

Dad's character, 'Beast', had to wear a kipper tie that was covered in palm trees. To delight Paul, Dad found out where the wardrobe was getting their ties from and went out to buy some more of his own. One night, Dad walked into his scene with Scofield wearing a new tie with a nude woman on. Scofield took one look at Dad's tie and squeezed 'What the fuck is that?' out of the side of his mouth.

The following year Dad was walking down South Street Avenue in Mayfair and bumped into Paul Scofield on his way to work. 'Don't say hello, then,' Dad said. He asked him what he was doing and Scofield said that he was in *The Potting Shed* by Graham Greene, which, as a dark psychological drama, was about as far away from *Expresso Bongo* as you can get. 'What's it like?' Dad asked. 'Oh Barry, no fucking overture.'

SAVILLE THEATRE

BY ARRANGEMENT WITH S.T.P. (THEATRES) LTD

OSCAR LEWENSTEIN and NEIL CRAWFORD
(for Oscar Lewenstein Ltd.)   (for Strand Productions Ltd.)
PRESENT

PAUL SCOFIELD

IN

EXPRESSO BONGO

A MUSICAL PLAY

From an original story by Wolf Mankowitz

Book by Wolf Mankowitz and Julian More

Music by David Heneker and Monty Norman

Lyrics by Julian More, David Heneker and Monty Norman

DIRECTED BY
WILLIAM CHAPPELL

Decor by
LOUDON SAINTHILL

Orchestrations by
TONY OSBORNE

6 D.

Expresso Bongo programme, 1958. Dad played 'Beast', the leader of a skiffle group.
Lock up your bongos…

The great Paul Scofield in Expresso Bongo. *'Don't say hello then.'*

Expresso Bongo left Dad on a high and feeling good at the start of 1959, having forged a new career despite the brief interruption and eruption of his eczema. He even booked a stint singing at the Café de Paris earning a hundred pounds a week. As the Café de Paris was a more straightforward music nightclub, he wasn't even having to tell jokes. A TV appearance on ABC's *Bid For Fame* followed, where one of the panel picked him out as a future star. This was now enough to convince producers in Blackpool to give him a summer season and, when he returned to London, he was straight back to work as an actor in a new musical called *The Quiz Kid*. In terms of Dad's creative development, the musical was described by

Jimmy Logan pictured with Vera Lynn and her manager Leslie MacDonald in 1960, the year Jimmy helped Dad begin his career as a TV writer.

the *Stage* as 'amateurish, but enjoyable', which is about as good a description of Dad's professional style as I've heard.

He was on the up and looking forward to his next challenge. However, the winter of 1959 saw his eczema return, perhaps because of his frenetic work schedule. It stopped him in his tracks and resulted in him spending a very miserable Christmas Day in hospital in Barnet. He was on his own, wrapped up in bandages rather like the Invisible Man. Denis King, who was on the bill with him in Dublin the previous year and had become a friend, visited with his family and brought some gifts, cards and, as he put it, 'most importantly cigarettes'. Dad never forgot that generosity and when Denis was a guest on Dad's *This Is Your Life* in 1995, he was asked to tell that story to Michael Aspel. It was a rather moving perspective on a troubling time.

His inability to perform meant Dad was now spending more time writing, mainly because it was the only way he could see of making a living. The natural aptitude he'd shown in revue for small-scale sketch comedy meant that the move from stage to TV was an obvious one. He just needed a catalyst to give him momentum again and that came from an unlikely and unfortunate intervention.

By 1960, Dad was living in a bedsit on Kildare Terrace, Bayswater, West London. We have a saying among the family that Dad had a 'bedsit mentality', which is to say that he was frugal in most things and didn't allow for anything resembling an extravagance. His domestic habits didn't really change much for the rest of his life and, ultimately, Dad didn't need or want much, aside from his family, friends and work. So long as there was a radio, a pen, a packet of Consulate cigarettes, a typewriter, a copy of the *Evening Standard*, salted snacks, a pub and a train station nearby, he was generally happy. At this point, however, his performing career had all but disappeared, though his eczema hadn't. He was starting to get quite low. Ted Dicks' revue *And Another Thing...* was still lurking in the background, but there was no other work coming in.

After Dad died, I talked to Mum about his battle with eczema, and she mentioned an incident during this period that I'd not heard before. Another tenant in his block who Dad had made friends with, Douglas Camfield, had said that he once smelled gas coming from Dad's flat and rushed downstairs to turn it off. Dad told Mum that he was so depressed by the state of his skin and its effect on his career that he'd 'experimented' with the thought of taking his own life. I prefer not to speculate on how close he came to this resolution, but he was asleep and Douglas's abrupt entry woke him up.

He, understandably, kept this fact from us as a family, but rather than feel shocked at this revelation, it only deepens my respect for my father's resolve and resilience in the face of such adversity. He was twenty-five, living far away from home and plying his trade in an uncertain profession while struggling with a skin disease.

Whether or not Dad intended to go through with his plan doesn't matter to me. What matters is that he bounced back from this moment. But the intervention of Douglas Camfield needs to be acknowledged properly and although he is no longer with us, I'd like to salute him. The incident proved to be a turning point both personally and professionally. Douglas, who worked in TV, realised Dad needed something to focus on and suggested they write some sketches together.

Although originally born in India, Douglas had some Yorkshire credentials, having studied at the York School of Art and served in the West Yorkshire Regiment of the Territorial Army. It may have been this that initially bonded the two young men, but it was a shared love of quick, punchy visual comedy that persuaded them to write together. Douglas hadn't dreamed of being a TV writer, he was hoping to be in the SAS, but an injury led him to look around for slightly less dangerous work. This sense of being trapped by a condition may also have drawn them together.

Douglas, who was working as a floor manager for the BBC at the time he met Dad, knew that *The Jimmy Logan Show* needed material. Jimmy, a great Scottish comedian (and friend of Stanley Baxter, who Dad would go on to write for), was a perfect choice for Dad, as he had a music-hall style but with a down-to-earth manner. The first series had been filmed in Scotland but with the second planned for the Riverside Studios in London, Jimmy was looking for some fresh English talent. All four of their scripts were accepted and suddenly, Barry Cryer was a television writer.

The moment was significant for Douglas too, as the Riverside Studios were where *Doctor Who* was to be filmed and where Douglas would ended up directing. It also brought Dad and Douglas into contact with soon-to-be *Doctor Who* writer Terry Nation. Terry was represented by Associated London Scripts (ALS), the famous writers' cooperative set up by Spike Milligan and Eric Sykes in the mid-1950s, that also included Galton and Simpson and Johnny Speight. Many people assume that Dad was part of that collective in the early years, given his close ties with many of the main protagonists, but working on *The Jimmy Logan Show* was probably the first time he'd encountered many of their clients.

Their most famous, Tony Hancock, was about to provide Dad with his next professional opportunity. Hancock writers Ray Galton and Alan Simpson were a huge part of Tony's success, but incredibly Tony felt he could do better on his own. Tony's brother, Roger, who'd gone from stage management to being an agent at ALS, set up his own agency to accommodate the move. Dad joined Roger soon after (on a handshake) and remained with the Roger Hancock agency until the end of his life. Jimmy Perry and David Croft, Willie Rushton, various Pythons, Goodies and much later David Renwick, were all on the Hancock books at various points. Terry Nation also joined Roger just after the agency was set up, and Hancock was largely responsible for engineering Terry a merchandising deal (for his creation of the Daleks) that proved to be very lucrative.

Dennis Spooner was another Jimmy Logan writer who went on to help establish *Doctor Who*. Dennis ended up living four doors down from us in Hatch End and he and Dad became good friends. Dennis even once arranged to have lunch with Boris Karloff and invited Dad to join them. Dad was a huge fan of Karloff's but sadly, the lunch never happened. Boris was taken ill and died a few days later, although I understand that Dad and Dennis didn't take it personally.

When you look at the other writers Jimmy Logan recruited, people like John Junkin, Brad Ashton and Dick Vosburgh, you can start to see a pattern of potential writing partners emerging for Dad. However, as we've seen, the reason Dad was writing at all was down to eczema making it difficult for him to perform. The fact that he made a success of writing was testament to his resilience to the disease and a tribute to his strength of character. Along with a bout of depression, he'd taken a potentially debilitating moment in his life and turned it into not just a second career, but also one that would eventually come to define him. Once again Dad had taken a new professional opportunity with alacrity and turned it into something meaningful. It's worth retracing our steps at this point in our journey to go back to the Ted Dicks revue *And Another Thing...* One night, West End legend Danny La Rue came in to see the show. He was in the market for new writers for his residency at Winston's nightclub and asked Dad and Ted to join the team. It was to be a pivotal move as it was the job that saw him perform again and subsequently introduced him to a woman who would change his life.

A man in a hospital gown and a drip on wheels walks into a pub. He orders a double whisky, which the barman gives him. The man drinks it all. 'I shouldn't be having this with what I've got.'

'What have you got?' asks the barman.

'Fifty pence.'

7

Dad and Ted Dicks started work with Danny on the revue *This Is Your Night Life* at Winston's nightclub in the spring of 1961 and when they arrived at rehearsal, it was to see a tall, striking redhead standing at the piano going through some warm-ups. Her name was Terry Donovan and she, like them, was new to the club. Ted Dicks quickly took a shine to Mum but was disappointed to learn that she was seeing Lonnie Donegan's guitarist Les Bennetts. That relationship was a legacy of Mum's role as Prince Charming in *Cinderella* at the Nottingham Theatre Royal the previous winter, where Lonnie was playing Buttons and his band, including Les, was drafted into the cast to play various smaller roles.

It was here that Mum first met Danny, who was playing one of the Ugly Sisters. Bryan Blackburn had written Danny's revue (and would go on to write many other Danny projects) but was unavailable for this one. The company the previous year had included a young comedian called Ronnie Corbett and singer and dancer Ann Hart was there too, who'd go on to be Ronnie's wife. The most repeated line of Dad's about his relationship with Mum was: 'I met my wife and Ronnie Corbett on the same day. I tossed a coin… and married her instead.'

Danny had been in residence at Winston's since 1957 and had managed to push the style of nightclub revue at Winston's towards the vogue for the more satirical, but as far as his patrons were concerned, it was never at the expense of the sophisticated filth they'd been used to. Each revue ran for three months before Danny refreshed the show, which just meant putting some of the older jokes in a different order.

The most important thing to remember when taking on a nightclub job in the 1960s is that these shows usually started at 12.45 a.m., meaning they often finished around 3 a.m. Almost all the performers, including Danny, had jobs in other West End shows and came to Winston's afterwards. When you consider that the nightclub shows refreshed every three months too and therefore needed regular rehearsing (at 11 a.m.) then you can see just how intense this lifestyle was. You had to commit to it wholeheartedly and both Mum and Dad took a huge amount of pleasure in belonging to what they felt was a very special community of people. Now in his late twenties and with a 'scene' to call his home, Dad was beginning to move on from the disappointment of *See You Inside*.

As a freelance performer, becoming part of a new cast can feel like gaining a second family and when a show is also tied to a location it can add some security. When my parents lived in Maida Vale in west London, they would cycle everywhere, to Danny's rehearsal, and then afterwards Mum would often go off to her show in the West End, or Dad to the Players' Theatre. Then they would go back to the club at around 11 p.m. to start all over again. Danny was the mentor or 'mother figure' at the heart of it all. Dad said that he was a tremendously loyal and supportive man, whose criticism, though direct, wasn't harsh and was usually constructive because he was a good listener. Danny's greatest skill as a producer was being decisive in terms of tone or running order in an environment that was often chaotic. Nightclubs reacquainted Dad with a kind of heckling and distraction he'd not experienced since the Windmill.

Born Daniel Patrick Carroll in Cork in 1927, Danny and his widowed mother moved to London when he was nine and they were evacuated to Devon during the war. Towards the end of the conflict, Danny joined the Royal Navy and it was here that he began to take part in concert parties. One thing that he and Dad shared was a period working backstage at a theatre, which is what Danny did in Exeter after touring the Far East with an all-male revue. It was pantomime that really allowed him the platform to fix his persona, elevating the cross-dressing dame from a figure of fun and mockery into something altogether more authentically feminine. Danny hated the term 'drag', preferring 'female impersonator' instead, as he dressed, groomed and styled himself not to exaggerate but to imitate. However, the duality at the heart of the persona was never far from the surface. He used to open his act with a deep bass holler of 'Wotcha mates!' before fixing his smile and parading around the stage with full regal elegance. He'd then lock eyes with a man in the front row and say 'I know what you're thinking. I've been doing this long enough that I just whistle and it goes away on its own.'

The careful balance between the sacred and the profane was not the only sign that he was an Irish Catholic, because he also kept a shrine to the Virgin Mary next to his 'falsies' in the dressing room. This balance between respectability and depravity was a carefully trodden path and Dad loved the challenge of capturing that on stage. Like a lot of his writing and performing, it's that magic moment when an audience sees that something is falling apart. The atmosphere created was of a party and the material veered from the knock-knock joke, via nursery rhymes and parodies, to satirical sketches with sharp edges. It was a real mix of influences and styles that suited Dad's meandering 'butterfly' brain. Once Dad's eczema had improved, he started providing warm-up for the evening as well.

It is easy to dismiss Danny La Rue as an eccentric curiosity in the history of the West End. However, when my parents first worked with him, he was about to become Britain's highest-paid entertainer with his West End shows selling out for months. Celebrities such as Princess Margaret, Richard Burton, Elizabeth Taylor, Marlene Dietrich, Judy Garland and Grace Kelly would all go to his club to pay homage (Grace Kelly's laugh was 'filthy' apparently) and also see themselves parodied or sent up. Dad remembers Margot

Fonteyn and Rudolph Nureyev snorting with laughter at a private viewing of a show featuring Danny as Fonteyn and Ronnie Corbett as Nureyev. Nureyev had an interpreter and Dad said it was the only time he got three laughs per joke.

Composers and songwriters also came in for parody where Bill Solly would rearrange the music and Dad would alter their lyrics. They once took aim at Noël Coward's musical *Ace of Clubs*. The song 'Two Juvenile Delinquents' was ripped off as 'Two Most Successful Call-Girls', with Danny and Toni Palmer. When Coward came backstage to congratulate the company, he patted Dad on the head, saying '*Nearly* as good as mine'. Dad then introduced him to Mum, who was very pregnant with my eldest brother Tony. Coward patted her on the stomach and said, 'Here's to a wonderful opening.'

Lionel Bart was also a regular visitor to Winston's when *Oliver!* and *Blitz!* were running in the West End at the same time. 'Who's This Geezer Hitler?' was one of the catchier tunes from *Blitz!* And, with the great Elizabeth Taylor epic *Cleopatra* still playing in cinemas, Dad thought Danny could play the Egyptian queen with Ronnie as her Julius Caesar. The song they sang was 'Who's This Geezer Caesar?' Bart came backstage and was delighted. 'That's better than mine,' he said. 'It rhymes for a start.'

Dad's parodies even had the power to see the future. He and Danny developed a character called Lady Cynthia Grope, who was a Conservative campaigner with big bouffant blonde hair, twinset and pearls. Her hectoring of liberal values would shortly be made real in the form of women like Margaret Thatcher and Mary Whitehouse. The eventual progression to Cupid Stunt in the *Kenny Everett Show* can also be seen in the way Lady Cynthia would protest innocence, but then unleash a torrent of double entendres. Not everyone approved, however. Dad was once halfway through his opening monologue when he was heckled: 'This is satire, I suppose?'

Dad looked over at a table containing Peter Sellers and Lionel Bart but saw only smiles. He fired back into the darkness: 'It's nightclub filth. You need to get out more.'

Turned out it was John Lennon.

A few years later, Dad was working on a David Frost TV show, when he bumped into Lennon in the green room (it was that kind of show).

'Where do I know you from?'

'Danny La Rue's nightclub probably.'

'Was I a pig that night?' Lennon said. 'I was out of it in those days, I don't remember much about them.'

Dad's relationship with Danny would continue unbroken for fourteen years overall, surviving the move from Winston's to Danny's own eponymous club and beyond, into his West End theatre shows. Of course, to make sure Danny felt at home onstage, he'd need women of suitable presence to compete with his energy. Alongside women through the years such as Anne Hart, Toni Palmer, Barbara Windsor, Val Walsh, Valerie Wolf, Clovissa Newcombe and Jenny Logan, was my mother, Terry.

When Mum first met Dad, she was the bigger star, having been a regular fixture in West End musicals and a professional singer and dancer for nearly half her life. She was born Teresa Margaret Elizabeth Agnes Donovan on 11 April 1932, meaning that she was (whisper it quietly) nearly three years older than Dad and, if you hadn't guessed by her full name, she too, like Danny, was from an Irish Catholic family. The O'Donovans had made their way slowly to Brighton from Ireland over several generations via a protracted stay in Bristol, losing the 'O' in the process.

By the time my mother's grandfather Charles was born, the Donovans had one of the most famous photography studios in town and his father, Thomas, had become something of a celebrity. His studio in St James' Street, Brighton did not close until the early 1920s, which is when his grandson Teddy and his wife Mary welcomed my Aunt Patricia into the world. A son, Anthony, followed four years later and my mother became their youngest child (just like Dad) in 1932.

Due to her age and location, Mum's experience of the Second World War was very different from Dad's. Teddy, her father, was captured in the Great War at thirty-one and served time in a prisoner-of-war camp in Westphalia. When war came to Brighton's

shores again, his age meant he could only serve as a special
constable on the Home Front. His day job was as a draughtsman
for the power station and when he returned home, he would take
his children out on fire-watch walks in the evening.

Unlike Leeds, where Dad was comparatively safe, Brighton
occasionally got the bombs that the Luftwaffe hadn't dropped on
the East End of London. It was known as the 'Brighton Blitz' and
many people were evacuated. The fact that the Donovans stayed
put, with children who were nineteen, fifteen and eight, must
have meant they were deemed too useful to the cause. As the
very real prospect of a German invasion neared, it was decided
that the army should remove parts of the Palace and West Piers,
lest they be used as landing stages. Mum remembers sitting in
her father's coat and watching as the British army blew up the
Palace Pier. At home, Mary had bags packed with tins of food in
case they had to move quickly and Mum spent this part of the
war dreaming of a life on a Scottish isle that she decided they
were going to live on.

Mary suffered panic attacks from time to time and Teddy was
still dealing with shell shock and the after-effects of his time in a
prisoner-of-war camp. Mum has vivid memories of them sitting in
their individual rocking chairs, ebbing away the stress in silence.
Another memory she has is of my grandfather's hand trembling
so much that my grandmother had to rest hers on top, attempting
to calm him as much as she was steadying herself. There's a
photograph by Steve Ullathorne of my parents at their golden
wedding anniversary that focuses just on their hands. My dad's
hand is resting on top of Mum's as they sit listening to music, much
as Teddy and Mary had done seventy years before.

My youngest daughter is fifteen. She is old enough and mature
enough to get the bus to and from school by herself, get on the
train to go and meet friends or explore London with her sisters.
However, if she announced that she was leaving school to join a
concert party tour of Britain with a bunch of strangers, it seems like
something my wife and I might be a little uncomfortable with. My
mother was fourteen and a half (the half is crucial) when she was

Danny La Rue and Ronnie Corbett mid tango at Winston's nightclub in the early 1960s.

asked to do just that. A convent schoolgirl, Mum found singing, dancing and drawing to be things that engaged her and occupied her time.

It wasn't without precedent as there was a performing streak in her family. Teddy was an enthusiastic baritone at local amateur concerts and Mum's aunt Mabel Tebbs was married to a famous film actor called Edmund Willard. Mum herself competed in music festivals, regularly winning certificates for singing, dancing and stage design. Such was the time she spent watching and taking part in Brighton Beach concert parties that the mother superior at the convent suggested she might as well join them full time. Which is what she did. Not just that, but my grandmother let her.

This nervous, watchful mother had allowed her young daughter to go to Glasgow all on her own to sing polite songs about English gardens. By the way, I'm not knocking Glasgow; it could have been Uttoxeter (and before there are letters from Staffordshire...). That's a remarkably bold step at such a formative age. I'm a youngest child, so I understand just how loose the hand can be on the tiller, but this points to a wilful bravery on my mum's part that obviously convinced her parents it was a viable option. I'm happy to say that this wilfulness is something Mum maintains to this day. Something else to bear in mind is that this is all happening in 1946 and the can-do spirit of the war is fuelling the national debate with ideals of building a future free from fear. In other words, the family needed the money.

Back then, she was billed as 'Terry Donovan, the singing sensation from the South Coast' and the next few years were a whirlwind of touring concert performances, pantomimes and, eventually, musicals. One of her best friends at convent school, Jackie Jefferson, who was similarly smitten with performing, joined her on auditions. Jackie wasn't Catholic and used to do her homework instead of going to Mass, with prep sessions supervised by a nun who was particularly cruel. Jackie couldn't wait to leave school as well and Mum turned out to be her ideal partner in crime. They became something of a force, and after Mum's concert tours, regularly got jobs on shows together.

They toured with *Bless the Bride* in the corps-de-ballet when they were just seventeen, but their big break was the tour and West End transfer of *Carousel* in 1951. On this show, Jackie met Edmund (Ted) Hockridge, a granite-jawed Canadian (think of Howard Keel without the bombast) who was one of the West End's biggest stars of the 1950s. Jackie was nineteen by this point, with Ted thirteen years her senior, meaning Mum was often asked to be a chaperone. Despite this, Mum and Jackie decided to form a cabaret double act in 1952 called the Taylormaids and began touring the UK. It was an invaluable period of professional growth for Mum, introducing her to many important producers and stars in the industry as the two women booked spots in the summer season, cabaret and variety. The Taylormaids performed many times on TV with *The Billy Cotton Band Show*, *The Tommy Trinder Show* and the Joe Loss Orchestra. A surprise invitation to entertain American troops whisked them off to Germany and, as a good Canadian, Ted assumed the Americans wouldn't behave themselves. Mum said they were very polite. Read into that what you will.

On their return, Mum moved in with Ted and Jackie and they lived in Soho for a while before Mum found herself travelling again. This time it was to Nottingham and the Theatre Royal production of *Cinderella*. It was here that she met Danny La Rue, who introduced her to a quirky northern comic with jet black hair and nice line in rollnecks. He was going to write shows for the club while she was going to convince him that he looked like Joseph Cotten. Dad was also in a pair of sunglasses at the time because his eczema had returned and the fact that it also caused him to have a stiff neck only heightened his mystique. Mum wasn't aware of his skin condition at first and thought he was either a drug dealer or a gangster (or perhaps both). It didn't help that one of the first songs Mum sang at the club was Dad's parody of the old Johnny Mercer number 'That Old Black Magic', which he'd changed to 'That Old White Magic'. *Barry Cryer: The Edgy, Dangerous Bohemian Years* had begun.

I don't know how long Mum's relationship with Les Bennetts lasted, but Dad was keen enough to start inviting himself over to Ted and Jackie's flat, which he said was charming and amusing and she said was irritating. This dynamic of misunderstanding would be played out many times over their marriage. Dad started sending Mum notes and when Mum started to see how silly and joyful he was in them, including little cartoons, she started writing her own back. Dad went back to Leeds to recuperate once the show was up and running, but not before Mum and Jackie had a party. Mum danced with Ted Dicks and not Dad. Dad travelled north with this moment fresh in his mind, suitably fuelled by jealousy. Like all red-blooded males, Dad decided he needed to act – by writing letters instead of notes.

TERRY
DONOVA
as
"PRINCE CHARMIN

JILL WESTLAKE as "CINDERELLA"

HERE MAY 7th for a 3 week season
TOM ARNOLD & LESLIE A. MACDONNELL
(by arrangement with Williamson Music Ltd.)
present
DAVID WHITFIELD
in an Entirely New and Spectacular Production of
"THE DESERT SONG"
Book and Lyrics by Otto Harbach, Otto Hammerstein II and Frank Mandell   Music by Sigmund Romberg.

*My mother when she was a giant caped superhero (or Prince Charming in the 1960
production of* Cinderella, *where she met Danny La Rue).*

Apparently, Dad knew that things were progressing well when Ted Dicks noticed the way Mum was looking at Dad during a rehearsal. Ted whispered to him: 'Looks like you've won.' They were now officially an item and, as the letters indicate, dog walking became a good opportunity to spend time with each other. When Mum and Jackie first moved to London, they lived above the famous 'Two i's' coffee bar in Old Compton Street, which was named after two brothers named Irani. Apparently there were 'Three i's', but legend had it that the third Irani was in prison. Coincidentally, the 'Two i's' formed the inspiration for the coffee bar in *Expresso Bongo*.

Danny, in typically understated mood, admiring his collection of Lord Chamberlain figurines.

Jackie owned a poodle and these two convent-educated girls from Brighton would innocently take it for a walk up and down the Soho streets late at night, little realising that owning a poodle was code, in those parts, for a very different type of working sisterhood. It hastened the purchase of a terrier named Pidge (after Pigeon from *Lady and the Tramp*) who began a long line of dog

ownership that lasted all the way through Mum's life to the late
1990s. It seemed that if Dad was going to truly win Mum's heart,
he'd have to start walking some dogs. About six months into their
time at Winston's, they were walking someone else's dogs (as well
as Pidge) in Hyde Park. It started raining and Mum started looking
miserable so, to cheer her up, he proposed.

Bristol, 4 March 1962. The Day The Earth Stood Still. Until it was
time to get back to rehearsals...

'What do you think?' he said.

'That's a big question. I'll have to tell you tomorrow.'

They were out with the dogs again the next day when Mum said,
'The answer to your question is "yes".'

Dad looked blankly back at her: 'What question?'

Dad claimed she threw a dog at him.

By 1962, Mum's parents had moved to Bristol and Mum
wanted the wedding to be at St Bonaventure's Catholic Church in
Bishopston. However, before that could happen, Dad insisted on
asking her father Teddy's permission to marry his daughter. As they

walked along Bristol Suspension Bridge, Dad nervously managed to spit the words out. Teddy stopped for a moment and considered what he'd just been told before turning back to Dad: 'If we both hold hands, we can jump off together.'

It wasn't just Dad's mother who did a nice line in deadpan twinkle.

Mum and Dad married on 4 March 1962. In keeping with the frenetic lifestyle of the time, they were in a Winston's show the night before. Mum, Dad and a few mates from the show, including Ronnie Corbett and Audrey Jeans, caught the early train from Paddington the following morning. They'd only had two or three hours of sleep, and Dad always winced when he looked at the wedding portrait. 'Those dead eyes,' he'd comment.

Dad used to say that it was Mum who made his eczema better. He had serious thoughts about giving up the business because it was making his life so difficult. Based on the moment when Douglas Camfield had to turn off the oven in his flat in Bayswater, Dad must have had some darker thoughts as well. He'd spent time in hospital, 'all bound up like the Invisible Man' and even had to be carried there twice on a stretcher, due to his locked limbs. We've looked at Dad's relationship with his skin in an earlier chapter, but it is worth reminding ourselves just how disastrous it could have been for him at this stage of his career. Dad claims there was a man on his ward in Barnet who hanged himself due to the amount of itching he was doing and this haunted him.

There is no question that Dad's skin did begin to get better after he met Mum, but it didn't completely leave him and the next sixty years were spent using any number of different ointments and creams to stay on top of treatment. However, the stability that Mum provided, supporting him, raising his children (sometimes single-handedly) and forgoing her own successful career in the process, was enough for him to know that his skin would never return to haunt him in quite the same way again. Of all the pivotal moments in his life where he met key individuals who transformed his fate, it is safe to say that Mum leaves the rest easily at the starting line.

Dad was now back performing at Winston's and life was returning to normal. If you can ever really describe the 1960s cabaret culture as 'normal'. There is one story, told to me by David Sherlock, Graham Chapman's former partner, that sums up both the scene at the time and Mum's sense of humour and perspective on it. The Corbetts used to throw big parties at their house in south London and one night they'd invited the cast of *Showboat* along (we've all had nights like that). Denis King was at the piano and while someone was singing 'Can't help loving that man of mine', a rather large man who no one could quite remember the name of, whispered in Denis's ear. He wanted him to play 'The Stripper'.

After a couple more drinks the man became insistent, and Denis gave in. All very innocuous and amusing until the man started disrobing. What was a fun evening had just become a little awkward. The man continued taking his clothes off down to his pants and the piano got quieter as the crowd became more uncomfortable. The joke had unfortunately backfired. Eventually, Denis stopped altogether and the man gathered up his discarded attire. Everyone turned to discover that Graham Chapman had also got undressed. Only Graham had managed to complete the task and sat there, straight-faced, stark bollock naked, smoking his pipe. Danny La Rue quickly took out his handkerchief and started to go 'Now you see it, now you don't'. There was another silence, broken eventually by my mother: 'Well, I thought it was very well formed.'

It seems impossible to condense all my parents' rich abundance of character into a solitary chapter, but I will attempt to follow my father's example and sketch their truth on the back of a fag packet. He wasn't the type of comedian to do long observational sets about the nature of a relationship, nor would he glibly indulge in 'my wife' stereotypes. Instead, his desire for a certain amount of privacy, but more likely his need for emotional economy, meant Dad used to do a few set lines about Mum and their marriage that read like dialogue from a longer play. They remained largely unchanged for many years. He'd say: 'People always ask me about our secret. The truth is, we argue every day. I was in the car with her recently and said, "We disagree about everything, don't we darling?" And she said, "No we don't!"'

Graeme Garden said he always liked staying at Mum and Dad's house because he enjoyed these little exchanges between them. There are some friends, he'd say, where there might be dark clouds threatening the atmosphere, but with my parents, it was always playful bickering. They always kissed and made up (not in front of Graeme, I hasten to add). Dad was devoted to her and expressed it in small tokens. He always called her when he got to a venue to perform and she'd get another call (whether she wanted it or not) when he was on his way home. He'd leave little notes for her and their late night chitchat as they went about getting ready for bed was a joyful chorus of giggles, misunderstandings and low wattage outrage.

When Dad was dying in hospital, we managed to get Mum to his bedside in a wheelchair while navigating an NHS hospital that was undergoing refurbishments. It was an ordeal. We stroked his brow, held his hand, my sister Jack and Mum sang with him and we joked as best we could in a respiratory ward at the tail end of a pandemic. When we got Mum home, we asked her when she wanted to return. 'I've said goodbye,' she replied. 'That is not the man I married.'

Another of Dad's emphatic statements on their marriage was: 'The secret to our marriage is that we don't understand each other.' She understood him all too well. Only one woman would pull up to the roundabout at Elstree Studios to pick him up and, when she found him dancing naked on the roundabout arm in arm with Bob Todd, not divorce him. Though she did drive off.

Mum would go on to repeat these well-rehearsed lines about their marriage at Dad's funeral and hearing her say them gave us a fresh perspective on each one. Here she was, the consummate performer at her own husband's funeral, giving his material wings Dad had long since neglected. Ironically, another running joke was that Mum didn't even get his jokes and Dad's greatest fear was to walk out on stage one day and see Mum sitting in every seat. He should be so lucky.

One of the questions I am most frequently asked is: 'What was Barry Cryer like at home?' My usual response is: 'I was told off like everyone else, just with better timing.' However, I realise that kind of glibness won't suffice in a biography. Even one about Barry Cryer. The short answer is that he was often the same, which was sometimes fun and sometimes frustrating. The tools that made him successful professionally were often a weakness privately. As with any family, we had serious conversations, but Dad would invariably hide away behind a joke or a facile remark when an opinion was sought. His obsessive nature, which was what made him such a brilliant mental archivist and detailed crafted comedian, could sometimes make him a petty or mean point-scorer. Where Dad could read a room in a comedy club, he could sometimes be tone-deaf at the dinner table. He could also be self-absorbed and incapable of talking about anything other than work. He was rarely 'off' and in public the instinct to find an audience to perform to was sometimes stronger than the need to remain with his family. However, this desire to express and create also made him sweet, warm, eager, gentle, kind, enthusiastic and most of all, silly.

For me and my siblings, Tony and Dave, my brothers, and my sister Jack, the abiding sound of Dad during our youth was the clacking of the electric typewriter coming from either the upstairs study or the kitchen. When he was working at home with people like Peter Vincent, David Nobbs, Dick Vosburgh and Graeme Garden, the other enduring sound that accompanied him was laughter. Lots of it. You could use it to find them in a haze of smoke, which was pipe smoke for one eccentric period of Dad's life. Yet, even surrounded by the buzz of a busy house, his mind was often on tour, in a TV studio or a radio theatre.

Since Dad died, I've reflected on how reluctant he was to actively parent and give direct advice. Very often he'd fall back on the old axiom that whatever decision we made as children, he just wanted us to be happy. When I started taking my own steps towards writing and performing, I was obviously keen to secure his approval, but I was also hungry for some guidance and wisdom as to how to navigate the business. Initially, it didn't come. I'd take him a short play or a sketch of my own and ask for his opinion. Usually, he'd find an excuse not to comment at all or at most praise it without much constructive insight. I quickly learned to rationalise this absence by looking at Dad's own upbringing. He didn't have the language or experience of his own father to feel comfortable playing with such machinery.

Later in his life, when I started working with him, it was a lot easier for me to observe at close quarters how that brilliant mind turned and, for his part, he'd be duty-bound to respond to my contributions without having to focus on any kind of parental judgement. We were working, after all, and not discussing life lessons. To him, that was a more palatable exchange and I probably learned more about him as a person during those years (albeit speaking in code) than during much of my childhood. I'd also made many of my own adult decisions by that point and he felt like he wasn't risking my future prosperity by giving bad advice. His need for approval often meant he didn't want to be held responsible for someone else's fortune. As a parent myself, I can easily relate to that dilemma, even if I don't agree with his dealing of it.

However, when he wasn't working, as I mentioned above, he was an eccentric and obsessive creature of habit. One memory I have is of him preparing the tea tray each night before going to bed and alongside the mugs, the small jug of milk, the sugar bowl and the tea bags was half a bread slice. Usually, it was a crust spread thinly with marmalade or a cream cracker with an industrial piece of cheddar on top if he was feeling skittish. He would take that up to bed, watch a movie and, incredibly, still manage to sleep like a (full) baby. The movie would be watched on a Sony Trinitron television (the one with a dial and a pop switch that made a satisfying clunk).

One of my regular pleasures was squirrelling into Mum and Dad's bedroom, grabbing a cream cracker and sitting down to watch a movie on the Sony Trinitron TV. I saw my very first Marx Brothers, Hitchcock and Mel Brooks movies on that screen, which for those of you that don't remember, was about the size of an exercise book, but the experience was no less thrilling for it. I always thought the colour balance was off and it took me a few years to realise that *Vertigo* was meant to look that gaudy. The Basil Rathbone Sherlock Holmes entered my life in that room and the main attraction for me was the joy Dad got from sharing his passion. Conan Doyle's books and Jeremy Brett came later, along with the shared love that led to us collaborating on a series of Mrs Hudson stories, but it all started with the films on Friday nights. On Saturday mornings, we'd re-enact Holmes and Moriarty's tussle at the Reichenbach Falls. That would be followed by silent movie and early comedy viewings and he had the same enthusiasm for Laurel & Hardy, Harold Lloyd and Buster Keaton as he did for the Marx Brothers. Our podcast *Now, Where Were We?* was inspired by conversations with Dad on those nights at the end of this bed.

He was like it with music too. I'll talk about his more personal relationship with music later, but given what we've learnt about his dalliances with jazz bands at university, his recording career in the 1950s and his musical theatre forays, not to mention marrying a singer, this all meant that music played a vital and pivotal role at home too. I'm pretty sure that's how and why my sister became a singer and I know she values the way he infected her with his enthusiasm.

The general memory is not of Dad as an authoritarian father, not by any stretch, but more as someone to be found pratting about in the kitchen doing a Wilson, Keppel and Betty routine (they were a music-hall trio that made an Egyptian sand-dance routine famous) with a tea towel. He was less an expert at teaching you the mechanics of a hatchback and more an authority on the surprise knee grasp. Left unprotected, a well-placed pinch just above the patella could quickly render you incapable of speech. I would've believed someone if they'd told me Dad had been a spy, but only if it was MI6 policy to torture Russians through sustained leg grabbing. He was also practised in the ancient art of spoon hanging. You could say he was born to it, given he had a particularly well-shaped nose for the sport, but he would still challenge you at the table to take your dessert spoon, place it on the end of your nose and see who could keep it hanging for the longest. If there's any justice, the best tribute we can pay my father is to lobby for it to be a test event at the next Olympics.

I don't know if you're familiar with the oeuvre of Willie the Worm, but it was particularly fashionable in the late seventies and early eighties. Our main protagonist would excitedly begin stories with everyday adventures, like painting a house, watching a football match or driving a car. Still, he soon learned he was hopelessly unsuited to them because he was a worm with no opposable thumbs to grab things or feet to kick things. His optimism would soon turn to frustration as he slipped out of a seat, fell down a drain or simply couldn't see over a dashboard. Besides, seatbelts weren't designed to restrain members of the annelid species. Nor were cars small enough for that matter. His progress was cruelly thwarted at every turn, but he kept trying, and his stories only ever ended if the listener (me) fell asleep.

Dad tried reading me stories at bedtime to get me to go to sleep but soon learned that these kinds of silly stories, made up on the spot, were much more likely to work than reading books plucked from my shelf. Alongside improvised stories, his other party piece (usually on holidays) consisted of sticking two pieces of paper together, cutting strips out of the top sheet and sliding them side to side to make his cartoon drawings of tigers disappear as if at the zoo. Only later did I realise that these playful indulgences were the same talents he employed as a storyteller and a comedian.

At Dad's memorial celebration in July 2022, much mention was made by Dad's friends of his phone calls, usually on their birthdays, but Saturday mornings were also time for the ring-round of friends. In researching this book, I came across an interview with the late great Bernard Cribbins:

> Phone calls from Barry were great fun. The phone rings and I pick it up and he says, 'Hello, Cryer here, I have got a couple for you!' He then passes on the jokes. The other day, we had a little joke swap, and I gave him one which crippled him.
>
> The best joke from the Cryer household was not Barry; it was his son Robert when he was quite young, many years ago. I rang. Robert picked up the phone and I said: 'Hello, who is that?'

'Robert.'

I said, 'Hello Robert, how are you?'

'Fine.'

'Is your daddy in?'

'Yes.'

And he put the phone down. Which I just thought was brilliant.

Had I been a bit older, I would have recited the Archbishop of Canterbury joke instead.

A man says to his doctor: 'I think my wife is going deaf, but I don't want to mention it because it might seem tactless and insensitive. Is there any way I can find out, without her knowing?'

The doctor replies: 'There is and it's quite easy. Choose a moment when she has her back to you, say something in a normal voice and if she doesn't answer, move a few steps closer and say it again. Keep going until you get an answer and then you'll get a good idea about the state of her hearing.'

So, the man comes home from work and sees his wife standing with her back to him in the kitchen. He says: 'What's for dinner?'

No answer. So, he moves a few steps closer: 'What's for dinner?'

Again, nothing. He moves in again: 'What's for dinner?'

Still nothing. By now he's practically right behind her, so he tries one more time: 'What's for dinner?'

She turns around and says: 'For the fourth time – chicken!'

8

There's a framed photograph in the hallway at Mum's house of a garden scene. The year is 1967. A group of people are posing with a trophy, rather in the style of a team photo. Although, instead of footballers or rugby players, we have a collection of production staff, writers, comedians and singers. Youthful, excited and celebratory, they variously hold champagne glasses, cigarettes, jaunty poses and silly grins. It is 1967, there is even a pipe or two. The back row consists of, among others, Dad, Terry Jones, Michael Palin and Dick Vosburgh (a long-time collaborator of Dad's). In front of them, crouching in no particular order, are Graham Chapman (owner of a pipe), John Cleese, Eric Idle, Antony Jay (future co-writer of *Yes, Minister*), Neil Shand (another of Dad's co-writers), Julie Felix (folk singer), Sheila Steafel (comic singer and actress), Marty Feldman and Ronnie Barker. They had all worked on a show called *Frost Over England*, which was a special compilation of sketches from the BBC's satirical series *The Frost Report*.

As the line-up proves, the show was a remarkable breeding ground and meeting point for some of the finest British comedy writing and performing talent. The proof of that was in the trophy held in the front row. It is the prestigious international TV award the Rose d'Or (also known as the Golden Rose of Montreux) and in the middle of the photo holding it is the 'team captain', presenter David Frost (the picture was taken in his garden) and the 'manager', producer James Gilbert. This gathering was just the tip of the iceberg as far as *The Frost Report* is concerned, as there were some key figures from both in front of and behind the camera who were missing that day. These included Bill Oddie, Tim Brooke-Taylor, Nicky Henson, Spike Mullins, Peter Tinniswood, Keith Waterhouse, Willis Hall, David Nobbs, Frank Muir and Denis Norden. However, there's one person who leaves a rather larger hole (cue obligatory 'diminutive size' gags): Ronnie Corbett, who was performing in Great Yarmouth that day, and it's with him that the story really begins.

When Danny La Rue came to see the sketch revue *And Another Thing...*, he liked it so much that he invited Dad to write for him at Winston's nightclub in 1961. Fast forward to 1964 and lightning strikes for a second time. Jenny Logan, the actress, singer and, I'm sure she won't mind me saying, future Shake n' Vac advertising legend, was part of the cast that left Winston's in 1964 to work at

The iconic Frost Over England *Montreux Rose D'Or winning team photo from 1967. An embarrassment of talented riches.*

Danny's new club, which opened in Hanover Square. It probably wasn't a long meeting to decide the name, but the new happening place in Mayfair was now called Danny's. The Beatles, Noël Coward, Zsa Zsa Gabor, the Kray twins and Judy Garland all filed through the doors in the wee small hours. Another guest was Jenny's boyfriend at the time, David Frost.

Frost had become a household name in 1962 with the satirical TV show *That Was The Week That Was* (or TW3 to its friends) and was considered by some as part *enfant terrible* (he was twenty-three) and part kingmaker. He was known for making the careers of writers and performers he used and breaking the reputations of some of the high-profile guests he interviewed. The show, quite unlike anything seen before or since, was a blend of songs, sketches, cartoons drawn live (no, really), monologues, interviews and studio debate. It's still revered as a benchmark in British TV sixty years on but, incredibly, ran for only two series. However, not everyone shared the enthusiasm at the time, with author Kitty Muggeridge describing Frost as a man who has 'risen without a trace' and his great rival and friend Peter Cook suggesting he wasn't perhaps the most original of thinkers when he described Frost as the 'bubonic plagiarist'.

Most people also know the famous story of Cook saving Frost from drowning and subsequently describing it as his 'greatest regret'. It is true that Cook was the man Frost most wanted to be like and TW3 did little to dissuade people from that notion. It also relied heavily on a writing brains trust borrowed from *Private Eye* magazine (where Cook was a co-owner), which included Willy Rushton, Christopher Booker and Richard Ingrams. Frost's talent, alongside his interviewing, was as a producer. He was a brilliant motivator of talent, although some have unkindly said that by including himself in the line-up of performers, he instantly lowered the bar for others. He also had a keen eye for spotting talent and blending their voices successfully. This is how Dad remembered him best when he met people on Frost shows like Graham Chapman, Eric Idle, Michael Palin, Neil Shand, David Nobbs and Dick Vosburgh. As a result, Dad called Frost a 'practising catalyst' and hailed the meeting with him as one of the most important of his life.

However, if it hadn't been for Jenny Logan, Dad might not have had that meeting at all. Frost, a former cabaret performer himself, had been in to see Jenny in the show at Danny's new club. Following the calling of a general election in 1964, the BBC had taken TW3 off the air for fear of it compromising their impartiality and Frost was in the process of putting a new show together, called *A Degree of Frost*. He particularly liked Dad's writing and invited him to submit some material for the broadcast. The programme itself was most famous for an interview with Paul McCartney where he opened up about life in the Beatles. Original TW3 writers like Bill Oddie, Christopher Booker, John Cleese, Frank Muir, Denis Norden and Janette Scott also contributed, but as it was a one-off, no writers' room was developed for it. However, Dad now had one foot in the door with David Frost.

The other foot joined in 1965. Frost returned to the club because he'd also been rather taken with the comic brilliance of Danny's leading man, Ronnie Corbett. The Frost writer Dick Vosburgh had also urged Jimmy Gilbert to see him and Jimmy was similarly impressed. Frost invited both Ronnie and Dad for a drink to see if they would be interested in joining his show, *The Frost Report*. However, there was an immediate problem. Recording was pencilled to start in the spring of 1966 and Ronnie was already playing Will Scarlett in Lionel Bart's new musical about Robin Hood called *Twang!!* at the Shaftesbury Theatre. Bart was on a roll after successes with *Oliver! Blitz!* and *Maggie May* (*Twang!!* had stolen its exclamation mark), so another hit would immediately rule Ronnie out of *The Frost Report*.

It's rare for a performer to wish their show not to succeed, but I wouldn't be surprised if Ronnie didn't at least breathe a sigh of relief when *Twang!!* closed early after forty-three performances. He'd received great reviews for his performance but the musical itself didn't fare so well and he was now free to take up a career-defining TV role on *The Frost Report*. This ripple was also felt by Dad, who even though he'd already proved himself to Frost and Gilbert, might not have joined the show without Ronnie's involvement. Another important consequence of this moment was that *The Frost Report* was where Corbett and Ronnie Barker worked together on TV for the first time. Spare a thought for Lionel Bart in all this, as he'd invested a lot of his own money into *Twang!!* and it nearly ruined him financially, but had it been a success, he could've been responsible for preventing the creation of a British cultural institution. One door closes, another opens.

The crew and writers of *The Frost Report* all met up for the first time in a Methodist Hall on Crawford Street in Marylebone, west London, sometime towards the end of 1965. Dad, no doubt a bit apprehensive on his first day at a new school, surrounded by comic talent old and new, did something that day that he felt was very natural and obvious but to others it made quite an impact. He greeted the younger writers, like Michael Palin, Graham Chapman and Eric Idle, who he noticed happened to be more nervous than he was. As we'll see, that act of routine civility had a profound effect on them. Dad was only thirty-one himself, so hardly a veteran, whereas people like Muir and Norden were in their forties. With that act, he took the energy that had been passed on to him by people like Johnny Gunn, David Nixon, Arthur Askey, Frankie Vaughan, Vivian Van Damm, Danny La Rue and now David Frost, and passed it on.

He'd set in stone a feature of his personality that remained with him to the end: making people feel welcome and spotting when they needed a lift. Barry Humphries, his contemporary, acknowledged this quality in a special tribute episode of *Now, Where Were We?* It was recorded just after Dad's funeral and was an incredibly moving and affectionate account of my Dad's place in the industry. The behaviour he detailed was made even more poignant when Barry Humphries himself died only a year later.

'In a sense, psychologically, he knew somehow when one was a bit down and when one needed cheering up. I'm surprised really to know that he ever really thought about himself. He was totally unusual in the business ... because we are all narcissists, we're all totally selfish, but Cryer was always thoughtful and supportive. I still can't believe he's no longer with us.'

That sentiment could be said of both men. I will treasure the time and consideration he gave me on the day we recorded the podcast, as well as his beautifully crafted testament at Dad's memorial. Michael Palin and Eric Idle both remember well that act of kindness on their first day on *The Frost Report*. As Palin recalls: 'It was Barry and Marty [Feldman] who first came over and said hello and made me feel at ease straight away. This was a key thing because I think my memories of Barry throughout my life were of him putting me at my ease. There was no bullshit from him, you know? He knew how to talk to people. He knew how to encourage people and he was terribly good at following up on gigs and when you were doing things.'

Idle adds: 'I loved him dearly and he was very good to me and sweet to me. I always thought he was much older than me, but I don't think he was. He was a professional writer. We'd only just come out of Oxford and Cambridge. It was an amazing team with people like Keith Waterhouse and Willis Hall and great writers who'd go on to write some of the best sitcoms and comedies on the BBC. And we were very young, so what he did was very sweet.'

In truth, he was only about seven or eight years older than those soon-to-be Pythons, but a combination of the fact that he was born before the war and had already been working meant that he seemed much older. To them, however, he felt like the product of a different age. There's a photo we have of him, aged around three or four, where he has a quiff and a rather knowing smile. He looks like a teenager.

Dad joked that there were two types of comedy writer: those that got it right and those that got it done by Monday. He was firmly in the latter camp, as he tended not to over-analyse his material. Denis Norden even once said of Dad: 'Baz delivers a script when we want it. It may not be great, but it's there.' Incredibly, Dad used to quote that line about himself all the time. By being honest about the quality of his work, he was obviously maintaining his reputation for humility, but he was also underlining his pride in being a diligent worker. A safe pair of hands. It's one of the reasons why he worked so successfully in an industry that relies on execution. Dad was someone who delivered.

Cryer and Palin in a sketch from Late Night Line Up *that no doubt ruined Dennis Potter's evening.*

Dad believed the former kind of writer was prone to losing the magic by overthinking. This kind of approach made it very difficult for Dad to write with John Cleese (they did try) as Cleese liked to pore over every syllable. Dad's most important quality on *The Frost Report* was his speed. The show was live, after all, and often situations changed on the day that needed a quick fix. The quick material needed in Vivian Van Damm's office was continuing to bear fruit. John Cleese was insightful when he was asked to reflect on Dad's qualities while working on *The Frost Report* when he was interviewed for *The Barry Cryer Scrapbook* (which Dad produced with Philip Porter):

Frost Report *writer's meeting, 1966: Corbett, Chapman, Cryer, Idle and Frost, among others. How times have changed. Not a latte in sight.*

I think the fact that he could write funny material of almost any kind is the first thing. The other thing about him is he was such a generous-spirited man. I could never remember him getting possessive about material and that is the greatest quality in the world because, particularly the young writers, they are always convinced, like I was, like Terry Jones was, that what we had just come up with was priceless and had to be thrust upon the public and could never be cut. Whereas Barry was always very relaxed. He had done so much but, if somebody didn't like anything, he couldn't be bothered to fight – he would just come up with something new. I don't ever remember him getting into arguments about material. He just wanted to help and if he was playing three lines in a sketch with Marty, Tim and me, he would enjoy it and would be a pleasure to be around. I never saw him angry. It's not that he was naive at all; he was very observant of people and he would occasionally make a remark that reminded one that he was a good observer – a little, very gentle, hint that somebody's personality was not perfect in every possible way but never in a mean way.

So, I think everyone loved having him around.

I'm rather humbled by this testimony and it speaks volumes, obviously of Dad, but also of John Cleese's forensic analysis of character.

Each week Frost took a different subject or theme and examined it with the help of illustrative sketches from his writing team. At rehearsals, script editor Antony Jay would read his script for Frost's opening monologue, known as the Continuing and Developing Monologue (or 'CDM' for short – which soon became known as 'Cadbury's Dairy Milk' instead). The show's basic narrative would be hammered out and jokes and sketches would slot in according to the theme. Marty Feldman would also act as a script editor during this process. Apparently, Feldman once suggested 'Holidays' as the theme of the week and then promptly disappeared on holiday. The show's first episode was on the subject of 'Authority' and by episode five, it had reached 'Class'. Here, it created its first classic sketch. Now known simply as the 'Class Sketch' and written by John Law and Marty Feldman, it featured John Cleese, Ronnie Barker and Ronnie Corbett representing each layer of the British class system. For the uninitiated, it used the differing heights of each performer to satirise their respective places in society.

At lunch, they'd all meet up again to play football in the hall in Marylebone with a tennis ball. Apparently, Frost was always in goal, and I once asked Dad what he was like as a keeper, but unfortunately, his performances were not memorable enough to earn a review. This is surprising, given that Frost was once offered a contract at Nottingham Forest. During this period, David Frost had become so successful and celebrated on both sides of the Atlantic that he soon became the butt of jokes. It must have been fascinating for him because if there's one thing that divides Britain and the US, it's the countries' different attitudes to success.

Frost had an open-top car at the time and Dad used to joke that if it started raining, he pressed a button on the dashboard and it stopped raining. That joke is a perfect example of Dad's deft ability to benignly skewer a subject without really landing a hurtful blow. Frost was not renowned for being the most self-aware person, but neither was he so blinkered he didn't take part in self-parody. In fact, to borrow from Oscar Wilde (he's generous like that), for Frost, at least, it meant he was still being talked about. Overall, he was an exciting person to be connected to and it led to one of the most dynamic writing periods in Dad's career. One of Eric Idle's favourite reminiscences of the Frost years was when Eric, Dick Vosburgh and Dad were sitting in the studio during a recording of *Frost On Wednesday*. Their job? To write Frost's ad-libs, which is just as absurd as it sounds. Eric said that Frost carried off these apparently improvised remarks seamlessly and that Dad was particularly adept at providing them.

It was only after Dad died that I truly reflected on his reluctant parenting style and realised that he often left clues in plain sight. They were coded and hidden in his anecdotes. By choosing to talk about certain people and giving his opinion of them, he revealed quite a lot about his philosophies and approaches to life. The things he decided to leave out of a story were as important as the things that he decided to talk about. A classic example was to compare David Frost and Simon Dee. Like Frost, Dee was slick, confident and brash, but Dee possessed an ego that was sometimes capable of crass misjudgements. He could be cruel. Frost was much more civil by comparison. Dad also likened the different approaches taken by Max Bygraves and Des O'Connor when being mocked by Morecambe and Wise. During a sketch about Napoleon, Vanessa Redgrave's Josephine turns to Eric's Duke of Wellington and says:

Vanessa: What will happen to Napoleon if he accepts the surrender terms?
Eric: I'll tell you what happens to Napoleon if he accepts the surrender terms. He will be dragged out by the

dragoons. Not a pretty sight. I wouldn't look if I were you, it would put you off your dinner.

Vanessa: I've never heard anything so terrible.

Eric: Oh, you must have done. What about Max Bygraves singing 'Deck Of Cards'? That takes some beating.

Bygraves responded by getting his agent to write Morecambe and Wise a letter asking them to show a little more respect. Then, the following week, Bygraves was on stage at the London Palladium and, instead of the usual choreography at the start of his routine, he had the dancers parade his gold discs in front of the audience while aiming some shots back at Morecambe and Wise (including calling Ernie Wise 'a short fat poof'). By contrast, when Eric and Ernie started doing jokes about Des O'Connor (Ernie: 'I've got some good news.' Eric: 'Has Des O'Connor got a sore throat?'), Des greeted them warmly and joined in the joke.

The truth was that he and Eric had been friends for a long time and although the jokes had started in private, the way Des dealt with the abuse in public was a perfect example of how not to take yourself too seriously and profit in the process. It cemented Des in the audience's affection and led to a broader appeal that lasted a long time.

Frost was very loyal to the talent he nurtured on *The Frost Report*, and after that first series many of them soon found their way into some new projects that he was producing. He used his bargaining power with the independent TV broadcaster Associated-Rediffusion to greenlight three new projects. *At Last the 1948 Show* was launched in February 1967. It took Tim Brooke-Taylor, John Cleese, Graham Chapman and Marty Feldman as its stars straight from *The Frost Report* and into a more conventional sketch show format. It's often credited with laying some of the groundwork for Monty Python, and even features the debut of the catchphrase 'And now for something completely different'. It heralded an interesting move back into performing for Dad, as he cropped up in various small roles, including the wine waiter and the only Yorkshireman in 'The Four Yorkshiremen' sketch. It's another sketch that was reworked for Python.

The second project was *The Ronnie Barker Playhouse*, which aired in April 1968, and, as the title suggests, Frost was keen to showcase the talents of an actor who was already being seen by many as a successor to Peter Sellers. As performers, they were both fine comic character actors with reputations for immersing themselves in their roles, but as people they couldn't have been more different. Where Sellers had an extravagant international lifestyle that garnered four wives and a plethora of neuroses, Barker was a more diffident presence off-camera. He was married to Joy for nearly fifty years and a large part of his domestic life was eked out in suburban Pinner, north-west London.

Ronnie Barker actually played quite an important role in the growing Cryer family's evolution. The year before *Playhouse*, 1967, when Dad was working with Ronnie on *The Frost Report*, Mum and Dad were thinking of moving out of their flat in Maida Vale. My grandmother Jenny had moved in to help with childcare for my two brothers, Tone and Dave, who were four and two at the time, and things were beginning to get a little crowded. Plus, my sister Jack would soon be along to join them all. Barker heard about Dad looking for new digs and took him out in the car around Pinner and surrounding villages to look for houses. He helped Dad find what ended up becoming our family home in Hatch End for close to half a century. It was a big, solid family home, dating from around 1900, and it was on the market for £11,000. In a rare act of financial swagger, Dad managed to push them down to £10,400. It is an age ago and, talking of these figures, I'm weeping as I type. That'll soon be the kind of money you place on a gas bill.

Dad and Ronnie stayed in regular touch over the years, most notably, of course, when Dad was writing for *The Two Ronnies*. He was present at a dinner for writers of the show when mysterious sketch contributor Gerald Wiley was unveiled by Ronnie Barker as... Ronnie Barker. Dad is reputed to have exclaimed 'No one likes a smart arse'. It turned out to be an act of hubris on Dad's part as karma struck when he tried to trick Ronnie at a book signing.

Dad thought it would be funny to go in disguise as a fan. Pulling up the collar of Mum's biggest coat, he donned dark glasses, a hat and put on his best American accent. Dad asked Ronnie to sign a book to 'John Smith'. He then smugly trooped off home to brag to Mum. She laughed at the tale, opened the book and read the inscription: 'Piss off, Cryer. Can't you see I'm busy?' It's only a shame he didn't write 'No one likes a smart arse'.

Frost created another show for his *Frost Report* stars in 1967 and it's by far the most significant one for Dad. He's not usually associated with the form, but it was a sitcom called *No – That's Me Over Here!* Frost saw that Dad and Graham Chapman hit it off during rehearsals of *The Frost Report* and suggested they write together. The show was designed to be a vehicle for Ronnie Corbett who, unlike Barker, didn't indulge in transformative character work. Dad and Graham celebrated this by having Ronnie Corbett play a character called Ronnie Corbett. It's a feat they managed to repeat in 1971 when they all reunited for another sitcom, *Now Look Here*, all about a young man called Ronnie Corbett living at home with his mother. Keen-eyed observers over the years have spotted the similarities with that other mother/son sitcom of the 1980s, *Sorry!* by Ian Davidson and Peter Vincent. Dad would be the first to acknowledge that his and Graham's dynamic was a much less nuanced affair and certainly didn't attract anything like the success of the latter show. Dad was even a huge fan of *Sorry!* and went on to work with both Ian and Peter.

The third instalment of the Cryer, Chapman and Corbett trilogy was a classic fish-out-of-water story called *The Prince of Denmark*. I'm pretty sure none of them ever used the term 'trilogy' but this show was at least a sequel to *Now Look Here*, with Ronnie reprising his character (although, because they're all called Ronnie Corbett, it's hard to tell). It's set in a pub called the Prince of Denmark, which was apt because it was also largely written in a pub. Dad and Graham were experimenting at the time with the little-known technique of 'method writing'. Ronnie plays a ridiculously inept landlord who consistently ignores the advice of experts (including his wife – the wonderfully understated

Rosemary Leach returning as Laura) to run their hospitality business into the ground.

Once again, there are obvious parallels here with a later sitcom and this wasn't lost within BBC Light Entertainment. John Cleese himself recently unearthed a letter from Iain Main, the Light Entertainment Comedy Script Editor in 1974 when *Fawlty Towers* was first broadcast. The note was sent to Dad's great friend Jimmy Gilbert (former producer of Frost and *On The Brighter Side*), and then Head of Comedy at the BBC. Referring to *Fawlty Towers* it said: 'I'm afraid I thought this one as dire as its title. It's a kind of "Prince of Denmark" of the hotel world. A collection of cliches and stock characters which I can't see being anything but a disaster.' Proof, if ever there was one, that rejection is often the kernel of greatness. It's only a shame those doubting voices didn't have the same effect on *The Prince of Denmark*.

Dad absolutely loved working with Graham and, although he'd written the odd thing in partnership up until this point, this was his first proper creative relationship. It's unfortunate that most people think of alcohol when they think of what it must have been like to work with Chapman and there's no question that Graham's mercurial mind, behaviour and, let's face it, his drinking, could be challenging. Dad most often found it thrilling and inspiring. It's often forgotten that Graham was dry for the last ten years of his life; however, Dad said that at the time he wrote with Graham, he would arrive at 10.30 in the morning to write and Graham would greet him with either a gin or a vodka in his hand. They'd chat for an hour and a half before Graham would say, 'Shall we go to the pub?'

While it may seem on the surface that Dad's willingness to go to the pub to write was the act of an enabler, there's everything to suggest that for Graham, beer in the pub, surrounded by people and convivial chatter was eminently better for him than drinking spirits alone at home. For about an hour and a half in the pub each day, Graham was at his brilliant best, before the beer took him off in a different direction. He was particularly good at constructing narrative, while Dad would provide the one-liners

Ronnie Corbett talks to critic Jack Tinker about his starring role in Dad *and Graham Chapman's 1974 sitcom* The Prince of Denmark. *Graham is in the background.*

and character detail. The general working culture was perhaps not ideal, but such was the friendship between the two men that this period was productive, playful and largely positive. Their strengths obviously dovetailed and they managed to get the best out of each other.

The thought of Dad working with a Python might seem incongruous but they had a shared love of wordplay and silliness. My favourite story about their friendship concerns a black-tie charity dinner at the Dorchester Hotel. As was the custom at these kinds of events, a toastmaster would announce each pair of guests as they entered the dining room. Graham, seeing that their names weren't written down on the list, leant into the man's ear and whispered. He and Dad then strode down the stairs, arm in arm, with the toastmaster proclaiming: 'My Lords, Ladies and Gentlemen, Mr Enoch Powell and Mrs Harry Belafonte.'

Initially, Dad and Graham were joined on *No – That's Me Over Here* by fellow soon-to-be-Python Eric Idle, who remembers the mischievous chaos of Chapman in those early Frost years:

Your dad and I were writing the Ronnie Corbett thing, and he lived in Elgin Crescent at that point, so we'd meet there. Graham wasn't there and we had assumed he was writing with *The 1948 Show* lot because he was working on both shows at the same time. So, we called them up because we had a plot point we wanted to talk over with him. And we spoke to Tim Brooke-Taylor, who said, 'Oh, he is not here. He's with you.' I said, 'Actually no, he's not with us. He's with you.' And then we found out that he was, of course, playing both ends against the middle as he was with his boyfriend [David Sherlock] up in Hampstead.

This brilliantly distils the rashly impulsive side of Graham but it also highlights Dad's reputation for reliability. For Dad at least, Graham's mercurial nature wasn't without its benefits. The work that they created was a lot more complex and character-driven than Dad had been used to up until that point. Knowing Ronnie Corbett well from the Danny La Rue years obviously helped, as did the discipline of now writing narrative for a sitcom format. However, Graham's surreal worldview was beginning to free Dad from some of his more traditional impulses. Though not everything Graham suggested was even remotely possible in the seventies. As Dad remembered: 'Graham and I used to write: "It's morning. We discover Ronnie wanking." And we'd laugh for about half an hour.'

If only they'd both lived long enough to see Jesse Armstrong manage to get exactly the same thing into an episode of *Succession* and win an Emmy. However, this wasn't the only example of their rather roguish spirit on *No – That's Me Over Here*. They would solemnly write other ridiculous things into the script like, 'Ronnie enters Mr Robinson's office. Mr Robinson is standing wearing a posing pouch'. They'd also often make the actor Ivor Dean (who was playing Mr Robinson) say things like, 'Corbett! What the FUCK are you talking about?' and that would make everyone laugh at the read-through. They also started writing an action for a goat that was never seen and in one wedding episode, it went: 'The sandwiches have been nibbled by the goat. We cannot see the goat as it is outside in the garden' or 'The goat is now just outside the front room door'. It became such a running gag, that at the last recording of the series, Dad and Graham arrived at the studio to find the crew had brought in an actual goat.

When Graham died in 1989, Dad's simple response when interviewed about him was to say that he couldn't think about Graham Chapman for more than five minutes without laughing. What did go into their shows was very often based on the characters who came into the Angel pub in Highgate (which they frequented at lunchtime). There was the bank manager from over the road, who used to come in with his wife, Judith. His name was Brian and for many years he claimed to be the inspiration for the eponymous hero of the Pythons' third film, a fact made credible by the fact that Brian's love interest in the movie is also called Judith (Iscariot). John Cleese claimed that the main reason they chose the name Brian was that they wanted to use the most boring name possible, so perhaps the bank manager's brag might have been a little double-edged. However, Brian's presence was felt in an even more constructive (and profitable) sense, as he also looked after the accounts of several Pink Floyd members, who went on to contribute not inconsiderable funds to the Pythons' second film *Monty Python and The Holy Grail*. Not a bad contact to have just over the road.

Dad remembers a young writer joining their circle at the Angel. He was something of a protégé of Graham's and had started helping him with various bits and pieces. Graham rewarded him with a small wage. The young writer made the mistake of arriving a little late for lunch one day, meaning that a couple of rounds had already been bought. He was left with the onerous task of buying drinks for the whole group and, because he was just starting out in the business, couldn't really afford it. Apparently, he even asked Brian the bank manager for a loan to buy the round. The young writer's name? Douglas Adams. Needless to say, a few years later when he revisited the Angel, he was not only able to buy Brian a drink but also probably the pub.

Another regular visitor was Keith Moon, the drummer of the Who. Keith came in and sat down with Dad and Graham and was having a pretty normal chat until he noticed a group of people whispering and pointing in the corner. He said: 'I suppose they're going to want some Mooning.' Without a pause, he let out a scream and threw his pint glass to the floor. The group were thrilled that they'd seen a legend in the flesh, in his natural habitat, behaving exactly as they expected. They left a short time afterwards, so Keith leant over to the barman and said: 'How much do I owe you for the pint glass?'

Perhaps Graham's greatest legacy for Dad, aside from the work they generated, was the instrumental part Chapman played in starting Dad's friendship with Yorkshire literary titan J. B. Priestley. Dad revered him and would let anyone who would listen know about his love for the man he called 'the great JB'. Dad and Graham were having lunch one day and Graham said, 'You know you're a bore on the subject of J. B. Priestley? Why don't you ring him?' Dad was stumped by this logic and blustered at the idea, but Chapman persisted. Dad then remembered a woman at Yorkshire Television who had made a documentary with JB and, before he knew it, he was calling the Priestley home. A woman answered the phone, who Dad later found out was the housekeeper and, with Graham at his elbow, said 'Is Mr Priestley in?' There was a short period of silence and then a very familiar voice said: 'Hello. Who's that?'

Dad stuttered: 'My name is… erm, Barry Cryer.'

'Are you indeed. I've heard you on the wireless,' said JB. Dad's confidence soared and suitably emboldened, asked if they could meet for tea. 'You're mad,' came the unexpected response, but Priestley consented. 'I'll have you know I'm giving up my walk,' he said. Dad then asked if his friend could join them. 'Who's your mate?' said the great man. It turned out that not only was JB a big fan of Monty Python, but he knew they were doing their (very first) stage show at the Belgrade in Coventry the following week. The Priestleys lived in Alveston outside Stratford-upon-Avon, which is about half an hour away. JB had even been infuriated that the BBC had stopped showing *Flying Circus* in the Midlands.

It didn't take too long before the other Pythons heard about the plan and the following week John Cleese, Michael Palin and Graham's partner David Sherlock were all packed into a car heading to Priestley's home, Kissing Tree House. After an initial mix-up that saw the Priestley housekeeper encounter a kneeling Michael Palin (who was checking the letterbox for signs of life), Priestley eventually greeted them warmly at the door and, although he looked pleased to see them, the atmosphere was a little stilted at first. It turned out Priestley was as nervous as they were. Graham took out his pipe and started filling it. Priestley did the same and the two men began comparing their tobacco. The afternoon shifted into an easy camaraderie that encouraged Priestley's wife, Jacquetta, to emerge from behind a bookcase to join them. Apparently, she'd been hiding there because she thought it might be *This Is Your Life*. Dad became friends with the Yorkshire writer after that and used to take him regularly to the Café Royal for lunch. They stayed in touch until Priestley's death in 1984.

To most of Dad's peers, Pythons excluded, J. B. Priestley was a creature from a bygone age, but Dad was always quick to champion his relevance, believing that good comedy and good writing transcended generations. Of writing generally, Priestley knew there were plenty of clever young writers, but wondered if there was 'too much genius, not enough talent'. As a result, Dad was never comfortable with comedy that was trying to be too clever, tricksy or ornate. It was a turn-off. Rather it was well-crafted silliness based on years of hard work that appealed to him most.

There were two comedians at the time who typified this approach better than anyone and Dad was about to experience their craft at first-hand: Morecambe and Wise.

A doctor was in a pub relaxing when a man came up to him and said: 'I know you're off-duty, and I must apologise for bothering you, but I'm getting these frightening migraines right across my forehead and I don't know what to do. I've tried aspirin and paracetamol and ibuprofen but they just don't seem to do anything.'

The doctor said: 'It's fine. In fact, I had exactly the same problem until recently. I tried all of the pills you mentioned too and just couldn't shift it. Then one night I was in bed with my wife and I put my head between her breasts and suddenly the headache just disappeared overnight. It has never happened again. Give it a go.'

Three weeks later they met again in the pub (as people do in jokes) and the doctor remembered the man and said: 'How's your headache? Did you do what I suggested?'

'I did,' replied the man. 'Haven't you got a lovely home?'

9

One of the high points of Dad's writing career was working for Morecambe and Wise. He and John Junkin wrote several sketches for them in the 1970s and 1980s, as well as two Christmas specials, in 1972 and 1978. Dad always felt the key to his writing partnership with John was that they were both performers. They even shared a similar introduction to the industry, as John had spent much of his early career alternating between writing and performing. John got his first break as a writer when he sent a script to Spike Milligan and ended up writing not only for Milligan (on his Australian radio show *The Idiot*) but also (with Terry Nation) for Peter Sellers, Marty Feldman, Frankie Howerd, Ronnie Barker, Ted Ray and Harry Worth.

In 1960, after a recommendation from Harry H. Corbett, he started acting at Joan Littlewood's Theatre Workshop, and eventually went on to take roles in *Till Death Us Do Part*, *On the House*, *Doctor in Love*, *Heavens Above!* and *The Wrong Arm of the Law*. He's probably best known as an actor for his role as the Beatles' road manager, 'Shake', in Richard Lester's *A Hard Day's Night*. Dad always respected John as an actor and his skill in this regard gave their partnership a dynamic that perhaps wasn't there with other writers he worked with, apart from Graham Chapman. Being able to perform in a writers' room isn't necessary but it can help the flow if one or other of you is able to vocalise the dialogue in the style of the person or people you're writing for.

While Dad also took various acting roles down the years, acting itself as a skill was not something he ever thought he was capable of. He saw those who could act as different animals, touched by an inspiration that he could never experience himself. I disagreed with him about this, as I could see he had all the necessary talents to develop a performance. As a writer, he was brilliantly intuitive with character and very particular with language, two things I think that he could have used to his advantage as an actor. 'It's the lines,' he'd say. 'They just won't stay in my head.' I think another reason he shied away from calling himself an actor is that he felt he'd be subjected to proper scrutiny. Much easier to say that he was a writer who did bits here and there.

However, knowing and understanding performance was key to his writing, even if the doing was transient. 'To be able to hear the voice of the person you're writing for is important when creating material for them. We're like a tailor making suits. We even use the same word – material,' he used to say. Dad and John were therefore required to mimic the people they were writing for and they would perform for each other. John did a very good Eric Morecambe impression (it helped that he smoked a pipe) and Dad would imitate Ernie Wise (it helped that he was from Yorkshire).

Dad worshipped Eric Morecambe, describing him as a 'one-off'. When talking about the quickest wit of all the people he worked with, he'd usually cite Eric. For example, when a man cornered Morecambe at a party and began pontificating on the qualities needed to succeed in show business, the man said: 'I always say you need three things...' to which Eric fired back: 'If you've got three things, you should be in a circus.'

This is not to say that Dad underrated Ernie. Not at all. A fellow Leeds man (and yet another example that explodes the popular myth that mirth belongs exclusively to the west side of the Pennines), Dad would show solidarity and celebrate Ernie's generous ability to help Eric shine. After all, they'd been together since they were teenagers and Eric openly acknowledged that he

Dad and longtime friend and collaborator John Junkin. If something wasn't nailed down, John would hang it round his neck.

felt vulnerable without him. Eddie Braben, their main writer (Dad used to infuriate John Junkin by calling Braben the 'A Team'), was conscious of this vulnerability from the start of their working relationship, which is all the more remarkable when you consider that Eddie wasn't actually that much of a fan of theirs to start with.

Braben had fallen out with Ken Dodd and was looking for a new gig. Bill Cotton, then Head of Light Entertainment at the BBC, got Eddie together with Morecambe and Wise. To Eddie, they were just a run-of-the-mill and conventional double act and he took a while to warm to the idea. Even though they were already stars, Eddie started to see something special in the intimate, almost fraternal bond between them. Eddie's innovation was to change them from 'Morecambe and Wise' where they were a knockabout hapless stage double act, to 'Eric and Ernie', where they became more down-to-earth, if still silly, sitcom-style flatmates. He stitched them at the hip and, while the change was a subtle one, the new dynamic was powerfully felt. Eddie even wrote a line for Eric to say when Ernie left the stage: 'Don't be too long, Ern, when you're not here I feel a cold draught all down one side.'

Phrasing the connection in terms of temperature was apt as warmth seemed to be at the heart of this new relationship for Eric and Ernie. They might sometimes be at cross purposes in a sketch but they were always inseparable. Eric trusted Ernie, especially when they began to ad lib. This was something that they'd been doing since the start of their careers and had become a key part of their appeal. Eric needed someone generous like Ernie to play with, someone who knew his mind and where it might be going if he went off script. There was great joy to be had in witnessing them both broadening their smiles as the exchanges become more and more informal.

There's a wonderful example of Eric's quick wit in one of their regular wig sketches. The set-up, written by Braben, sees Eric wearing a wig as an advertisement for the treats in store for the audience, to which Ernie says:

Ernie: 'You can't advertise on the BBC. Nobody can advertise
         on the BBC. Even Lord Hill [then chairman of the
         BBC board of governors] can't say what kind of pipe
         tobacco he smokes.'
Eric: 'And no wonder, it's mine. It is well known along the
         powers of corridor…'
Pause. Ernie smiles at the mistake and corrects him…
Ernie: 'Corridors of power.'
Eric: 'Ah, don't forget – he walks backwards.'

It was a fluffed line but Eric's brain and Ernie's heart turned it into a magical exchange. You can see the exhilaration in their eyes as they get back on track.

Dad's favourite sketch that he and John wrote for Morecambe and Wise during their tenure was also based on a more informal moment. Eric once wondered what would happen if they had a guest on the show who didn't know what they were supposed to do. Dad and John hit upon the idea of having Vera Lynn on and getting Eric to mispronounce her name (see Andrew Preview). Vera then goes to sulk in her dressing room and refuses to come back on:

Ernie: 'How can we get her to sing?'
Eric: 'I don't know, just short of starting another war, I've no idea!'

In a neat piece of symmetry, it echoes one of Dad's favourite Ken Dodd lines (probably written by Braben): 'I knew there'd be a war because I've just walked past Vera Lynn's dressing room and heard her gargling.' Which lyricist Don Black later turned into this musing: 'I think the Second World War was started by Vera Lynn's agent.'

Apparently, the first time Dad worked on a Morecambe and Wise Christmas show (in 1972) Eric said: 'We don't need sketches with trees and reindeer and Father Christmas or anything.' Dad and John were puzzled. How is this a Christmas show, then? Turns out Eric always worried the show wouldn't be repeated at Easter if it was too styled for Christmas. Sure enough, he was right, and Dad and John were grateful for the repeat fees. It's staggering to think that those shows generated audience figures in the 20 millions – famously peaking in 1977 (sorry Dad, you just missed by a year) at 28 million. That was half the population at the time.

For John and Dad, their Christmas specials presented them with huge exposure, an amazing opportunity but also a huge amount of pressure to match Braben's standard. I think it's safe to say that not everyone has been that kind to their material on the 1972 and 1978 shows since, but I love the rudimentary silliness of them. Tongue-in-cheek knockabout gags were typical of the style of a lot of Dad's stuff with Junkin, and Morecambe and Wise suited it perfectly. They would be the first to say that it would've been a mistake to attempt to copy Braben's more complex style that explored the pair's relationship. Instead, Dad and John stuck to their strengths. Old-fashioned variety gags, which Eric and Ernie were obviously comfortable with, mixed in with bold, anarchic, visual set pieces.

By the time I was on the scene, Mum and Dad had slowed a little in their celebrity entertaining. My siblings have some good stories about those times, helping to hand round drinks to people like Frankie Howerd, Kenny Everett, Peter Cook and Ronnie Barker, but I think it must've been around 1980 (when I was nearly seven) that I met Eric Morecambe. I was obsessed with being a goalkeeper at the time and, when I wasn't at school, would wear my black and yellow goalkeeper's kit morning, noon and night. Gloves included. My parents threw a birthday party for Dad that year and there was a real mix of local mates and showbiz pals, all arriving to position their cars on the street outside our house. My job was to sit behind the curtain of a window at the front of the house and tell one of my older brothers that a car had pulled up. They'd then run outside and direct them to a side street where there was extra parking. That was it. A simple job, even for a six-year-old. What I hadn't worked out was that, as the house filled up with people, my job would become more and more redundant. But would I move from my post? Not on your life. A sentry man must remain vigilant at all times! You never knew who might turn up late (usually Peter Cook).

I'm not quite sure how close it was to my bedtime, but as I sat there, looking out into the street, the curtains next to me started to move. They suddenly parted a little and I was greeted by this big smile and a familiar pair of glasses. I say familiar, I had a vague idea who he was but my viewing habits were a little different back then. Had it been Johnny Ball I probably would've fallen through the window. However, emerging through the curtains was, of course, a speciality of his. Eric leaned in. 'Have you seen much of the ball yet?'

Dad said that Eric in private was very different from his screen persona. Although he'd happily give a waggle of his glasses to people in the street, he was essentially quite shy. It was quite telling that when he came to the house that night, Dad said he spent most of the evening talking to a guy from the local pub who, as the result of a rugby accident, was in a wheelchair. He wasn't really interested in comparing notes with other celebrities.

In 2017, my friend Neil Forsyth (*The Gold, Guilt, Bob Servant*) wrote a one-off film for BBC Four about Eddie Braben called *Eric, Ernie and Me*. It starred Stephen Tompkinson as Eddie, Mark Bonnar as Eric and Neil Maskell as Ernie. Rufus Jones played Johnny Ammonds, the double act's long-suffering producer, forever trying to keep the peace and protect them from the BBC. Rufus captured Johnny's forensic eye for detail. Dad once claimed that Ammonds's favourite piece of music was Stravinsky's *Rewrite of Spring*.

Neil told me he'd written a scene in the film in which 'Barry Cryer' does the warm-up for Eric and Ernie's studio audience. Neil drew Dad's appearance from a 1973 *Omnibus* documentary about the duo called *Fools Rush In*. His turn only includes a couple of lines from his act, followed by his handover (delivered in the high-pitched BBC voice he was sporting at the time): 'And now may I welcome two gentlemen who I may hazard a guess you have come to see. Will you welcome and say good evening to Mr Eric Morecambe and Mr Ernie Wise.'

Neil asked me if I could talk to Dad and get some more of his warm-up material from that time. He wanted to flesh out the warm-up scene a bit as he had Eric, Ernie and John Ammonds chatting nervously about the recording in the wings in the foreground. I told Neil I'd speak to Dad before asking him if they had anyone in mind to play the role. 'Funny you should mention it…' he said. I called Dad and asked him what sort of stuff he was doing back then. We joked about how it was probably not that dissimilar to the stuff he was doing now, just with more outdated references. Then he confessed he could barely remember any of the jokes he did, or was doing, back in the day. He certainly didn't have them in a file somewhere.

They say American comedian Don Rickles never wrote down his material, as it was all stored in his head. The same was pretty much true of Dad (and that's where the similarity with Rickles ends). Despite Dad being a writer for most of his life, when it came to performing, he'd often prefer to work out material for a TV show, one-man show or after-dinner speech in a series of beats or bullet points. Famously, he'd often do so on the back of a cigarette packet. Graeme Garden offered that the reason he used Consulate as his brand of choice was not because of the taste but because it had the largest amount of white space on its packaging to make notes on. Dad described them as his File-O-Fags. He needed to jot something down quickly as his most creative moments usually came when he was away from his typewriter and either improvising or reacting. He said that he enjoyed *I'm Sorry I Haven't A Clue* best for this reason, when 'the wheels were coming off'.

When it came to Neil's request, I therefore had to do some digging around, partly from my own memory. There was one joke I remembered he used to do at the top of his act that started by addressing the audience. He'd say: 'You're clearly an educated crowd. Only just now in the bar, I overheard a man ordering a "Martinus".' The barman said: "Surely, sir, you mean a Martini?" The man said, "If I'd wanted two, I'd have asked for two."' When I reminded him of it, he was delighted. 'Of course! Martinus!' It was like I'd suddenly reunited him with an old friend. I even asked him if he'd start using it again. 'Probably not,' he said, citing it as being quite specific to an after-dinner circuit that he was no longer on, 'but it's nice to know it's still there. Frank Muir was right. He once told me that all the material is all still there, it's just that some get pushed to the back.'

I provided this kind of service often for Dad when he was older. His memory was such a powerful weapon in his armoury that when it occasionally slipped, it troubled him, and he immediately sent for reinforcements. He was very reliant on others to fill in those gaps. Famously, the legendary Dick Vosburgh, an American-born British comedy writer (and writing partner of Dad's), played a role now inhabited by IMDb. Dad would be watching a Hollywood western from the 1940s and wouldn't be able to identify the second lead, which infuriated him. He had a whole row of *Halliwell's Film Guide* sitting behind him, but he would immediately call Dick.

'Who's playing Bull McQuade in *Rogue's Gallery* on BBC 2 right now, Dick?'

Dick's New Jersey bass-baritone would chime back straight away: 'Hmmm… Bull McQuade, eh? Noah Beery Snr if I'm not mistaken.'

Colin Sell, who toured with Dad on stage for many years, often found himself in a similar position when it came to remembering material. As Dad got older, he would ring Colin up before they did a show together to jog his memory:

'It's important to say that he very rarely forgot anything, but occasionally he'd call and say: "What was the joke about so-and-so?" and only fifty per cent of the time I'd have a memory of it. "Oh, that's great. Thanks. You really are an encyclopedia, Col." "I'm not really, Baz," I'd say. Mainly because I don't remember jokes very well. I told him that I only really remember the openers or the punchlines and that was because I'd sat there for so many bloody years, listening to him tell all those jokes. However, sometimes he wouldn't tell a joke for quite a while, and I wondered if he'd just lost interest in it.

'There was then sometimes a lovely moment when he'd remember one in the middle of a show and because he was a bit rusty, he'd forget an element of it. There was this joke about a man who goes into a restaurant and orders an Aylesbury duck. The idea is that the man is supposed to get his finger and put it up the duck's backside. He'd say: "No, this is not an Aylesbury duck. This is a Suffolk duck. Get it right." The waiter goes back to the kitchen, and the chef in the kitchen gets very cross and sends out another duck. Same routine. Finger up the backside of the duck. "No, this is a Norfolk duck," the man would say. "I want you to get it right." Eventually, a third duck appears, and he gets his finger, and puts it up the backside of the duck. "Ah! This is an Aylesbury duck!" The man starts eating it. He calls the waiter over again. "Not only is it an Aylesbury duck, but it's one of the best Aylesbury ducks I've ever tasted! Please send the chef out as I'd like to congratulate him." The chef comes out but he is still pretty pissed off with the way he's been treated. They chat for a little bit and the guy says to the chef, where did you train? The chef tells him. "And tell me, where are you from, originally?" So, the chef drops his trousers and says, "I don't know. You're the expert. You tell me!"

'Now, on one occasion he, Barry, forgot to do the finger up the duck's backside bit of the joke at the beginning. I'd learned enough by this time to know that when you're on stage with a comedian, do not tell them how to sell a joke, because that's a good way to die. I thought, maybe, he's found a new way of doing this? Maybe somebody came up to him in the bar after the show one night and told him there was a different version? So, I didn't say anything and waited in anticipation. He didn't do the finger up the duck's backside at all. He got to the punchline and said, with the air of triumph that all comedians have: "You're the expert. You tell me!"

'...and his sling was full of shot!' Dad warming up the studio audience for Harry H. Corbett's TV show Mr Aitch in 1967.

'There was absolute silence in the audience, apart from the pianist (me) who fell off his stool laughing. And Barry said, "What?" I said, "Well, you didn't do the finger up the duck's backside!" And then Barry realised he hadn't. So, he started to laugh as well and then the audience got it. It was then one of the most confusing jokes you've ever heard, but it worked wonderfully well because the audience got it by piecing together all the missing parts. And it was just the sort of thing that Barry loved because the wheels had come off.'

A few moments after I'd reminded him of the Martinus joke, Dad started to remember lots of little lines and asides he used to do in warm-ups. 'Hello, my name's Barry Cryer, one of the better cheaper acts.' 'I don't play golf. I like women.' 'I don't really tell jokes; my big thing is magic... but that's just my opinion.' That kind of material. Although most were cleaner than that last one.

He then asked me who was playing him in the film. I hesitated. I don't know why, but I think I wanted it to be a surprise. 'Well, you were about thirty-seven when you did that warm-up for Eric and Ernie, weren't you? I'm forty-three. I thought I'd have a crack at it.' He beamed. I was a regular on *Hollyoaks* at the time, and management had said that I could have two days off to film *Eric, Ernie and Me*. However, due to a change in the availability of the venue for the warm-up scene, the dates moved and this magical window, where I could've played Dad in a film written by a friend of mine, abruptly closed. I put away my black glasses and white wig, closed my collection of Baz warm-up material and sloped off back to Liverpool.

'Why don't they just stop messing around and give *you* the part?' I said.

He laughed and then said: 'Do you think they would?'

John Culshaw ended up playing 'Barry Cryer' and did a great job. It was the perfect solution to our disappointment as not only was he a long-time fan of Dad's, but he'd become a friend of his as well.

The tone of warm-up is subtly different from other forms of comedy. In short, the job is to go out into the studio just after the audience has arrived and chat with them, explain how the evening is going to work and, usually, tell some jokes. You're not the main event, so a degree of humility is required, as you're really cheering for someone else. Much of the job is obviously to set the tone for the recording, so a good understanding of the show's style and a feeling for its audience is essential. However, I think the biggest thrill would have been to see Dad's quick wits tested, as he needed to fill in if there was a technical error or even shorten a set if the problem was fixed early. In short, Dad fitted the job description perfectly. Upbeat, enthusiastic, humble, flexible and confident – he was in his element as a warm-up man.

However, I believe Dad's formal introduction to the skill needed for a warm-up spot came when he started playing the role of old-time music hall chairman at the Players' Theatre in London. A chairman is a slightly different role from a warm-up act, but they do share a lot of the same responsibilities and it's not uncommon for the same type of comedian to work both roles. Those of us that remember *The Good Old Days* will associate the role of chairman with Leonard Sachs. His extravagant style was typified by long, verbally dextrous runs of ornate, florid and sesquipedalian word usage (you get the idea). Above all, his energy was very rapid and rhythmic, like a cross between a Gilbert and Sullivan patter song and a market trader. As well as *The Good Old Days* (which was filmed at Dad's alma mater the City Varieties in Leeds), Leonard was instrumental in establishing the Players' Theatre Club and inaugurated a music-hall revival show called *Ridgeway's Late Joys* upon which *The Good Old Days* was based.

There's a great documentary about the history of music hall from 1968, called *A Little of What You Fancy*. It charts music hall's humble architectural beginnings from the back rooms of pubs to the 3,000-strong 'grand hall' heyday of the late Victorian period. The evolution of the form is also examined by looking at the singers and acts of the day, intermixed with footage of the contemporary performers who helped its revival in the sixties. Right towards the beginning of this section is Dad at the Players', all thirty-two years of him, heavily made up, with tight black curls on his head and even tighter white gloves on his hands. There's a lovely exchange where he asks a young couple in the stalls if they've set a date for their wedding. When the woman says that they haven't, Dad responds: 'I hope he's not like one of these new soap powders, dear. Works fast and leaves no ring.'

This documentary holds a special resonance for me and Dad as one of the buildings featured is Wilton's Music Hall. I've performed there quite a few times as an actor and I can safely say that it's my favourite venue not just to play, but to spend time in. Dad and I also collaborated with Spymonkey Theatre to interpret our book *Mrs Hudson's Diaries* for Wilton's first Christmas show in 2014. When it came time for the inaugural artistic director Frances Mayhew to step down in 2015, she asked Dad and me if we'd help with the reopening ceremony (following a £4.5 million restoration grant) the following year. Simon Callow would be our hyperbolic chairman and introduce magic from Morgan and West, and a cabaret number from Gwyneth Herbert and Frances Ruffelle.

Remembering *The Good Old Days*, when he and Bernard Cribbins put routines together, Dad suggested we sing the old music-hall audience participation favourite 'My Bonnie Lies Over the Ocean'. Every time you sing a word beginning with 'B', the audience stands up, and when you sing another 'B', they sit down. And so on and so forth. Well, the song has more Bs in it than a hive, and soon descends into chaos with the audience bobbing up and down, in Bernard's words 'like overtime in a yo-yo factory'. It's a lot of fun and would be perfect for such a celebratory occasion. What we'd forgotten is that Wilton's royal patron would be guest of honour. King Charles was just a lowly prince in those days, but we were suddenly tickled by the thought of him pogoing in the front row.

We decided to open with Dad turning up late, leaving me to fill in onstage by making copious excuses for his terrible behaviour. Dad enters, claiming he'd been into several pubs nearby (admonishing the audience for getting the wrong idea along the way), but couldn't find the Prince of Wales (see what we did there?). He then spots Charles sitting in front of him. Dad then leans into the old variety standby of: 'They say you only play Wilton's twice in your career, once on the way up and once on the way down... It's nice to be back.' Next, we go into a bit about choosing songs and then sing 'My Bonnie Lies Over The Ocean'.

I didn't expect the future king to jump around like a squash-filled toddler, given the amount of security detail we were told would be there. However, he and Camilla joined in with the spirit of things and before long, we had our very own mink-lined mosh pit. In the meet-and-greet afterwards, Charles said to me: 'My grandmother would've loved that up and down song,' adding: 'It must be such fun working with your father.' I was tempted to say: 'Yes. It must be such fun working with yours.' But I resisted the temptation. I told him that it was a lot of fun working with Dad because silliness was in short supply. It is a very happy memory, an experience I wish Dad and I had got to do more of on stage when he was alive, but I cherished it all the more because of its rarity.

In 1966, a couple of years before the documentary was made, and just as Dad was beginning his life as a Frost writer, David approached him to ask if he'd like to try warm-up. As Frost had seen him performing at Danny La Rue's show, he thought Dad's easy-going manner and quick brain might be a good fit for recordings. Dad wasn't sure, as he didn't really know what was involved, but David assured him it was no different from the stuff he was doing at Winston's. Dad was glad he accepted, because in those early days, especially when Frost went to ITV with *The Frost Programme*, he ended up doing three shows a week. It was a good source of income at a time when writing wasn't covering all the bills.

David then started booking Dad for other gigs too. Dad remembered the occasion when he really felt he was beginning to master the craft. During a recording with Noël Coward, who was being interviewed by Frost at the Mayfair Hotel, a camera froze. Dad was asked to fill in. Now, one request that Coward always made when doing such shows was to have a bottle of champagne in a bucket of ice sitting to the side of his chair. Dad walked onstage, had a scan of the room and for some reason looked to the ice bucket for inspiration. He then turned to the audience: 'Oh look! Monogrammed ice cubes.'

It didn't always run so smoothly. At least according to Dad. He was once warming up for Spike Milligan, when, unannounced, Spike walked on behind him and exclaimed: 'Van Gogh was Jewish!' Dad was a huge Goons fan growing up (as were many of his contemporaries) and Spike's rhythm was so unique that it would be understandable if he had just let the audience enjoy the moment and ride it out. However, he chose to accept the challenge and added to the line: 'Well, that explains everything; the rabbi clearly had a terrible sense of direction!'

To me, that's a great retort, fully in the spirit of improvised comedy. Dad's listening, building on the image and clearly respecting the other performer's contribution, yet Spike glowered at him, unhappy that he'd trodden on his energy. Spike was an idol to many of that generation, but to clash swords with him, no matter how benignly, could leave you open to ridicule. Even the then Prince Charles found this out to his cost when Spike called him 'the little grovelling bastard' on accepting a lifetime achievement comedy award in 1994. I think this sensitivity on Dad's part goes back to a moment when he was backstage in the green room of a chat show, and Spike jumped up, spread-eagled himself against the wall and said: 'Cryer's here. Take my jokes. Just don't hurt me!'

One group that easily fitted into the Spike fan club (again, it's difficult to find an exception in that era of comedians) were the Pythons. When they came along, featuring as they did many Frost writers, it didn't hurt that they remembered Dad doing warm-ups for *The Frost Report*. In fact, he was drafted in to do warm-ups for their first series. However, there was a significant disparity between the expectation of Dad's work for a Python recording compared to a Frost one. TV companies these days often try to match the audience to the show, but when Python began, they were in the habit of bussing in audiences, regardless of the content. So early Python audiences were sometimes made up of a disparate group of people, some of whom came to the first recording thinking it was about an actual circus. Then the sketches started and there were dummies falling from buildings, undertakers lugging dead bodies around in bin bags and prat-falling Gestapo officers. In Dad's words: 'There were these dear old souls regretting going: "Oh yes, a circus, that'll be interesting!"'

After a time, the Pythons relieved Dad of warm-up duties because, in Michael Palin's words, 'he was getting more laughs than we were'. Tongue-in-cheek, of course, but Dad admitted that the styles were a mismatch. Dad's approach was well suited to a general audience, while the Pythons were very much more an acquired taste at this point.

Dad's adaptability made him a good fit for the role of warm-up, if not on this occasion. Just like his experience in revue, Dad was now self-aware enough to know that his warm-up routines were made with an orthodox stance. Welcoming the audience, he'd tell them a bit about the show, do some jokes and then bring out members of the cast to fool around with and generally keep the energy in the room. Dad's warm-up approach could accommodate most styles of comedy, but instinctively, Dad felt this slant cutting across the direction of this strange, quirky new sketch show and he was bold enough to admit it. He continued to work with Pythons on other projects, of course, and remained friends with them all until the end, perhaps because of, rather than despite, this moment of honesty.

One of his favourite warm-up stories came when he opened for the great Danish musician and raconteur Victor Borge in the seventies. It was a real thrill when he was asked to call Tito Burns, Borge's agent, to confirm the gig. The first thing Dad did (he did it for after-dinners too) was ask for Borge's CV, so he could talk about his career to the audience. Dad went on and told them his life story, throwing in a joke or two along the way. Then he got the signal that Victor was ready, so immediately wrapped up: 'The reason we're all here tonight is Victor Borge!'

The show began and was only a few minutes old when a camera went down. Victor wasn't best pleased. Before Dad trots on again, he says to the director: 'I can't tell jokes while this man is playing,' but the director insisted. Dad went on, and rambled for a while, trying desperately to avoid telling too many jokes (which for Dad must've taken a superhuman effort). When they were ready to start again, he welcomed Victor back onto the stage and Borge sat down at the piano. The camera failed again. Victor was now simmering. Dad filled with polite observations, but again, a few jokes: 'For the third time tonight, the reason we're all here... Mr Victor Borge!'

Dad backed off deferentially, but just before he made it to the wings, Borge grabbed his arm and led him back into the spotlight: 'Now you know the reason why I'm here tonight... to fill in the gaps between Barry Cryer.'

It was a pivotal moment for Dad. He was now shoulder-to-shoulder with a man he admired hugely and who he had seen perform on countless occasions; Borge was one of the first people Dad saw when he first came to London, and one of the reasons he wanted to stay. He was a hero. Yet here he was, pulling Dad back in front of his own audience to compliment Dad's patience, humour and respect. Dad felt that rare thing as a young comedian: acknowledgement.

Warming up an audience is like a lot of those seemingly straightforward performance skills. It takes a lot of craft and a lot of hard work to make it look that effortless and, by all accounts, Dad excelled in both departments. However, as soon as he started to make a name for himself, the warm-up work began to diminish. As I pointed out earlier, one of the key attributes of a warm-up is being able to hype the profiles of those performers and shows you're there to help. It's therefore another of those unsung jobs in show business that is not always appreciated, even less understood. To demonstrate, I'll leave you with one of Dad's favourite stories about the art form:

> A young comedian years ago at Granada TV was in front
> of the audience and got on to the subject of astrology. He
> said to them: 'Shout out your star sign and I'll tell you your
> main personality traits.' A man shouted: 'Aquarius!' The
> comic responds: 'Big mouth, always wants to get in first!'
> Later on, the comedian was in the bar with the producer
> and the producer said: 'You're good, I'd like to use you again.
> I especially loved that astrology joke you did. How did you
> know somebody was going to shout "Aquarius"?'

Two men are walking along the street, and one has his dog with him. The dog keeps pulling on the lead to one side and the man says: 'Do you mind if we stop so he can pee?'

'Of course not. Go ahead,' says the other man.

The man takes his dog to the side of the street and the dog gets up on its hind legs, puts its front paws up against the wall and starts peeing. The other man says: 'That's incredible. How did you teach him to do that?'

'I didn't. He's been doing it himself for a while.'

'Really?'

'Yes. Ever since a wall fell on him.'

10

For Dad, the 1970s were full of expressions like *Hello Cheeky* and *Jokers Wild*. Questions like *Who Do You Do?* and *What's My Line?* were asked. However, by the end of the decade, there was only really one answer: *I'm Sorry I Haven't A Clue*. Now in his late thirties, the most important shift for Dad was that he moved away from being the beneficiary of individual acts of kindness and mentorship from people like David Nixon, Frankie Vaughan, Danny La Rue and David Frost, and was instead becoming his own man. He'd also found himself beginning to perform a lot more after his hospitalisations with eczema had ceased.

Apart from walk-ons in *Python* and *1948 Show* sketches, one of Dad's more significant contributions during the late sixties was playing notorious fraudster Emil Savundra on *The Frost Programme*. Savundra was in the public eye as the owner of the unsecured Fire, Auto and Marine Insurance Company that swindled hundreds of thousands of British motorists out of their premiums when the company folded. Dad, Dick Vosburgh and Eric Idle wrote a sketch where Dad played the head of a similar company called the Fire Renewal And Universal Debt (yes, FRAUD, for those at the back).

After the sketch went out, Savundra phoned David Frost personally to compliment the show on Dad's portrayal. The British newspapers of the time had been hunting Savundra for weeks to try to get him to confess his crimes, yet here he was voluntarily speaking to Frost (most probably out of vanity). Frost used the call as an opportunity to invite Savundra onto the programme to defend himself. What followed the next evening was one of the most iconic (and electric) television exchanges of that or any era. All because Dad had mocked him on television (well, it wasn't ALL because of Dad, but it's his book, so I'll give him some extra credit). It clearly inspired a talent for satirical portrayals of high-profile fraudsters in Dad, but not one that was triggered again until 1993, when he found himself unexpectedly approached to play Robert Maxwell in *Maxwell: The Musical*. More of that later (no, really, I'm not kidding).

The writing work, following on from his partnership with Graham Chapman, had grown exponentially. In 1969 alone, he'd written for Ronnie Corbett, Max Bygraves, David Frost, *Doctor in the House* and Les Dawson. The 1960s generally took in work for Tommy Cooper, Jimmy Logan, Danny La Rue, Stanley Baxter and Kenneth Horne. Dad always batted back the description that 'he' wrote for people and was quick to add that 'we' was usually the correct way to describe things. While writing alone was true of the first half of the 1960s, by the seventies, Dad's creative relationships began to evolve.

The attraction for him was obvious. The sociability and the camaraderie were necessary elements for a man who'd essentially grown up alone and thrived on companionship. The playful exchange of ideas and the chance to elicit a laugh were equally essential for someone who'd spent much of his apprenticeship as a performer. Partnerships became the default setting for Dad during this busy period and remained the bedrock of his output for the rest of his career. Due to his visibility as a performer (compared to other writers of the same era), there was a temptation for people to attach sole authorship to the material he created for so many comedians. It's a great testament to Dad's humility that he would always be the first to credit his collaborators.

The constant in those partnerships was usually Dad's responsibility for the line work – gags, jokes and character detail. He tended to work with people who were better at construction, like story arcs, research and sketch structure. When I worked with Dad, I saw it as my job to provide a strong platform upon which Dad could play around and subvert the narrative I'd created. The fun was in testing each other's work and teasing each other's sensibilities, with the joy being that whatever your role, you were only there to make something silly. He often talked about 'walkers and typists' and 'worriers and loungers', but the golden rule was always the same: never be precious. The material wouldn't make it if the other person didn't laugh.

David Nobbs (another Frost writer) was his writing partner on the Les Dawson vehicle *Sez Les* during the mid-seventies. Together they wrote sixty-eight episodes or, as David put it, 'just missed sixty-nine – the story of my life'. Their writing culture seemed to follow a similar pattern to working with Graham Chapman, as one where they'd work at home in the morning, go to the pub at lunchtime and use the renowned powers of that type of social lubrication to 'improve the edit'. By the time David Nobbs moved to Harrogate in the late nineties, he and Dad would stay in Nobbs's garden to write if the weather allowed. Not because they'd had an attack of sobriety, but because the pub was now next door, and the pints could be passed over the wall. Writing for Les with Nobbs also saw the inaugural use of a favourite creative writing tool of Dad's. He wasn't one for spreadsheets, whiteboards and workshops, but instead would go to the bookcase, open a dictionary (yes, readers, remember *them*?) and he and David would write a sketch inspired by the first word they came across. Not foolproof by any means, and with plenty of false starts, but Dad maintains that the sketch they wrote for Les about an ostrich was one of the best they produced.

What's most intriguing is that John Cleese became a big part of the *Sez Les* show. The accepted notion is that Cleese was an Oxbridge prodigy who was a natural fit for the satire boom, found a like-minded tribe in Monty Python and then emerged from that formative experience like an angry, nuanced butterfly crafting pitch-perfect farce with *Fawlty Towers*. On the surface, of course, that's true but it's only part of the story. You'd think the university satirist Cleese and the traditional variety comic Dawson would be contrasting characters, at least from a social background standpoint. Still, nothing could have been further from the truth. Dad said that introducing them to each other was a joy. They were both avid readers and deep thinkers with intellectual and philosophical views on life who approached their performing work like writers.

Dawson had originally wanted to be a writer in the mould of Jack Kerouac, and hitchhiked his way across Europe. The legend has it that he found work as a pianist in a Parisian brothel, playing Charlie Chaplin's 'Limelight' every evening. The reality is that he tried to sell some poetry and came back after ten days. However, while the bohemian adventure of his youth may have been a touch fabricated, it is true that Les was most happy in a convivial setting rather than in a studio. Dad would invariably find him entertaining a group of people in the bar and had to coax him back to rehearsal. Les was always very giving of himself, and Dad often felt this selflessness greatly burdened his health. Though his time in Paris (however it panned out) gave way to a more conventional path as a comedian, his intellect, meta-theatricality and verbal dexterity endeared him to Cleese, who described Dawson as 'an autodidact, a very smart guy who was fascinated by words'.

Dad and David Nobbs attempted on a couple of occasions to write Les's monologues, but he ended up writing them himself. Dad was always honest when it came to admitting someone was better equipped to do a job. He and David were quite happy to concede the monologue when they heard lines like these: 'In awe, I watched the waxing moon ride across the zenith of the heavens like an ambered chariot towards the ebony void of infinite space wherein the tethered belts of Jupiter and Mars hang, for ever festooned in their orbital majesty. And as I looked at all this, I thought... I must put a roof on this toilet.'

Following the success of Cleese, a precedent was created to put Les with an unlikely sparring partner. They cast Humphrey Lyttelton as Sherlock Holmes opposite Les as his faithful sidekick, Dr Watson, and their partnership lasted across several sketches. Dad was obviously delighted as Humph was in full sail as chairman of *I'm Sorry I Haven't*

A Clue by this point and the leap to TV sketch performer was an unexpected one. Les, famously, used to play the piano very poorly, but the speculation was that it was all part of the performance, and that he was actually a very good pianist. Les liked the idea that people would say it took a brilliant pianist to hit the wrong note at the right time. Dad discovered this was a little generous when he and David Nobbs worked 'Bad Penny Blues' (the jazz track Humph wrote and made famous) into a Holmes and Watson sketch. During rehearsals, it soon became apparent that Les couldn't play the boogie-woogie piano required, and he became frustrated. He wasn't a bad player but couldn't play in the key that suited Humph's trumpet. They rewrote the sketch so that when Les talked to Humph, he slid off the piano stool to let musical director Laurie Holloway take over. They even made a feature of the joke, but Dad could see Les was a bit embarrassed.

Les Dawson's second volume of his autobiography is called *No Tears for the Clown*, but despite this and because of his trademark lugubrious expression and often grumpy onscreen persona, Les was forever being asked about melancholy behind the scenes. A journalist even asked Dad (for a documentary about Les): 'Was there a dark side to Les Dawson that we never saw?' Dad replied: 'Well, if there was, we never saw it.' Apparently, the take had to be scrapped because the cameraman was laughing too much.

As we discovered when we talked about the Frost years, the chemistry between writing partners was just as important as that between the performers above on *Sez Les*. Dad's greatest asset as a writer was his quick wit, ability to improvise and agility in the edit. John Cleese, as we've mentioned, was meticulous and deliberately specific when it came to writing. They attempted to write together a few times, but the differences were amicably insurmountable. Michael Palin recalls a similar experience with both men:

'I wrote occasionally with John on certain things and found it difficult. But that went back to my way of writing and that was probably why I didn't write that much with Barry. Barry was great at jokes and knew how to manufacture how to create a joke, the precise skill of putting across the humour, at just the right moment and with the right pitch. It was a brilliant thing he did.'

Dad and Michael wrote some sketches in the mid-sixties (along with Robert Hewison and Terry Jones) as part of *Late Night Review*, a comedy companion piece to the hip cultural discussion show *Late Night Line Up* presented by, among others, Joan Bakewell. On one occasion, Dad and Michael, dressed as trainee Supermen, jumped off chairs to silence in a church hall. Dennis Potter (who was being interviewed straight afterwards) was so enraged by the sketch that he complained live on air about being driven all the way from Gloucestershire to sit through 'this rubbish'. Michael and Dad weren't asked back, and their brief collaboration wasn't repeated, except across the lunch table at regular intervals, with fellow Yorkshireman Alan Bennett. Michael's point about Dad's style is that where he'd found John Cleese's approach too specifically targeted, Dad's, though gentler, was too traditionally consequential. Of course, Michael already had a writing partner in Terry Jones, where he could indulge a looser, more abstract and whimsical style. Overall, it's the perfect example of how, despite good personal chemistry, similar methodologies are important to comedy partnerships.

Dad and Nobbs, on the other hand, were like chalk and chalk, both alike in personality and in their attitude to writing. Although Nobbs was born in Kent, Dad often described him as an honorary northerner, who eventually fulfilled his calling by moving to Harrogate. *A Bit of a Do*, his brilliant comedy-drama series from 1989, was even set in a fictional Yorkshire town and mirrored the class tensions and social geography that Dad must've recognised from his upbringing.

At Dad's eightieth birthday celebration, which I organised for him at the Palace Theatre in the West End, I asked Victoria Coren Mitchell to read a tribute David Nobbs had written about Dad (in *Punch* magazine) a few years earlier. Victoria knew Dad through her father, Alan Coren, and her husband, David Mitchell. However, it was their daughter Barbara who cemented a friendship when she and Dad began swapping earnest video calls during the Covid lockdown of 2020. Barbara was five at the time, but Dad treated her messages with the same consideration he gave an old friend. When it came to the eightieth birthday celebration in 2015,

Victoria preceded her tribute by delivering a wonderful account of her father Alan's friendship with Dad. It also happened to be the eighth anniversary of Alan's death and David Nobbs had only just died earlier that year. Nobbs's tribute to Dad ended: 'Eyes light up and spirits lift when he enters a room. Knowing him is a joy.' There were one or two tears, not least from Victoria herself, and I couldn't have asked for a better expression of a network of friendships past, present and future. The celebration highlighted Dad's uncanny ability to find kinship regardless of age, geography or background, especially in a business so synonymous with transience.

In order to put the evolution in Dad's TV career into some kind of context, it's worth noting that the medium, just like the society it was serving, had significantly changed its personality by this time. It was no longer a realm dominated by stuffed suits and antiquated production systems (stop sniggering at the back – there was *some* change), but an influx of fresh minds from different media backgrounds made it an exciting time to be working in TV comedy. As Dad would always continue to do, he seemed to roll with the times and benefited from keeping an open mind to the increasingly eclectic creatives he was now starting to work with.

It began with a director on *Sez Les* called David Mallet, who although only twenty-eight on that show, had already made a name for himself back in 1969 when he was just twenty-four. He'd been working as a director for the talk show diva Simon Dee (who I mentioned earlier in the Frost chapter) for a couple of years when he met Mike King, the guitar-playing third of successful sixties hitmakers the King Brothers. Mike was now branching out into TV production and needed a director for a new panel show he'd devised with Canadian writer-performer Ray Cameron.

Ray was a different animal entirely, not just because his frame of reference was North American, but because his background in music was a little less conventional than Mike's. As a comic in the sixties, Ray had regularly compèred music festivals and gigs, opening for people like Roy Orbison, the Animals and the Rolling Stones. After a while, he began producing and writing music too and, if doing the warm-up for Mick and Keith hadn't been prestigious enough, he opened the new decade by helping birth the Clive Dunn saccharine masterpiece 'Grandad'. Ray first worked with Mike when they wrote a couple of songs for another Ray, actor Ray Brooks' album for Polydor. Barry 'King of the Segue' Cryer would no doubt approve of the convoluted journey to their meeting – in fact Ray Cameron once said of Dad, 'I just wish I could mention something without it reminding you of something else.'

The new show, for Yorkshire TV, was based on US shows like *Stop Me If You've Heard This One* and *Can You Top This?* The concept was simple: pick a theme at random and get a team of comics to riff a joke on the subject. However, if the joke-teller paused for too long (like *Just A Minute*), another comedian could buzz in and take the joke in a new direction. The show obviously needed an unflappable chairman to keep six competitive comedians in check, one with experience but without the kind of profile that would intimidate them. Mike's brother Denis, the piano-playing King Brother, remembered a comic he'd worked with in Dublin a few years earlier. The same comic had gone on to become a chairman at the Players' Theatre and a writer-performer at Danny La Rue's club, where he'd proved adept at controlling an audience with his quick wit and general bonhomie. His name? It'll come to me...

And lo! *Jokers Wild* was born. The pilot aired on 15 April 1969, and it ran for 150 episodes, concluding in 1974. The importance of its success wasn't lost on the Cryer family, as by the time the series came to an end, I'd arrived (in 1973) and the wisdom of the move to a bigger house in the suburbs, now that there were six of us, had become all too clear. It's symbolic too that the early seventies also saw the end of Dad's writing duties for Danny La Rue, as the club in Hanover Square closed its doors for the final time in 1972. The Theatres Act of 1968 meant that the Lord Chamberlain no longer had the power to censor the West End and a new kind of liberated and more confrontational voice was now being heard. Innuendo, that great staple of cabaret and Danny's nightclub shows, not to mention one of Dad's great weapons (if you pardon the, ahem, innuendo), was now seen as quite quaint. Double entendres were being shafted by singles.

The list of contestants on *Jokers Wild* also reflected that change. The guests were quite mixed (albeit not particularly diverse by today's standards) and ran from traditional comics like Les Dawson, Arthur Askey, Ted Ray and Bob Monkhouse, to comic actors like Sid James, Jon Pertwee, June Whitfield, Roy Kinnear and Warren Mitchell. One of the original ideas for *Jokers Wild* was that the comics might feel more inspired to contribute if the format challenged them to improvise rather than doing back-to-back spots. There were also writers like Eric Sykes, John Junkin, Tim Brooke-Taylor and, reuniting him with Les Dawson, John Cleese.

Jokers Wild, *the show Dad chaired in the 1970s, proving just how far we've come in gender equality on panel games. Dad and Isabella Rye are surrounded by Ray Martine, Charlie Chester, Les Dawson and Ted Ray in the pilot episode.*

Dad said one of the best bits about doing *Jokers Wild* was getting the morning train up to Leeds with all the comics. Breakfast was conducted to the tune of the kind of back-and-forth joke-telling you'd think they'd save for the show. On one particular journey, John Cleese admitted that he felt like a fish out of water and, without wishing to appear rude, retired to a quieter corner of the carriage with a book. Dad went over to ask if he was okay. John said: 'I'm fine. I just won't have any material left for the recording if I start chatting.'

Dad looked at the scene with his chairman's hat on and thought about how he could use the dynamic to the show's advantage. Returning to John, Dad suggested John read a book during the taping as well. John thought about it for a while and then agreed. Where they'd failed to combine as writers, what followed is a good example of a meeting of both of their other qualities – Dad's generosity with other comics and John's impeccable focus when executing a concept. When it came to John's turn during the show, Dad invited him to speak and was ignored. John continued to read his book. 'Mr Cleese,' Dad said again.

'What?' said John.

'It's your turn,' said Dad.

Cleese then sighed, carefully replaced his bookmark and took to the floor, before delivering a linguistically dexterous avalanche of nonsense (very much in the vein of Stanley Unwin's gibberish). The older comics are seen doubled over in the background.

If the contrast in performance styles was a defining feature of the show, then the key to its success was Dad's ability to calmly straddle different generations and comic approaches. The show's broad-church format even seemed to find space for appearances by Hollywood star Stubby Kaye and screen siren Diana Dors. This shift in profile for Dad was a meaningful one for a couple of reasons. Firstly, he was able to use his position to bring David Nixon in as a team captain and repay David the favour shown to Dad ten years earlier. Secondly, Dad was now a 'face', being beamed into people's homes at the incredibly family-friendly time of 5.10 in the afternoon. While Ronnie Corbett may have been right about Dad staying on his rung, a little visibility became useful in reminding people that he was still a performer, even if he was doing so in writers' clothing.

You'd be tempted to think that after hosting *Jokers Wild*, a career of light entertainment hosting and presenting beckoned. Yet as we've seen before, Dad was too skittish and too clubbable to remain in one pigeonhole. His relationship with Ronnies Corbett and Barker led to his next opening and a place on the roster of writing talent for their new show, which began in 1971. Incidentally, the inception of *The Two Ronnies* was by no means an inevitability, despite their obvious harmony on Frost shows. It was only when Bill Cotton, Head of BBC Light Entertainment, saw the two of them improvise adeptly during a technical hitch at the London Palladium during the 1970 Bafta Awards, that he thought they might be capable of a fully fledged sketch show. At the time, Barker was dressed as Henry VIII and Corbett as Cardinal Wolsey and the absurd nature of the situation didn't fluster either of them. It was the power (and height) dynamic not dissimilar to the roles Danny La Rue and Corbett had played in the club days.

Dad was therefore an obvious choice as a writer – one who knew how to exploit Corbett's talents. There's a belief that Dad was also responsible for the innovation of the news desk closing sketch that became their trademark. He'd be the first to say that he alone didn't innovate anything, as he always wrote in a partnership on that show too. Peter Vincent and Dad did write a newsreader sketch for Ronnie Barker that established the format of punnable fictional news stories early on, but this kind of detail would've been lost to the Barry Cryer of the time, due to the sheer weight of material. When you consider that Dad was one of the very few writers who was also writing for Morecambe and Wise at the same time, it's easy to see why *Jokers Wild* was a fun distraction rather than a bellwether for his career.

One of the aspects of Dad's career that people were most intrigued by was the sheer range and diversity of people that he wrote for. Three names in particular stick out from the list of British comedy greats in the seventies: Bob Hope, Jack Benny and Richard Pryor. They're usually listed on his CV without context, but the eclectic credits all came from his time working on a version of *The Des O'Connor Show* that would go out on US TV. Often writing with Neil Shand, Dad would be in the green room at the ATV studios in Elstree, ready to talk to the guests and translate British idioms or give them an update on the topical talking points at the time. Benny, a real idol of Dad's, delivered a monologue before sitting down to talk with Des, the host.

As Jack was leaving to get into his car to go back to the hotel, the floor manager came up to him to say that there had been a technical issue. As a result, his monologue hadn't been recorded properly. They then nervously asked if he could come back the following day to re-record it. Without an audience. Benny was flying back to the US but, amazingly, agreed to change his flight in order to fulfil his obligation. Dad was so bowled over at this act of generosity that he offered to come back the next day as well to witness some more Benny magic at close hand.

He told me that what followed was educational. Jack came in, and delivered the monologue, practically word for word, to an empty studio. Dad then went upstairs with him to the edit suite to sit with the engineer who was dubbing on the laugh track. Benny would grade the laughs he was mixing in. He'd say things like 'That joke is not strong enough for that laugh. Make it lighter.' He also kept stopping the engineer from adding laughs at certain points, usually the punchline. 'They haven't got it yet. You see here, where I pause, that's where the laugh is.' Steve Martin used to call these 'icebox laughs'. You don't laugh immediately, but later, when you're standing at the icebox choosing your dinner, you'll get it. Incredible to think that Jack Benny's instinct could still tune in so well without an audience. The humility, the dedication and the sheer talent were instructive. Dad said it was nothing short of a masterclass.

Dad's interaction with Bob Hope was briefer but no less profound. It happened backstage at *Parkinson* during the same period, this time at the BBC. Dad and Dick Vosburgh had been drafted in to rewrite the lyrics to Hope's signature tune 'Thanks for the Memories' (I believe they were working from the sandstone cuneiform texts of the original). By the time Hope was on the show, he had fallen out of favour in America (Vietnam had changed the mood for flag-waving celebrities like him), and Dad chatted with him for a while in the dressing room, and was surprised to see him looking so down about his career. 'But you're Bob Hope,' Dad said.

'Sure,' Bob said. 'Back home, I'm the friend of the President, the hawk, part of the old guard. People still say, "Here's the great Bob Hope." If you don't make them laugh in the first two or three minutes, they will say, "Oh, *that's* the great Bob Hope, is it?"' It was a cautionary tale to Dad of just how quickly things can change in the business and, if you're too cosy with the establishment, how your strengths can soon be turned against you.

Richard Pryor was also a guest on *The Des O'Connor Show* when he met Dad. He was charming, polite and, if Dad was honest, didn't really need his help before the show. Besides, Dad's racially satirical material was a little underdeveloped at this point. Instead, he felt it was his duty to chaperone Pryor. They were all sitting in the bar at Elstree waiting for the audience to file in when Pryor starts remonstrating with a guy over in the corner. Dad gets worried as they begin to go at each other and Pryor still has a show to do. Thankfully, the argument plateaus and the two men leave the room. Dad is now worried that Pryor is going to walk out, so he follows him into the corridor. There he is, with the guy he was just arguing with, laughing his head off. Apparently, they were old friends and this was their way of winding each other up.

Mentioning Richard Pryor also gives me an excuse to tell Dad's other favourite story about him, although not one that Pryor was personally involved in. This oft-repeated story was told to Dad by Ross Noble (you can join in with the ending if you like). Nicholas Parsons was talking to Ross after a BBC Radio 4 recording of *Just A Minute* and he asked Ross who his favourite comedian was. Ross replied, without hesitation, 'Richard Pryor'. Nicholas was intrigued, so Ross regaled him with a blow-by-blow account of his biography. An outrageously funny man, but with an outrageously tragic life to match. His mother was a prostitute, he grew up in a brothel run by his grandmother, had spells in prison, had problems with drink and drugs, as well as a litany of mental health issues. Not content with this, he once set himself on fire and ran down the street after unsuccessfully trying to freebase crack. Nicholas Parsons was in shock. He had no idea. A while later, Ross passes Nicholas as he's chatting with another guest: 'Have you heard about Richard Briers?'

Dad loved telling that story and it was typical of the kind of obscure show-business gossip he liked to garner for retelling. And the first person he called when he heard that story was Richard Briers, who laughed.

I've found that one of the great sorrows of a parent dying is not so much revealed in a lost relationship but in the absence of little routines that seemed inconsequential. Every now and then I'd call Dad up with snippets of gossip or jokes I'd heard from actors or writers and hope that he'd retell it (I'd usually know I'd been successful if Simon Hoggart mentioned it in his *Guardian* diary each Saturday). There are things that I hear now and want to call him about, only to remember that he's no longer around.

One such story came from Colin Sell when we were talking for this book. He was backstage in front of a tray of BBC sandwiches with Ross Noble (he's the gift that keeps on giving) and Ross told Colin about another time he was standing in front of a tray of BBC sandwiches. When Ross was just starting out as a stand-up, like Dad, he did a fair amount of warm-ups for TV and radio recordings. Ross was in the green room, looking at the lunch table and was about to put his hand out to take a sandwich. A producer stopped him: 'Prawn is for the talent.' Colin and I had the same thought: Barry would have *loved* that.

In 1971, while still at ATV, Dad was in the canteen with American director Barry Levinson (I know, pick the names up as we go), who was working on *The Marty Feldman Comedy Machine*. They were chatting when Dad suddenly spotted the elderly Groucho Marx sitting in the corner. This was a few years after an ill-fated British run of a show called simply *Groucho* but anglophile that he was, Groucho saw fit to return and record an interview for another show.

For reasons known only to serendipity, Dad had a copy of the book *The Groucho Letters* in his dressing room and ran to get it, so Groucho could sign it. When Dad returned, he suddenly lost confidence about approaching Groucho. Instead, Barry Levinson took the book over and Dad watched as they chatted. Groucho smiled, took out a pen and duly signed it. Levinson came back, but quickly realised that the inscription only read 'From Groucho'. Dad was happy, but Levinson insisted on going back. He then asked for Groucho to add 'To Barry' but also to add 'Marx' as well, after 'Groucho' (as if there were any other Grouchos at ATV that day). Groucho with good grace added to his previous effort. As a result, we now have a book on Mum's shelf with a title page that reads:

'To Barry Marx from Groucho Marx.'

Publicity shot for a series of Henri Winterman cigar commercials that saw Dad realise a lifelong dream. 'Go! And never darken my towels again!'

The seventies saw radio, Dad's first love, beginning to crop up again with increasing frequency. The sixties had seen him land a spot on satirical shows *Listen To This Space* (with Nicholas Parsons) and *Better Late* and these were either side of a rare acting outing in the sitcom *Sam and Janet*, with David Kossoff and Joan Sims. Dad would argue that you just go where the work takes you, but the transition back to radio more fully in the 1970s would be subtly transformative. It was in the consecutive Aprils of 1972 and 1973 that two radio shows were launched that not only reminded Dad of the innocent silliness of his earlier career in rag revue, with their requirement to write, sing, play instruments and generally muck about, but these shows would eventually come to define him in the public's affection.

Jokers Wild changed Dad's career; he was now an on-screen celebrity. Once he'd worked out how to hold the card up so you could see the subject.

A newly married couple. The husband goes into the bathroom and finds a dead horse in the bath.

'Darling,' he calls. 'There's a dead horse in the bath.'

'So?' she says. 'I never said I was tidy.'

11

In 2020, it was announced to a shocked British comedy world that Tim Brooke-Taylor had died. Although there were many tributes, I never really felt he got the send-off he deserved. In mitigation, a major factor in the response to the news was that the country was dealing with a Covid pandemic, but even Tim couldn't have wished for such understatement. Granted, his wife Christine and their sons Ben and Ed always seemed more important to him than any public adulation, but his legacy was worthy of greater fanfare. Tim was the longest-serving collaborator of Dad's career, starting with their meeting on *The Frost Report*, through BBC adventures like *At Last The 1948 Show* and *The Two Ronnies* to ITV's *Jokers Wild* and even Kenny Everett. Their fellowship even reached as far as a US/UK co-production called *Assaulted Nuts* in the 1980s, meaning they worked on projects together almost every year from 1965 to 2020.

Given the amount of time they spent together professionally, it's not surprising that they didn't socialise much. Besides, Tim was a much more reserved and traditional presence off-screen and off-mic. Whereas Dad's energy often continued unbroken into a green room or a restaurant afterwards. However, Tim the comedian was a very different creature, able to tackle the grandest of Guignol with a stiff upper lip and an effortlessly gentle affability that made him seem forever young. There's a plaque at Mornington Crescent tube station dedicated to Willie Rushton in honour of the station's connection to the radio show *I'm Sorry I Haven't A Clue*. Opposite that is the now-renamed pub the Lyttelton Arms. I hope it's not too long before Dad and Tim are reunited with Humph and Willie.

In searching for the magic formula that drew Dad and Tim together in their joint pursuit of silliness, I've often thought it was down to their respect for each other's contrasting characteristics. Where Dad had the teasingly droll ripostes of a friendly landlord, Tim had the impish insouciance of a cheeky housemaster bunking off in his pub. One characteristic that united them was the well-practised English art of self-deprecation. They both revelled in getting their defences in first, just when you thought a show was coming across as too glossy.

In researching this book, I've discovered something else that bonds them. Tim also lost his father when he was a boy. As I've gleaned from my own father's experience, losing a parent when you're young can lead to a lifelong fear of abandonment. There are many different ways to deal with so abrupt a loss, but it seems that Dad and Tim both chose to seek approval and acceptance through laughter. I don't know if they ever talked to each other about this shared dynamic, but I take great solace in the fact that they had such a positive influence on not just audiences' happiness but each other's.

'Dear Hello Cheeky, I was wondering if you could help me. On second thoughts, if I'm writing to you, I must be beyond help.'

So begins a typical dip into the letters bag during the radio show where Dad and Tim were first pitched together as writers and performers in 1973. *Hello Cheeky* introduced listeners to the quartet (or '*ménage à quatre*' as the *TV Times* once had it) of Dad, Tim, *Morecambe and Wise* co-writer John Junkin and pianist and composer Denis King. The previous year, Dad had worked on another TV sketch show called *Who Do You Do?* again on writing and performing duties. The difference here was that it was largely a vehicle for impressionists (not the French *fin-de-siècle* kind, you understand – less Edgar Degas, more Freddie Starr) and, because it was a TV show, it was tightly edited. Dad hankered for something a little freer and more imaginative.

Hello Cheeky was a half-hour show pre-recorded in front of a live audience (which cut down on editing) but wasn't a traditional sketch show like *The Two Ronnies* or Dick Emery, more a loosely assembled mix of stream-of-consciousness puns, one-liners and dramatised jokes. To some that picked up the zeitgeist of Python and Spike Millgan's *Q*, but to Dad it was like going back to basics. Taking the irreverent approach summed up by Dad as '*Rowan & Martin's Laugh-In* but without the gloss', *Hello Cheeky* felt cosier than Python but still retained a requisite dash of Milligan. Tim was working on *The Goodies* at the same time and there's a little of the irreverence of that show too, daubed around the edges. The tone was of an informal conversation between old friends, riffing on themes and poking harmless fun at each other (both Tim and Dad never wanted humour to be cruel). Improvisation was encouraged and the occasional slip became part of the appeal. It was another voyage into professional amateurism.

Hello Cheeky *giving* Panorama *a run for its money.*

It was a very liberating creative expression exercise for Dad with tangents, ad libs and curiosities. It was the kind of thing he was doing even at school, let alone at university, and very much akin to the collage of ideas and styles that inspired his Danny La Rue writing. A typical show might feature advice on looking after an armadillo, teaching your dog to samba or making your very own space rocket from a yard of lint. Despite the potential budgetary restraint on their comic vision, Dad's position on the Yorkshire TV bandwagon (via *Jokers Wild* and *Sez Les*) meant that *Hello Cheeky* eventually made the move to the small screen as well. Whether that was a wise move is another story.

The TV show was recorded in Leeds and part of the fun, like *Jokers Wild*, was the journey from London by train. My dad never learned to drive, deciding after six lessons in his early twenties that he was likely to injure someone if he carried on. It meant that train travel was a regular feature of his routine. There were benefits, as it provided another opportunity to work on scripts, and there was often an impromptu audience to test material, should the need arise. After Dad died, a few people contacted me to say that they had no personal or professional connection to Dad, but had been regaled by him on a Tube to Uxbridge or on a fast train to Birmingham. J. B. Priestley's most famous novel, *The Good Companions* (one of Dad's favourites), focuses on a group of performers in a concert party as they traverse England between the wars. On those journeys up to Leeds, he must have felt a kinship with Priestley's travelling troubadours. It also meant that my mother (now of four children) had to do a hell of a lot of driving, whether he was away or not.

The TV show didn't really take off, mainly because there was little money available to make the often surreal visual aspects work for television. Besides, such was the turnover of characters and scenarios, an edit would have been needed to smooth down the transitions. 'Smooth' wasn't really in the *Hello Cheeky* dictionary. What you see onscreen is effectively the product of three men (King is usually on piano with his trio) running around long props tables covered in wigs, moustaches, hats, scarves and gloves. Half the time they'd trip over each other while trying to remember their

lines and the other half they'd spend either panicked or trying not
to laugh. One minute they were a mountain goat, the next Miss
Moneypenny, the next they were a policeman, Lady Hamilton or
an amnesia patient with a taped-on moustache. 'Can you perform
an operation on a false moustache, doctor?' asks Junkin at one
point, clearly improvising. The art of professional amateurism was
clearly a lot of fun for the performers (Dad always admitted as
much), but it was a work in progress for audiences. The show was
initially broadcast at 8 p.m., before being bumped to a later slot
and then no slot at all.

This could have been another pivotal moment for Dad. Following
a very successful run as a writer and performer, the inability to
transfer the success of the radio show to TV could have been an
unsettling moment. His general attitude to most of his career
high-wire moments often resulted in the same conclusion: it didn't
bother him at all. In his mind, success and failure were judged the
same and were a matter of luck. The result of the game should not
spoil your fun. As we've already seen with Dad's recording career,
Kingsley Amis's line 'A bad review may spoil your breakfast, but
you shouldn't allow it to spoil your lunch,' seemed to hold true in
most things.

However, another radio show was already in place to lessen the
blow. A year before *Hello Cheeky*, Dad's success on *Jokers Wild*
meant he was invited to fill the unexpectedly vacant chair of a new
BBC radio panel show. The producer was fellow Yorkshireman
David Hatch (also a Footlight and a *Hello Cheeky* producer), Tim
Brooke-Taylor was again involved and the show was called *I'm
Sorry I Haven't A Clue*. It was initially devised as a spin-off from
I'm Sorry I'll Read That Again, which had quickly developed a cult
following but grew into a favourite over the eight years it ran on
the radio. That show starred Graeme Garden and Hatch, alongside
John Cleese, Jo Kendall, Bill Oddie and Tim. In fact, Graeme
Garden said that he and Hatch only developed *I'm Sorry I Haven't
A Clue* as a response to the rigours of having a heavy script turnover
on *I'm Sorry I'll Read That Again*. They wanted a format where they
could just turn up and do it. A panel game was the perfect fit, but

they needed a twist. It needed to be different from the others. An antidote, if you will.

Veteran jazz trumpeter and Old Etonian Humphrey Lyttelton had been the first choice to be chairman. Graeme said that when he and David Hatch first suggested Humph's name, they instantly knew that it was both an eccentric choice but also a perfect fit. In the *Independent* in November 1997, Humph suggested he wasn't so sure:

'Driving to record the pilot for the show in 1972, I thought to myself, "What the hell am I doing? I've got a perfectly good career already. I'll just sound ridiculous trying to match the comics." I've tried to have that in the back of my mind ever since. "What am I doing here?" It gives me an image of being detached. The biggest compliment I got was when a reviewer called me a "comatose presenter". I thought, "I'm getting it across."'

Humph's 'perfectly good career' as an internationally respected jazz musician meant that he was unavailable for a few episodes at the start. They sent for Dad. The programme was very far from being an institution at that stage and, naturally, it had to battle against not just the vagaries of the schedule (it moved a few times across the week in its early years) but also the performers' other commitments. The permutation of the line-up on the first series largely hopped around the same performers as *I'm Sorry I'll Read That Again*. However, John Cleese wanted something more structured, and Bill Oddie wanted something a little less stressful. So once Humph returned, Dad moved to his left and remained in post thereafter.

It is sobering to think that even at this point, the show wasn't really considered a prospect and it nearly got taken off the airwaves a few times. With Willie Rushton joining in 1974 and Colin Sell in 1975, the four panellists and their much-abused accompanist settled into a pattern that would last for twenty-two years. Jon Naismith took the reins as producer in 1991, and *Clue* began its expansion into live shows and digital downloads. It entered an unparalleled period of success and stability that it has managed to maintain to this day, despite the loss of most of its 'founding fathers'.

The dynamic between the chair, panel and piano was obviously a big part of the show's original appeal. Dad saw Humph as the toff in a room of oiks or the head teacher unexpectedly found among the schoolboys. He was the model of the anti-host, pouring cold water on anything that might be mistaken for enthusiasm. When a round finished and there was applause, Humph once followed the silence with, 'Right, that's eight across, now for three down.' Graeme always said that Tim was the one the audience identified with, while Willie was the one most liable to cut against sentiment and say something outrageous. Graeme himself was the ticking timebomb of wit who would economically pitch interventions that the other panellists would be unable to top. I spoke to Colin about Dad's function within the show and Col believed that Dad was part cheerleader, part pacesetter:

> If they were all in the mood, it was because Barry had set the thing up. In a traditional panel show, the host drives the energy, but the point of *Clue* is that each host has had to undercut the energy. So, you needed someone to be like the team captain. Barry was always the one who would be making the quick quips and then you'd just wait. Eventually one of the others, like Graeme or Willie would come in with something which came in under the radar, which was very funny. The audience would usually be laughing because they were in a laughing mood. Barry had put them there. We were very lucky with *Clue* because everybody complemented each other. Everybody had a role to play, I think, without probably even realising it.

Dad liked it best when the show was 'falling apart' and if that sounds a bit like *Hello Cheeky*, then you can see that by the mid-seventies Dad had now found his persona. Tim agreed; in a piece about *Clue* for the *Liverpool Echo* in 1992, he said: 'The other big thing is that no one is trying to get one up on somebody else. Basically, we're all trying desperately to keep the ball up in the air and the others will or will not save you, and often when they don't, it's the highlight of the programme.'

As I reflect on my father's second-longest love affair (after my mother, if you please – you old gossip), it occurs to me that he didn't really talk much about the show at home. There was the physical presence of *Clue* everywhere: scripts, producer's notes, Colin's lyric sheets piled up on Dad's desk and regular phone calls about travel, but the only time he'd firmly bring *Clue* into the conversation would be if he was stuck on ideas for the 'Late Arrivals' or 'Uxbridge English Dictionary' rounds. So, if you had a particular favourite of Dad's that really made you laugh, then I'm happy to say it was probably one of mine.

He'd listen to the repeat on a Sunday and then he'd laugh at all the same points as he did in the recording, but he'd then move on. I think one of the reasons he didn't talk much about the show is that it had become such a good fit, he didn't really stress over his place in it or whether he should change anything to help. It had become so commonplace fixture in Dad's life that by the time I'd grown up (the show is only a year older than me) he didn't feel the need to pore over things in detail.

We'd go to recordings of the live show as a family, cheering along with the announcement of favourite rounds or jokes. Dad would say 'Was that all right?', as if two and a half hours of industrial-strength laughter had said otherwise. Professionally, he never ever took things for granted, but the older he got, the more his routine seemed to depend on the show. Like Dad himself, it seemed to defy politics, class or fashion and, also just like him, was written off several times, only to emerge funnier and more vibrant than before.

As the nineties rolled around and political correctness trained its crosshairs on the show, it didn't so much evolve as double down on its worldview. However, that didn't mean it saw itself as politically incorrect, it meant critics had probably missed the point. *Clue* was always committed to being what Pete Bradshaw of the *Evening Standard* (24 May 1995) described as 'this whimsical and hallucinatory game show pastiche'. It was always a parody of an establishment tradition, rather than a reinforcement of one. An apolitical show. For example, the debate in the nineties that surrounded first Samantha and then Sven, the show's mute scorers, seems quite quaint by today's standards. They were there to satirise the kind of excessive chauvinism demonstrated by game shows where scantily clad models would accompany the male host as he showed off that week's prize. Dad had even been through this conventional route when he was flanked by female scorers during the first series of *Jokers Wild*.

As recently as 2014, the BBC Trust was required to rule on a complaint that the show had 'failed to keep abreast of changing social attitudes and values relating to the non-acceptability of sexist humour and the sexual objectification of women' before deciding that Samantha and Sven's dynamic 'was a skit on both the misogynist and sexist programmes which were predominantly popular some years ago and the attitudes that led to them which still exist today'.

Catchy, huh? They don't write rulings like that any more, do they? This admission seemed self-evident to Dad, but he was nonetheless relieved to hear it proclaimed publicly. He had been stung by some of the accusations over the years that the show was becoming a bit of a dinosaur. However, the fact that anyone might have got hot under the collar when hearing about the salacious private lives of a couple of silent scorers now seems as absurd as the stories themselves. Unless, of course, these people were getting hot under the collar for an entirely different reason. You'd have to ask their therapist. I offer the following as evidence:

'Samantha nearly made it. She's been detained at the last minute in the city's Latin Quarter. An Italian gentleman friend has promised to take her out for an ice cream, and she likes nothing better than to spend the evening licking the nuts off a large Neapolitan.'

There are cars zipping round the circuit each year in Monaco that have poorer engineering. However, rather more difficult to defend was the singling out of Lionel Blair as the regular target of the introduction to the 'Sound Charades' round. Originally, the intros ran like this: 'In the original [charades], the players were not allowed to speak, resulting in much hilarity. Our version differs subtly in two ways.'

However, when the round began to draw its comparison more regularly with the TV version of the parlour game *Give Us A Clue*, the intros began to cut a little differently: 'Who could ever forget

opposing team captain Una Stubbs sitting open-mouthed as he
tried to pull off *Twelve Angry Men* in under two minutes.'

As with the line about Samantha, this is about as technically
exceptional a line as you can imagine. There's no argument from
me there. The rhythm, the compressed detail and the beautifully
earnest and unexpected choice of film title all conspire to create
what Humph called 'blue-chip filth'. That is the genius of the
well-crafted double entendre, to make the audience feel they were
making up their own jokes. It is a deftly trodden fine line. The
show didn't always get it right, particularly when it got personal
with Blair. However, Dad defended the show by saying that Lionel
loved and hated the attention it brought in equal measure. The
social politics of the show became a distraction during the more
sensitive nineties, but *Clue* could always point to its own absurdity
to absolve any malicious intent. Besides, Dad would never have
been comfortable had the humour become more obviously targeted
and if anything, the older the show got, the more brilliantly silly
it became.

Clue was so popular by 2002 that it even moved into the realm
of spin-off. *Hamish and Dougal: You'll Have Had Your Tea?* by Dad
and Graeme Garden was the more formal sitcom version of the
sketches that sprang from those Sound Charades rounds. Hamish
and Dougal were two Scotsmen (Graeme was born in Aberdeen,
Dad wasn't), forever misunderstanding each other and embarking
on comically bizarre adventures. The engine room of the show was
often a pun, a double entendre or the kind of absurd visual humour
that only a radio budget can deliver. It featured cameos by *Clue*
regulars, such as Jeremy Hardy as the local laird, Humph as the
laird's butler Lyttelton, and Sandi Toksvig as golf champion Sandi
Wedge. Added to the cast was their housekeeper Mrs Naughtie,
played by Alison Steadman, and broadcaster Jim Naughtie, who
played her son. Graeme told me that the writing dynamic on *Hamish
and Dougal* with Dad was based on trying to outsmart each other.

'He or I would suddenly go into a totally bizarre non sequitur
and find a way of making it work in the plot. The sheer range of
jokes he knew – he could use to structure the sitcom, which was

not just pinching the joke and putting it in but using that as a way of making ours work.'

It is a fine tradition. Dave Allen used to take the narrative of a joke and turn it into a sketch all the time. Dad used to call his jokes 'little plays' or 'short stories' and that kind of recycling was merely a form of the 'oral folk history' I mentioned in the introduction. Graeme said that Dad's use of the folk tradition extended to vernacular sayings he employed during *Clue* recordings.

> When things got out of control, he would say folksy things like 'You are now watching a family at war' or 'Is this too slick for you?' or 'My hair was black when I came in here' or 'That's why I don't buy green bananas any more'. We'd heard them a million times, but they always got a laugh. Later I realised it was because Jon Naismith [the producer] had cut them out of the recordings. So, every audience was hearing it for the first time.

Even if an audience had heard the joke before, Dad's great skill was, of course, telling those jokes with a freshness as if for the first time, which came from lots and lots of practice. He was no stranger to practice. As a family, we often got to road test material well before it was ready. Graeme believes Dad's rhythms were so hard-wired that he also developed a skill that few comedians would ever own up to. Telling the 'non-joke':

> He was so good at doing it, he could do that thing, which I've described as telling a thing that isn't a joke but makes a noise like a joke. There was one he used to do relentlessly on tour, sometimes in recordings, during the Uxbridge English Dictionary round (where panellists would give alternative definitions to words) which was 'rancour – a Japanese term of abuse'. The audience would always laugh. And as a purist, I'd say that doesn't work on any level. Because the Japanese have no problem with a W. Ls and Rs? Sure. But the audience still laughed. The thing about *Clue* was that it's always about trying

to make the other panellists laugh. And we try to make sure
that we don't tell everybody what jokes we're going to do before
the show so that we can surprise them. One of the things I miss
about your Dad is when we hear *Clue* in the car sometimes,
I miss his laugh. It just pealed out over everything because he
just loved it all so much.

In 2020, *I'm Sorry I Haven't A Clue* was voted the greatest radio
comedy of all time by a *Radio Times* panel. Of all the accolades
Dad garnered in his career, I think this was the one he was most
proud of. Graeme's summary of the show as 'always about trying
to make the other panellists laugh' probably gets closest to defining
why *Clue* achieved this place in the national consciousness because
despite its absurdity it essentially radiates benevolence. No other
programme that Dad was associated with came closer to matching
his own persona. Joyful, silly, archly brilliant and most importantly,
glib. The spirit he'd been nurturing since school fitted him like
a glove.

Clue also gave Dad the forum to indulge one of the passions
he was most celebrated for. Encouraging younger comedians.
Although Graeme puts a slightly different spin on it:

The tenor of the tributes after he died, there was a lot about
his generosity with other comedians. I think that was the most
obvious example. That he would laugh a lot. At anything that
amused him. He always took an interest in the young comics
and people coming up. I remember whenever we had a new
person on *Clue*, like, I don't know, Ross Noble or somebody
doing it for the first time. We'd all be in the bar in the hotel the
night before and Barry would monopolise him and sort of have
fresh blood to feast on. Maybe that's his secret. The comedy
vampire that was drawing blood from the new generation.

Clue also seemed to survive the generational bureaucratic purges
at the BBC, too. In a moment worthy of a round in the game
itself, the corporation once tried to block a live version of the show

Humph Tribute: Dad at The Memorial Concert for Humphrey Lyttelton at the Hammersmith Apollo on 25 April 2010, with fellow 'Clue' Rob Brydon, Tim Brooke-Taylor, Jeremy Hardy and Jack Dee. Dad would sing one of Humph's favourite songs, 'Doctor Jazz', at the drop of a hat.

The infamous Clue Lockdown Zoom: (clockwise from top left) Jon Naismith (producer), Harry Hill, Colin Sell, Graeme Garden, Dad, Pippa Evans, Tony Hawks and Jack Dee. Sandi Toksvig (centre). Dad's Luddite bafflement made everyone except Graeme laugh. It made him fall asleep.

from using the *Clue* name. They eventually relented, but not before Dad had carefully targeted a few entertainment journalists at *Oldie* magazine lunches. He informally mentioned the row, which up until this point had been behind closed doors, and this duly found its way into both broadsheet and tabloid diary sections. I'm not suggesting that Dad held any sway in the final decision, but I do remember him being quite proud of his use of the dark arts at the time. It's the closest I ever saw him get to being openly devious.

For all the excitement of meeting younger comedians, working with Humph was still the permanent thrill as Dad was a huge fan of his music. It would have been very intimidating working with Humph had they not already met some twenty years before. The story goes that while Dad was singing with a jazz band on the steps of Leeds Town Hall in 1955, Humph was stretching his legs in the city before a gig. Humph (who was thirty-four at this point and already a star) was playing a show in Leeds that night. Back then, he was even sporting the goatee and sideburns that all 'groovy young jazzers' seemed to have at the time.

'Humphrey Lyttelton,' he said, stretching out his hand, as if he needed identifying.

'I know,' said Dad, a little taken aback.

'Heard you singing with the band,' he continued. 'It wasn't difficult; you were quite loud.'

It seems Humph's trademark sangfroid was present even then. Another thing that didn't change was how generous he was with his time. One of the recipients of Humph's generosity was my oldest brother Tony's son, Evan. My nephew was about eight at the time, and a keen trumpeter, so Tony booked tickets for himself, Evan and Dad to go and see Humph's band, who were playing locally. Evan went clutching his trumpet manual. After the show, as was Dad's habit with performers he knew (and occasionally those that he didn't), he took them both backstage. Dad tipped Humph off about his grandson's passion and the great man strode over to meet him.

'Good evening,' Humph beamed. 'How nice of you to come and see me. Can I sign your trumpet book, Evan?'

He took out his pen and was about to sign when a man came over to talk business. 'Excuse me,' he said, politely. 'I'm talking to Evan.'

He drew a picture of a trumpeter and underneath he wrote: 'To Evan, from one trumpeter to another.'

You'll be pleased to know that Evan went on to play with Humph's band at Dad's eightieth birthday celebration and also played with Colin Sell at Dad's funeral.

Humph was rarely known to swear, but there is one story that Dad used to tell about him that proves that, in the right hands, a well-chosen curse word can be a thing of beauty. They were on tour in Harrogate and everyone was gathered around the hotel breakfast table. Humph sat in front of a bowl of prunes. He tasted the first one, grimaced, and then said: 'How can you fuck up a prune?'

Around twenty years ago, Dad went to the hospital to have his aorta repaired. It was a very worrying time for the family, but thanks to his surgeon, Sir Magdi Yacoub, he made a full recovery. Dad told Humph about this experience before Humph's own aorta surgery. 'Don't worry, it's only plumbing. You'll be fine.' Dad then told him about the time, a while later, when they gave his heart a full check over. The nurse asked if Dad wanted to see his heart on the ultrasound. 'Only if it's a moving picture,' Dad replied. Humph laughed, but Dad could see he was still a little nervous. He'd always been a resilient, hard-working professional who'd even postponed the operation so he could fulfil his touring obligations. When he couldn't make the very last show, he recorded a message: 'I'm sorry I can't be with you today as I am in hospital – I wish I'd thought of this sooner.'

Graeme Garden, who'd trained as a doctor, was more worried about the anaesthetic than the operation. It's quite common for complications to occur in older patients and Humph, despite his energy, was eighty-six after all. Remembering Dad's experiences with the ultrasound, Humph told Dad that when they asked if he wanted to see his heart, he said: 'I never watch daytime television.' He then said to Dad: 'If all goes well, this year's drama will be next year's anecdote.'

I remember Dad telling me about going to see Humph after the operation. He got a call from Humph's family to go back to Barnet Hospital. He saw his old friend all but hollowed out from the experience. He talked about how much it distressed him. He didn't recognise the old man in the hospital bed. Humph's eyes were closed, and it was very difficult to tell if anything was going on under the lids. Dad leaned over the bed and decided that he would try to not be too sentimental: 'I'm a very busy man, Humph, and this is all very inconvenient. Look at you, like Lord Muck, surrounded by all these nurses.'

He didn't say whether Humph responded, but Humph died later that evening and Dad was pleased he'd honoured his last moments with him by staying true to their relationship. He composed a poem (as he often did on such occasions) in celebration of his old friend:

Ode to Humph

As the trumpeter of eternity sits on the mute of fate
Today we join and celebrate
And sing in praise of peerless Humph
Looking at this sheet of bumf
I realise there's only one rhyme for Humph
But onward – 36 years of fun and laughter
1972, Clue was born, I joined soon after
...
Since then, he'd been our adjudicator
Tolerating 'we're going for a walk later'
One of a kind and standing tall
The thinking woman's Kenny Ball
...
No other chairman can compare
Well, Nicholas... this is a joke I swear
Turning up, like our own bad penny
Dispelling our blues, if we had any
Thank you for the friendship and fun
I raise my glass – oh, just the one
Cheers, Humph

Humph was a witty man in his own right, but the introduction of writer Iain Pattinson in 1992 crystallised the chairman's role into a fully fledged work of art. If Eddie Braben helped transform Morecambe and Wise from a great variety double act into a brilliantly nuanced character study, and Galton and Simpson elevated gifted comic actors like Harry H. Corbett or Tony Hancock into national heroes, then Iain worked a similar act for Humph. All within the restrictions of a panel game too, which is pretty impressive. Iain managed to craft double entendres that had no right to be there, let alone work so well, and these soon became a key feature of the show. Humph delivered them with as much innocence, naivety and ennui as he could feign in front of a snickering crowd. Pattinson wrote the introductions and links for Humph for sixteen years and then for his successor Jack Dee for a further eleven.

If Iain was the persistent driving force behind the Lionel Blair jokes, he was also relentless in pursuit of jokes at the panellists' expense. Dad was a huge fan of Iain's but occasionally the jibes about his drinking would grate. Humph once opened an introduction with: 'Barry's in a bad mood today. Some swine has cut the ring-pulls off his lunch.' Dad would bristle a bit, and he decided to talk to Iain about it. It was all very amicable, and Iain agreed to tone things down a bit, but not before pointing out that Dad was guilty of sometimes doing the jokes himself. Dad was famous for being a pub lover and often when they were on tour, he'd open his account at the bar with a cry of 'just the one!'

At one recording, Dad sported a bandage on his hand after burning it on the cooker. He held it up to the audience and said: 'This happened while I was leaving the pub last night. Someone trod on my hand.' Another regular saying was 'I'm the thinking woman's lager lout.' When he had heart surgery, he took a picture of a can of beer attached to his saline drip. It was his Christmas card that year.

He often displayed a lack of awareness of his own shortcomings like this and, despite his reputation for humility, at least latterly, as age took a toll on his hearing and reactions, he morphed into quite a difficult grumpy old man on occasions. For example, he used to make fun of Humph's age by saying things like 'Nurse, the screens!' and (shouting) 'We'll go for a walk later...' However, as he transitioned to elder statesman after Humph's death, it took him a while to be comfortable with such a dubious honour and it wasn't always easy to deal with. Pippa Evans remembers a mad Covid lockdown recording, where Dad kept taking his headphones off, meaning they couldn't get his attention: 'So me and Harry Hill wrote signs saying "Barry!" and held them up. Eventually, we had to call Barry's son [my brother Dave] to call Barry's wife and tell him to put his headphones back on.'

Technology was never Dad's strong point (he couldn't even stand it if people texted him) and Jon Naismith had to display great patience as *Clue* battled the vagaries of remote recordings during the pandemic. It was a low point for Dad, as he acknowledged how much he had lost touch with the art of being able to laugh at himself. I think the smile only returned when he thought of how graceful Humph had been at the end.

Happily, the show is now back in its element – rocking and rolling in front of full houses, with its wheels still coming off and falling apart. Maybe if you listen carefully enough, you can still hear Dad's laugh in the background. Losing Tim, Dad and Iain, all within two years of each other, looked to have opened a hole in the show's foundations that would be irreparable. However, as with Willie and Humph before them, the strength of *Clue* has never been in the show's individual performers but in the blend of talent and the format's DNA of inspired lunacy. After all, as Humph once said, 'If I go under a bus, I want no displays of loyalty.'

So it proved. Jack Dee seamlessly assumed the chairman's role with all Humph's drollery and added an extra dose of granite-faced apathy. Dad told me about one of the first shows they ever did with Jack. It was at the Rose Theatre in Kingston upon Thames and, in the middle of the recording, a man in the audience said very loudly: 'Not the same without Humphrey Lyttelton, is it?'

There was an uncomfortable silence before Jack said: 'Oh, dear Humph, I wonder where he is now. I envy him.'

He got a huge round of applause.

If Dad's school report cautioned against glibness at the start of his career, Lyttelton's legacy with Dad was his promise to 'never lose touch with silly'. The late seventies and early eighties brought him his silliest challenge to date and one that once again introduced him to another true soulmate.

A ventriloquist is stranded in the outback. He sees a farmer on his horse, with a sheep and his dog, and thinks he'll have some fun.

Ventriloquist: 'Mind if I talk to your dog?'

Farmer (puzzled): 'Okay. Sure.'

Ventriloquist (to the dog): 'How's it going, mate?'

Dog: 'Beaut, mate. Three walks and three meals a day. Plenty of bones to play with. Bonza.'

Ventriloquist: 'Mind if I talk to your horse?'

Farmer (still puzzled): 'Erm. Okay.'

Ventriloquist (to the horse): 'Hey horse, how's it going?'

Horse: 'Great. I get regular trail rides, fed tasty oats, brushed down at night and he keeps me in a barn to protect me from the elements.'

The farmer can't believe it.

Ventriloquist: 'Mind if I talk to your sheep?'

Farmer: 'That sheep's a liar.'

12

Most of the comedians that I know Dad admired as he grew up, people like Groucho Marx, Jack Benny, George Burns, Max Miller, Eric Morecambe or Tommy Cooper, all had warmth, a mischievous streak, or a combination of both. They were also outsiders. In the case of Max Miller, there is an additional element of a 'dandy' to his persona. Miller experimented with other identities, but it was only when an appearance in a grey lounge suit at the Palladium went badly that Max decided to stick to his brightly coloured image. Miller had apparently always had this eccentric bent, as a child he donned paper collars and top hats, as well as different coloured socks. Therefore, to Max, it must have seemed like a more honest persona rather than an artifice. Dad eventually went on to perform alongside Miller as part of *Midday Music Hall* in 1958 at the Playhouse Theatre in the West End. He remembered being surprised that Max insisted on wearing his full stage costume. This included a homburg hat, plus-fours and a floral silk jacket. 'Can't work in ordinary clothes, son,' he'd say. Dad was surprised because *Midday Music Hall* was a radio show.

Dad performed alongside Max Miller as part of Midday Music Hall *in 1958 and went on to impersonate his idol on* Who Do You Do? *In the 1970s.*

When he was writing for Morecambe, Cooper or Frankie Howerd, Dad would often step back and describe these performers as 'one-offs' with an 'other-worldly talent' or, in J. B. Priestley's terms, 'alien beings from another planet'. In other words, he didn't identify as being one himself. Perhaps the responsibility he felt to his mother to not get 'too big for your boots' was part of that, matched by the discomfort he felt putting himself forward as a leader. As much as Dad loved eccentrics and rogues, he just couldn't be one himself – it wasn't in his nature. However, he'd happily be the second person through the breach in the wall of good taste, which is an important quality if you're going to write for and support that kind of person. He was tremendously loyal to them in that sense.

When Dad first met Max Miller, while working at the Leeds Empire, it was in the position of stagehand and he saw the courteous, polite and helpful side of the man. When they worked together as performers on *Midday Music Hall* and Max insisted on wearing his stage 'clobber' for a radio show, there was an incident that perfectly illustrated his impish nature. Ray Ellington, the great *Goon Show* band leader, was on conducting duties for that recording and dared Max to tell his joke about a bus driver: 'This bus breaks down and the driver says to the conductress, "I'll fix this, love." A while later, with the rest of the bus getting impatient, she goes to check. "Do you want a screwdriver?" she says. "No, we're ten minutes late as it is."'

Ellington bet Miller a fiver that he wouldn't tell it on live radio. Max took the bet and the company, Dad included, stood in the wings, waiting for the big moment. Max went through his act and every now and again he'd shoot Ray a mischievous look as if to say, 'I'll do it now'. Max got to the end of his act without even mentioning a bus, let alone doing a joke about its driver. Ray Ellington went over to Miller to ask for his fiver in the pub afterwards. 'I was going to tell it,' said Max, 'but they flashed the light at me.' Both men knew full well he wasn't going to tell it, but by having the other performers gathered in anticipation, Max was creating an expectation that was just as exciting as the joke itself. That was the quality a 'Cheeky Chappy' like Max could exude.

On location with the undead version of Kenny Everett from the second series of The Kenny Everett Television Show *in 1983. The show wasn't immortal but that sheepskin coat was.*

Then by refusing to pay up, Max further extended the prank and added to that persona, no matter how annoying for Ray Ellington that might have been.

By the end of the 1970s, and now into his forties, Dad had tried on a variety of different roles but had settled into a very happy and successful professional groove in his life, mainly as a writer, servicing these rare talents. He was writing with an impressive array of brilliant collaborators like Spike Mullins on Harry Secombe specials, Neil Shand on Stanley Baxter Christmas shows, Graham Chapman on Ronnie Corbett sitcoms and the *Doctor In The House* TV series, John Junkin on *Morecambe and Wise*, Peter Vincent on *The Two Ronnies*, David Nobbs on Les Dawson and Dick Vosburgh on both Tommy Cooper and Danny La Rue projects as well as the *Carry On* TV series.

As a performer, *Hello Cheeky* and *I'm Sorry I Haven't A Clue* were now well established, and *Jokers Wild*, although finished by 1974, had made him a visible presence in people's homes. Whisper it quietly, he was becoming a bit of a 'celebrity' and this meant after-dinner speaking had overtaken warm-up spots, and personal appearances and invitations to charity events were now part of his regular routine. He also managed to find time to renew his friendship with Bernard Cribbins by constructing various double-act routines for *The Good Old Days* and was even starting to make 'top left' his own on a new panel game called *Blankety Blank* with Terry Wogan.

With professional relationships with Danny La Rue and Graham Chapman both on hiatus towards the end of the decade, and despite his own personal success, there was a feeling that Dad's need for another eccentric talent to inspire and champion was becoming obvious. The pioneering radio producer Angela Bond (she'd been one of the first female producers at Radio 1) invited Dad to lunch in the West End to talk about doing a radio series. Her reputation at Radio 1 was largely forged because of her role in discovering and advocating a young Liverpudlian DJ, whom she'd first heard working at Radio London. His name was Kenny Everett.

Angela got Kenny and Dad together to talk through some ideas and, although the radio series never materialised, the die was cast.

The two men got on immediately and it was clear from the outset that Dad had found someone that he wanted to work with in the future. Billy Connolly, a friend of Everett's, once said (echoing Dad's words about one-offs): 'I don't think there will be another Kenny Everett and I don't think there's supposed to be. These guys come in ones; you don't replace them. You count yourself grateful you saw it when it was there and if you were dead jammy you got to stand beside it when it was working. Kenny arrived as a fully fashioned rebel, did his rebellious work and buggered off.'

There was a chemistry between Dad and Kenny, and it would prove to be one of the great relationships of Dad's life. It was the same connection he had found with Danny La Rue and Graham Chapman. The common denominator, of course, was that all three were gay men. Growing up alone with a single mother and an imaginative flair for flamboyant performance was a situation Dad felt he shared with many of his gay friends. David Sherlock, Graham Chapman's partner, even described Dad to me once as a 'man magnet'. There were stories of him going on nights out to gay bars with Graham and Kenny and returning home with phone numbers scribbled on scraps of paper in his pockets. My mother found it all highly amusing. Kenny, whom Dad ended up just calling 'Ev', once said: 'Ooh Bar [Kenny's name for Dad], married for twenty-five years and four children. What a smokescreen!'

I always took it for granted that, just by virtue of working in the entertainment industry, my dad was bound to be socially liberal. However, I must keep reminding myself that, for most of the first half of Dad's life, homosexuality was illegal and the prospect of having an open conversation with anyone about their homosexuality was practically impossible. You'd have to imagine that when he was still living in Leeds, the first gay man Dad would've met would have been Cyril Livingstone (the founder of the Proscenium Players, the Jewish theatre company that performed some of Dad's early sketches) when he was at university.

While Cyril was undoubtedly flamboyant, it's unlikely the mores of the time would've allowed him to be fully open about his identity. This was the same Leeds, after all, that Dad's friend Alan

Bennett was growing up in and he once revealed in his memoirs that he never came out to his parents because it would have 'distressed' them too much. However, when Dad first moved down to London, this all changed dramatically. In fact, one of his first flatmates was the Scottish actor Angus Lennie, eventual star of *The Great Escape* and *Crossroads* (not at the same time, mind), who used to leave a vase upturned in the hall if he was 'entertaining'. Dad's education began in earnest when he came home early one night to discover that Angus had forgotten to turn the vase over.

In 1958, my uncle John, who had left the Merchant Navy by this point and was now living in London, came to see Dad in *Expresso Bongo*. Dad was keen for John to meet his new mates and gain his older brother's approval of his choice of career. John, who was ten years older than Dad and not from the same business, was bemused by the campy, bitchy jollity that surrounded him at the pub. When the two brothers left the pub, John turned to Dad and said, 'What are you hanging around with all these poofs for?' Needless to say, their relationship, though never close to begin with, didn't exactly blossom after that.

Dad talked empathetically about the sacrifices his gay friends made to protect their identities in the fifties and sixties. Some of the people he worked with, like Kenneth Williams, Jimmy Edwards and Frankie Howerd, were like 'tortured souls' for most of their careers. However, around the time that Dad started working with Graham Chapman, things were beginning to change. In 1967, after homosexuality was decriminalised in the UK, Graham held a coming-out party at his home in Belsize Park where his friends, including Dad, were invited to meet his partner David Sherlock. He then got on with his life, free from the burden of personal secrecy. Then, in 1972, jazz singer and writer George Melly, who described himself as gay in adolescence, bisexual in the navy and heterosexual in later life, invited an obviously drunk Graham onto his talk show to discuss a variety of topics. Halfway through, Graham casually announced he was gay (he'd never done so before on television). It was a low-key moment and not a surprise to those that knew him, but it was an important moment for gay rights in Britain. He was one of the first celebrities to make quite so open an announcement and as he did so, he attacked intolerance in general:

'I was in a pub the other day, and I overheard a conversation between some labourers, okay, and they were fine, but they were talking about how they had beaten up this poof in a pub. Now, what does that mean to them? What is the credit to them? It's pure prejudice. It's fear. It's fear. It's like white people have a fear of black people, like heterosexual people have a fear of homosexual people. There's no point to it. We should all love each other and do it in our own way. That is the only thing that matters.'

Around the same time, Dad and Graham wrote a pilot for a sitcom called *Frank & Ernest*, in which the lead characters were an openly gay couple. Unheard of at the time, Dad was particularly proud of how sensitively and honestly he thought they treated the subject. For Graham, it could have been a moment for him to make a personal statement through his work, but when they showed it to Humphrey Barclay, the producer, he said, 'I love this but it's too soon. We will never get this on.'

It's therefore not surprising that later in life, Dad reacted badly to the ITV sitcom *Vicious*, with Sir Ian McKellen and Sir Derek Jacobi, describing it as 'positively homophobic'. It was a truly surprising outburst, given Dad's reputation for being very supportive of other people's work, but the personal memories of his friends over the years obviously still hurt. 'A sitcom with two old gays could be really good and moving,' he said. 'With two great actors in Sir Ian McKellen and Derek Jacobi, it should be fantastic, but it was insult, insult, insult every other line. You don't believe in them. You don't like them, for a start. It made John Inman look restrained.' He was not alone. The *Evening Standard*'s Brian Sewell thought it 'a spiteful parody that could not have been nastier had it been devised and written by a malevolent and recriminatory heterosexual'.

One thing you could never accuse Kenny Everett of being was restrained. You couldn't really accuse him of being a comedian either, at least not in the strictest sense. Kenny was completely different from any other performer Dad had worked with. Dad was used to writing sketches for variety comedians and character lines for comic actors, but never for someone without any formal experience in sketch comedy. It was clear from his radio show that he was charismatic, silly and very funny, but he was still essentially a DJ who'd branched out into small, improvised sketches that relied on sound effects.

Music still defined Everett, and his friendship with the Beatles during the launch of *Sgt Pepper* (when he had only just joined the BBC) had brought him to a wider audience. However, it was at Capital Radio in 1975 and his influence on the fortunes of Queen's 'Bohemian Rhapsody' that made people realise just how powerful a communicator he could be. EMI thought it was too long and wanted it cut, but Kenny played it in full several times over one weekend and, it is said, that helped it become a hit. His summary was typically quirky: 'I love this song. This is so good; they'll have to invent a new chart position. Instead of it being Number One, it'll be Number Half.'

TV broadcasters were keen to cash in on his influence, but there was still a fair amount of snobbery surrounding his ability to transcend being a radio DJ. His TV outings thus far hadn't exactly fired the imagination either. He was recruited to a magazine show in 1968 with Germaine Greer (more in her Footlights guise than in her Warwick University persona) called *Nice Time* that although a modest success, never quite decided who its targets were. The fact that it was also produced by future *World in Action* editor and BBC Director General John Birt might tell you something about what a strange concoction it must have been. To anyone in the 1990s, the idea of John Birt and Kenny Everett collaborating would have been absurd. In short, Kenny quickly grew disillusioned with television and moved out of London to the Cotswolds.

Having been burnt by some of his other experiences, including shows at LWT, Kenny was in no hurry to rush back. However, any comeback depended on Kenny behaving himself. For example, later in his radio career, having been sacked by the BBC twice, he was offered a final olive branch. The producer said: 'Now Kenny, you're live on Saturday, for goodness' sake behave yourself.' Kenny's first words on air were 'I've just been told I mustn't say penis'.

Couple this with his infamous 'Let's bomb Russia' comment at the Young Conservatives conference in 1983 (when he was already a TV star) and you can see why this kind of behaviour would make TV executives nervous.

Off-screen, Kenny was quite shy but once comfortable with someone, he would become quite playful. Dad and his friends used to go to a Chinese restaurant on the Goldhawk Road to wind down after work, and Kenny became fascinated by a plaque on the door of the gents. It featured the figure of a dancing man, in the style of Fred Astaire, complete with top hat and cane. One night, they all sat down to order food and Kenny announced that he needed to visit the loo. When he returned, he was carrying a top hat and cane (that he'd nicked from wardrobe) and danced down the middle of the restaurant.

It's like a story Eric Sykes told Dad about Tommy Cooper. Eric and Tommy were making a film together and had decided to meet in a pub near the studios at noon. 'So, noon comes and goes,' said Eric, 'and there's no sign of Tommy. The pub is beginning to fill up and I, being a stickler for punctuality, am getting very annoyed. It's now 12.15 and I'm telling the producer that when Tom does arrive, he's going to get a very big piece of my mind. At 12.45 – the pub is totally full by now – the front door swings open and standing there is Tommy wearing a bowler hat and a pair of pyjamas. He walks up to our table and says: "I'm sorry I'm late. I couldn't get up."'

Tommy, like Everett, had been to wardrobe to make a casual throwaway gag work. It was that kind of dedication to playfulness at unlikely times that Dad loved about these kinds of eccentric one-off forces. However, for Everett, all that skittish talent was just sitting at home in the Cotswolds reluctant to get into a TV studio again. It just needed the right kind of vehicle to tempt Kenny back.

A young curate is giving his first sermon and asks an older vicar for his advice.

'Well,' says the older priest. 'You know that glass of water I sip from during my sermons? It's not water. It's neat gin. Get yourself a glass of that to calm your nerves while you're talking.'

So, the young vicar does his sermon, all the time drinking from his glass, and afterwards asks the older priest what he thought.

'That was one of the best first sermons I've ever heard. It had fire and authority and you held the congregation's attention,' said the older priest. 'Just three things:

'Don't tear up your notes and throw them at the congregation when you've finished.

'Walk down the stairs of the pulpit; don't slide down the banister.

'And, technically speaking, David slew Goliath. He didn't "knock seven bloody bells out of him"…

'… And his sling was full of shot.'

13

It took the advice of an eighteen-year-old for Kenny Everett to get his biggest TV break in 1978. Thames TV's Head of Light Entertainment, Philip Jones, asked his son who he thought should be a star but wasn't. The boy, who was a Capital Radio fan, suggested Kenny. Jones was very collaborative and open-minded, so his son's recommendation was treated just as seriously as those of any veteran producer. He hated the snobbery in the industry that looked down on those in light entertainment, so to him, Kenny was a perfect way to prove a point.

That same year, Jones had also poached Morecambe and Wise from the BBC and got Dad and John Junkin to write for them, including their much revered Christmas specials. Now that *Jokers Wild* had finished at Yorkshire TV, David Mallet was hired to produce and direct Kenny's new show and, because he'd enjoyed a great working relationship with Dad, suggested him for scriptwriting duties. You'd think that because Dad was already at Thames with Morecambe and Wise, they would have had no problem hiring him for Kenny. However, Philip Jones was chasing a younger audience, and Dad was made to wait. This was a crucial moment for Dad and similar in many ways to the difficulty he found himself in after his West End revue *See You Inside* was so poorly received a decade earlier. Then he was seen as old-fashioned, whereas now he faced the possibility that he might be too old. Apparently, forty-three was okay for Morecambe and Wise, but not for Kenny Everett.

Dad told David about the lunch he'd had with Kenny and how excited he'd been about his talent. Kenny's radio stuff reminded Dad of the quick bursts of jokes and sketches he'd been doing with Tim Brooke-Taylor and John Junkin on *Hello Cheeky* and with Bill Franklyn on *What's On Next?* If Philip Jones needed convincing of older precedents, then it was worth pointing out that Kenny's stream-of-consciousness, sound effect-laden nonsense reminded people of Monty Python, who in turn owed a lot of their inspiration to the Goons. David, still only in his early thirties at the time, could see those parallels too and fought for Dad to be included. In the end, he managed to use the age difference to his advantage by convincing Philip that Dad's experience would give Kenny a safe pair of hands. Dick Vosburgh, whom Dad had written with many times before on Danny La Rue and the *Carry On* TV series, was then added to the scriptwriting team as well to reinforce the point. Given Kenny's erratic reputation, this proved to be persuasive argument.

The Kenny Everett Video Show (later *The Kenny Everett Video Cassette*) was originally intended to be a contemporary music show with comic links, which is why David Mallet, who'd already directed music videos for Queen and Blondie, was chosen. They also wanted someone with a pop music background to join on the writing team. *Jokers Wild* yielded the answer once again, as David Mallet recalls. He and Dad were in the gents at Thames (always a good location for gossip), during a break in a meeting where no one could agree on what writer they needed. Dad and David remembered that before he co-devised *Jokers Wild*, Ray Cameron had been a stand-up, opening for rock acts. Ray was a highly innovative individual who'd grown up in Canada watching a lot of US TV, something Thames found attractive. Philip thought Ray would be perfect for the show.

The early recordings of *The Kenny Everett Video Show* were anarchic. Dad said that it was the only show he ever worked on where the camera script (the 'finalised' document for shooting) was sometimes full of blank pages. As it was originally only set up to be a clip programme (made up of links between music videos), there was to be no audience. Kenny used to make stuff up on the spot and if the crew laughed, it was in. In a regular comedy show, having the crew laugh would usually put the performers off, but seeing that the only performer was Kenny (who loved it) it soon became a feature of the show. Crews would fight to get on the show. They all enjoyed working with Kenny, and it was the only show Dad ever worked on where nobody said: 'Quiet!' before a take. There was no countdown, no schedule as such, they just started the cameras and waited to see what happened.

It's hard to imagine any of Dad's peers being quite so affable in the face of such anarchy, but Dad was back in his favourite element. Utter chaos. Just as he loved the cushion falling out of his shirt when he was playing Falstaff at school, or when the set was falling down in *Expresso Bongo*, or when the *Hello Cheeky* costumes got mixed up, or when *I'm Sorry I Haven't A Clue* was falling apart, Dad was once again practising the art of professional amateurism. The charm of that performance mode is that you are sharing your workings out with the audience (not to mention a camera crew) and that builds a trust and a rapport. When you eventually get it right, the audience at home (or in the studio or the theatre) feels part of the journey. It's easier to laugh if you trust that the process is being honest with you.

That feeling is perfectly preserved in one of Kenny's improvisations that Dad always claimed was his favourite. Once, when Everett was playing the leather-clad rocker Sid Snot, he grabbed some cigarettes from a cameraman just before filming and started throwing them in the air to catch them in his mouth. When he finally caught one, he beamed, and the crew started laughing. Just pure joy. Pure silliness. And nothing to do with what was written in the script. Dad said that those days at Thames were some of the happiest days he ever spent in a TV studio and it's easy to see why. It's an authentic, unvarnished moment, free from pretension or indulgence. David Mallet says now, looking back, that they didn't realise how lucky they were.

Given how extemporary a lot of the work was going to be, David suddenly saw the wisdom of bringing in Dad and Ray (Dick

Vosburgh also worked on four episodes of the first series). They both had stand-up experience and, as a result, were able to come up with jokes and ideas on the spot. Dad's ability to deliver in extreme circumstances was one of his greatest strengths as a writer. He was regularly hired because he usually delivered without bother, self-importance or, more importantly, procrastination. Dad fell back on that hard-earned sinew that came from having to consistently create new material from scratch for Vivian Van Damm at the Windmill, Danny La Rue at Winston's or David Frost on *The Frost Programme*. He was used to finding different ways of making things work in front of indifferent crowds on many occasions, whereas here he was preaching to the choir. A haven of silliness that just happened to result in pleasure for millions. At Thames, it was 'mostly' created in a positive, nurturing atmosphere of support and love… and old jokes.

The 1980s unholy trinity of Kenny Everett, Dad and Ray Cameron discussing the finer points of the Sid Snot oeuvre.

Old-school jokes, lovingly handcrafted by skilled, experienced jokewrights and being performed by expert variety players was a dynamic that Dad obviously knew how to handle. However, when you put those same old jokes in the mouth of Everett, in all his naive glory, bubbling with quirky, tongue-in-cheek archness, it becomes something fresh. There was a quality to the contrast, where although you knew you were hearing a hoary old chestnut (calm down at the back) it was delivered with such energy, celebration and warmth, that the ironic handling of it generated a second laugh. It was conspiratorial. Kenny was being bold and brash with something so hackneyed. In David Mallet's opinion, it was a perfect storm, and he remembers Dad as being pivotal to that spirit:

> It's not what you say, it's the way you say it. That's another old one. Barry would come up with these things from his memory bank and Everett would immediately put a spin on them. They just worked. Every single one of those Sid Snot jokes, if you analyse them, is really, I mean, they're virtually out of Christmas crackers. They're Windmill jokes with nothing else to them.

Mallet was responsible for making sure the show was technically daring, with Quantel Paintbox TV effects not only offering Dad and Ray different avenues of creation but also giving artists like David Bowie licence to do more than just sit strumming a guitar. However, despite the effects, the general feel of the show was still that of a live broadcast. Monty Python loomed in the abandoned punchlines and the early cartoon sequences also owed much to Terry Gilliam. The minds of *Danger Mouse* creators Cosgrove Hall were picked as Captain Kremmen (a Kenny character from the radio) became another animated feature. Dance troupe Hot Gossip was added to provide a visual for songs with no videos, and their louche sexiness led to one wag referring to them as 'Porn's People'. *Songs of Praise* this was not.

Sid Snot was just one of several Everett creations that balanced the rough, charismatic, contemporary feel of a music show with an old-fashioned spirit drawn from a music-hall age. Initially, the first series concentrated on the links to music videos or live acts (including an impressive array of talent such as Bryan Ferry and Rod Stewart), but the characters soon began to demand longer screen time, so the links got longer. Dad took pleasure in the amount of visual comedy they were allowed to do. It tapped into his childhood love of movie comedy heroes like Buster Keaton, Jacques Tati and Laurel and Hardy. He and Ray created Morris Mimer, the mime artist who drew simple cartoons and shapes on a white background, which usually came to life in 3D. All set to perky synth versions of J. S. Bach. Then there was the Spiderman sketch where he's climbing halfway up an office building but suddenly needs to pee. He clambers into a company toilet only to discover he doesn't know how to unzip his lycra suit. I remember the wet leg shake that Kenny did as he walked away was one of the most copied impressions in the school playground the next week. Dad was very proud of the sketch and loved the fact that people were copying it.

Brother Lee Love was a black-hatted American preacher with huge polystyrene hands, who used to come on to the backing of a gospel choir. One day, completely unscripted, Kenny threw off the fake hands, grabbed the autocue camera and spun it around to face the rest of the studio. All the usual detritus of a working studio was there: the brick walls, the coffee cups and the crew standing about with cables and clipboards. To the amusement of everyone, Kenny looked down the barrel of the lens and said, 'Oh, the glamour of it all!' Dad said it was pure Spike Milligan. Kenny's moment of inspiration was left in the show and, when broadcast, drew a lot of attention.

Yet it wasn't always rosy in the Thames garden. As Dad said: 'The boss was upstairs, and the joke was that if he ever found out what was going on down there, there'd be trouble.' Sid Snot was a big hit and the plan was that they were going to do a soap called *The Snots*. Unfortunately, news about this was leaked to Philip Jones who, for reasons known only to himself, wanted it stopped. As Dad recalled: 'We turned up and the studio was empty. We went upstairs [to see Jones] and Kenny said he couldn't work with these people.' To Dad, who hated confrontation and usually just wanted everyone to get along, this was a stressful moment. David Mallet described Dad's approach to negotiation perfectly: 'If you had to go and have a row, there would be me in front, Ray Cameron behind and Barry would be leading up the rear.'

Once again, Dad loved being with the mavericks but didn't want to be there when the grenades went off. Ultimately, Kenny was angered by the cancellation of *The Snots* and always hated the fact his show was scheduled at 8 p.m. on a Thursday, up against *Top of the Pops*. Where Morecambe and Wise had left the BBC to join Thames, Kenny went in the opposite direction and BBC's *The Kenny Everett Television Show* was born. The new slot? After *Top of the Pops*.

Dad worried that the BBC (or 'Auntie Beeb' as Everett had it, replacing 'Lord Thames' as the moniker for ridiculing his paymasters) would try to tame Everett's wilder moments. He said that they'd try to turn him into 'a BBC comedian'. However, he needn't have worried too much. Firstly, Kenny was not a comedian in the conventional sense and had no preconceived ideas of what he 'ought' to be doing. This is what helped Dad and Ray break so much new ground with him at Thames. He was just Kenny – daft, funny, brilliant, witty and always open to ideas. Secondly, he wasn't likely to listen to attempts to make him more mainstream. Kenny loved the fact that they could do the same stuff but with a higher profile 'establishment' TV channel that would also attract, on average, around 6 million more viewers. However, there were some red flags early on. They were doing a pre-record one afternoon and Dad said to Kenny, 'Do the camera gag again.' So, he did exactly the same thing, pulling the camera around to reveal the distinctly unglamorous studio, repeating the line he'd previously used at Thames. Bill Wilson, the producer, came down from the gallery. 'Very funny,' Bill said. 'But could we do it again? There was a shadow on Kenny's face.'

'We do tacky, Bill. I thought you knew that,' Dad said. 'Let's leave it as it is.'

Then the BBC started wanting the scripts in advance and any hint of improvisation was eroded.

What the show needed was a shake-up in the form of a bubble blonde loudmouth film starlet called Cupid Stunt. Aside from a deliberate attempt to tug at Auntie's bloomers, she was created because Dad remembers watching a young actress giving an interview to promote her new film, in which she had to do a nude axe-murder scene. She mitigated that to the interviewer by saying 'It was all done in the best possible taste'. Dad told Kenny and Ray this story and they both fell about laughing. When it came to shooting, Kenny thought of the 'Old Mother Riley' film comedies of the 1950s, where Arthur Lucan used to extravagantly cross and uncross his legs. The Cupid Stunt sketches would always take place on a mocked-up Michael Parkinson interview set, with a cardboard cut-out of the interviewer sitting opposite. The leg cross came as Kenny uttered the punchline and gave the viewers a flash of Cupid's red knickers. A sort of reverse Sharon Stone. As the sketches got more elaborate, some of Cupid's longer stories even cut back to Parky's skeleton.

Now, some of the sharper-eyed of you might have noticed that the name of the character contains a spoonerism perhaps unsuitable for 8 p.m. on a Thursday night. Indeed, this wordplay took the show's daring to a whole new level and Kenny attracted the attention of Mary Whitehouse, the campaigning conservative moral activist. She objected to many aspects of the show but reserved some particular bile for the dance troupe, Hot Gossip. David Mallet was rather proud that she had described them as 'poison being poured into millions of homes'. Dad once ran into her at a charity function, where he told her: 'You made us!'

After two series (I'm amazed it took that long), Bill Cotton Jr, Managing Director of the BBC, finally worked out the joke behind Cupid's name. He found Dad one day and insisted they change the name. Dad immediately agreed and they promised to alter it for the following series. To Mary Hinge. Cotton later caught up with Dad and said: 'You see? You don't have to be disgusting to get a laugh.'

My personal favourite sketch from Kenny's time at the BBC came in the first series in 1981. It was one of the many Dad and Ray wrote for Kenny and Billy Connolly. Kenny is coming down the stairs of his house when there is a knock on the door. He opens it. Billy is standing outside and speaks first:

Billy:	Yes?
Kenny:	What? What do you mean *yes*?
Billy:	Well? What do you want?
Kenny:	What do you mean what do *I* want? What do *you* want?
Billy:	I don't want anything – it's you who opened the door.
Kenny:	I know that, but what are you doing there?
Billy:	Listen, pal, what do you want? I haven't got all day.
Kenny:	I don't want anything!
Billy (abusive):	Well, why don't you clear off then before I call a constable? Go on! On yer bike!
	Kenny shuts the door. Pause. He opens the door again. Billy is still there.
Billy:	Yes?

A favourite sketch of Dad's featured Cliff Richard, appearing in what looks like an old piece of black and white footage. With careful wardrobe and make-up, they'd got Cliff to look pretty much like he did in his early 1960s 'Summer Holiday' period. He's singing away and then Kenny walks into frame wearing a bright red shirt and blue jeans. 'Get out of my old clip!' says Cliff.

Kenny had an amazing gift for learning lines after only a couple of run-throughs of a sketch. It used to unnerve some of the actors they hired when they arrived and Kenny hadn't learned the script. Veteran comedy actor Geoffrey Palmer once turned up to work on the show and, like the professional he was, was word-perfect. Geoffrey was slightly worried to see that Kenny had an autocue as he thought it might look like Kenny was reading. However, after rehearsals, Geoffrey was amazed at the speed with which he picked it up. Spike Milligan arrived one afternoon to be greeted by Kenny, with script in hand, casually glancing at it in rehearsals. 'I've been up all fucking night learning my lines. Remind me to send you an assassin for Christmas.'

The BBC years also saw the introduction to British screens of Anglo-Greco Brazilian model and actress, Cleo Rocos, who, when she wasn't sparring with Kenny on-screen, she was fast becoming Kenny's favourite companion (and nearly his wife) off-screen. When I was a young actor, one of my first jobs was to go to Paris to film the TV show *Highlander*. They were overlapping the filming of the series and quite often I'd get to meet the cast from another episode. One day, at lunch, this very striking woman with curly red hair came over to me and said hello. She said she'd noticed my name on the call sheet and wondered if I was related to Barry. We chatted for a little bit before she was whisked away to a different location. As she left, she said to me: 'Too much buttock juggling with your dad, by the way.' Now, as a twenty-two-year-old, I didn't really know how to respond to that, and I made sure that when I got back home, I'd break the bad news to Mum myself. Before I did so, I told Dad who I'd seen over in Paris and told him what she said. Turns out this was Cleo and Kenny's nickname for dancing.

In the years following the end of the Everett show, David Mallet and Dad would still occasionally meet for lunch at the same old Italian restaurant near BBC Broadcasting House that they'd always used. Anyone who has spent time in Dad's company, especially if they're in show business, will know that a joke is going to punctuate your conversation. When I talked to David he said the lunches with Dad were usually dominated by tales from the Everett years, with Dad often in a wistful mood: 'There's a very interesting point about that. And that is that after Everett, whenever we used to get together for our lunches, he was never jokey at all. Never jokes. Never. Okay, maybe one or two, but nothing like the normal Baz. It was always reminiscing. And we really had the best time of our lives.'

Kenny Everett was clearly more important to Dad than just a job. He was a friend and collaborator who stretched Dad's talent professionally and personally, and also stretched his horizons. The warmth Kenny exuded and the trust he put in him meant that Dad finally learned that these 'one-offs' were not just 'creatures from another planet'. Kenny's friendship humanised the industry a little more for Dad and he'd even begin to bring a little more personal recollection into his own comedy afterwards as a result.

However, there could be no more sobering reminder of the fragility of this kind of genius than when the decade closed with Kenny's HIV diagnosis. Paul Gambaccini once commented that due to the advances in medicine, had Kenny contracted the disease only a year later, he might have survived. When you consider that 1989 was also the year that Graham Chapman died, the personal toll on Dad meant that the next decade would feel a little less colourful.

Back in 1984, while still working on Kenny's BBC show, Dad and Ray managed to make a film with Kenny, called *Bloodbath at the House of Death* (with Vincent Price, no less), but they also worked on *Assaulted Nuts*, the TV sketch show Tim Brooke-Taylor was in. It mixed American and British performers and, without being overly critical, only the *Titanic* had a less successful journey across the Atlantic. The British actors were Cleo, Tim, a young Danny Peacock and, briefly, Barry Cryer. When the second series came around, Tim was double booked and couldn't join them, so they got the obvious replacement: a young comedy actress called Emma Thompson. The Americans were Elaine Hausman, Bill Sadler ('Death' in *Bill and Ted's Bogus Journey* and 'Red' in *The Shawshank Redemption*), and Wayne Knight (who later popped up in *Basic Instinct*, *Jurassic Park* and was Newman the Postman in *Seinfeld*).

These performing talents were matched by the writers on the show. People like David Renwick, Andrew Marshall, Paul Minnett, Brian Leveson, Ian Davidson, Peter Vincent and Dick Vosburgh all contributed sketches. I've had experiences as an actor where happy sets sometimes make for bland shows and that seems to be the case here. Everyone involved talked in glowing terms about it afterwards. Yet it couldn't succeed, and I remember Dad being particularly disappointed that even though they made two series, only one was shown in the UK (and that was at 11.15 at night). He'd long been a fan of US comedy and while he held no ambition to work in the States, he felt it was an opportunity missed to gain at least some recognition over there.

Dad may not have had ambitions when it came to working in the US, but it did nearly happen and in the most unexpected way. *Bloodbath at the House of Death* was not the first time Dad and Ray had written a screenplay for Kenny. Back in 1980, when they were all at Thames, Kenny was still a weekend DJ at Capital Radio. The story goes that American film director Stanley Kubrick, a UK resident with a house near St Albans, loved to listen to Kenny's show. When his movie *The Shining* was launching in the UK, Kubrick decided he didn't want the gravelly Hollywood blockbuster-style voice-over for the radio ads (usually Redd Pepper in the UK or Don 'In A Time...' LaFontaine in the US). Ever the genre contrarian, Kubrick felt that kind of voice would signpost *The Shining* as a horror movie a little too much and he wanted to keep audiences guessing when they went into theatres. He thought Kenny would be the perfect misdirection. He invited Kenny for tea, and it didn't take long for Kenny to agree to do the voice-overs. Making conversation, Kubrick then asked what else Kenny was up to besides his radio and TV shows. Kenny said that his writers, Dad and Ray, had written a film for him called *Suicide: The Movie*. Kubrick was intrigued: 'What's it about?'

'Well, there's this guy who's pretty down on his luck,' Kenny replies. 'His girlfriend wants to split up with him, his boss wants to fire him, and his family is generally embarrassed by him. In a panic, he pretends he wants to commit suicide and, suddenly, his fortunes change. People feel sorry for him. He gets married, gets a promotion, a raise and his family can't stop spoiling him for fear he'll get depressed again. He feels so guilty that people are treating him this way, and all because of a lie, that he starts to feel genuinely suicidal because of it. Don't worry, it's a comedy.'

Kubrick let this information tick over. 'I like the sound of it. Send me the script. I'd like to do it.'

Kenny went back to Dad and Ray and told them that Kubrick wanted to do their movie. Dad was bowled over with excitement, but Ray was less enthusiastic: 'It won't be our movie. It'll be Kubrick's.'

'Who cares?' said Dad.

'Besides, I want to direct it,' said Ray.

Kubrick hadn't done a comedy since *Dr Strangelove* in 1964 (unless you're counting *Clockwork Orange*, which I'm sure you're not), so it was plausible that so dark a theme might have tempted him. However, the only thing that came from that tea party was a voice-over gig for Kenny. A folder to put away in the 'what if' file of Dad's career. I like to imagine a parallel universe where Redd Pepper is intoning: 'From the people that brought you *Bloodbath at the House of Death*!'

When you consider that all the *Assaulted Nuts* writers I mentioned above were also writing on *The Kenny Everett Television Show*, it tells you two things. Firstly, Kenny's shows were now too big for Dad and Ray to handle alone. The writing talent they attracted was unquestioned, but the result was the authorship of the show became a little diluted. Secondly, it proved how much more brilliant writing talent there was out there to compete with. The longer Dad remained with just one show, the more likely it was that he might be left behind.

What was lazily dubbed at the time 'alternative comedy' had started making itself felt and was challenging the political status quo. Shows like *The Young Ones*, *The Comic Strip Presents* and *Not The Nine O'Clock News* brought comedians Alexei Sayle, Rik Mayall, French and Saunders and Rowan Atkinson to public attention, performing material by new voices Ben Elton, Richard Curtis and Peter Richardson. Just as with the satire boom, a lot of the values and cultures associated with the established (not to mention old-school) variety were now becoming unfashionable. This included the art of the 'joke'. The 'alternative' boom was no different from the other generational shifts in comedy, save for its political bias perhaps being more closely affiliated to a left-wing agenda rather than purely anti-establishment like the movements that came before it.

Typically, Dad paid little notice to the politics but for what must have seemed like the umpteenth time in his career, whether he liked it or not, he was being challenged to stick with his style or twist. Fashion didn't really bother Dad, as anyone who saw his shirts in the eighties would testify. He was always either too canny for that question or too stubborn (the answer is always too stubborn by the way). Dad was a born survivor, so continued to cast his net around the various variety wagons that were circling in the late 1980s and he didn't have to wait long for the call. It eventually came from Russ Abbot, one of the alumni of both *What's On Next?* and the impressions show *Who Do You Do?* that Dad had worked on in the 1970s.

After those shows, Russ became part of the cast of the LWT Freddie Starr vehicle, *Variety Madhouse*. When Freddie quit, Russ took over the show with Les Dennis and made it a family-friendly Saturday evening success. The BBC decided it needed a dose of those ratings for its own weekend schedule and, in 1986, offered Russ a contract. With the move to the BBC, a new creative team was assembled and *The Russ Abbot Show* now metaphorically had a card in the window looking for new writers.

However, in an offer that Dad could've taken as a sign that he was either 'over the hill' or 'comedy royalty' (let's go with the latter), he was asked to be a script associate and editor. He would still write the odd bit of material, but other people would send in sketches and new writers would be scouted. It was rather similar to 'The Comedy Corridor' set up at BBC Light Entertainment (Radio) in the 1970s and 1980s, where it seemed any writer with a good enough idea could walk in and contribute to shows. This included Douglas Adams, who we met in the Graham Chapman years. This democratic experiment spawned the most remarkable influx into the industry since perhaps Frost's heyday. At *The Russ Abbot Show*, although old friends of Dad's like Dick Vosburgh and Peter Vincent were there, the show also gave a chance to different younger voices, such as Paul Minnett and Brian Leveson (writers on *Assaulted Nuts*). It seemed the era of celebrity writers like Eddie Braben, Galton and Simpson, Muir and Norden and Johnny Speight was now moving to a more egalitarian era. Dad's hard-earned reputation garnered with shapeshifting tenures from Frost to Everett was starting to feel a little like a millstone.

The more the comedy-world plates shifted, the more some older writers, like David Nobbs, were forced to morph into literary fiction and TV drama. Others dug their heels in, like Bryan Blackburn, who helped Cannon and Ball regularly achieve over 20 million viewers with about as traditional a sketch show as was possible in the 1980s. For Dad, where Everett had been an unconventional agitator, lobbing stones at the establishment, Abbot was now seen by the 'alternatives' as a traditional protector of a threatened culture. In just the space of a few short years, Dad had switched horses from the avant-garde back to the older order of things, and it looked like he might be riding in the wrong direction.

In fact, Dad didn't see it like that at all. His lack of awareness of this cultural change in direction was born less of a misdirected belief in a golden age of comedy and more of an innate need to see the positives in any given person or situation. If you've never being fashionable in the first place, then you can never really go out of fashion. Suddenly, a utilitarian brand of apolitical silliness was a superpower. He also saw parallels between his own development from Frost to Everett and the likely route to be taken by the writers of shows like *Spitting Image* or the performers on *Saturday Live*. He regularly identified and reframed the new wave in terms of the past, cementing one of the key aspects of his personality that would be celebrated widely after his death. Remarkably, in an interview with *The Times* in 1986, he said: 'Ben Elton is a sort of latter-day Arthur English with his line of patter. Rik Mayall is the new Max Wall and Ade Edmondson is Norman Wisdom all over again. And these guys are often getting a tougher theatrical training. Ben Elton does a two-hour spot in the theatres. Max Miller would never have done more than 25 minutes.'

It's a remarkably generous observation, given the climate in the industry was urging a move away from his generation, but he did put it into practice. Dad was invited to a live TV debate on a programme called *Central Weekend* in 1986. It was chaired by Sue Jay and the focus was on the rise of alternative comedy. Jimmy Tarbuck had just signed a new £3 million deal with LWT and *Spitting Image* had satirised him and Bruce Forsyth as old-fashioned comedians who'd become little more than gameshow hosts with a golf membership. Dad was joined in the studio by

John Lloyd, Ben Elton, Stephen Fry, Michael Bentine and Neil Shand (who Dad had just finished working with on the Everett Christmas Special).

Before the show, Dad was having a pee (why are so many of his stories set in the toilet?) and in walked Ben Elton. They'd both worked out that the show had been set up as a polemic and realised that the producers wanted them to have a go at each other. They were probably after something like the intergenerational *Life of Brian* debate between Malcolm Muggeridge, the Bishop of Southwark, John Cleese and Michael Palin. Instead, Dad and Ben decided to agree with each other as much as possible to deflate the rhetoric. They just didn't see this kind of division as helpful to the industry.

Proof (if proof was needed) that Dad believed in a broad church of comedy.
Bobby Ball, Ben Elton, Tommy Cannon, John Inman and Dad at Comic
Relief in 1989. Together at last.

Dad's ability to suspend judgement on these changes and focus on his own work while applauding younger writers and comedians was not going unnoticed. By the time the final BBC *Russ Abbot*

Show aired in 1991, it was the last time that Dad would ever be hitched exclusively to one TV performer as a writer. That was as much about the changing landscape of central contracts and the rise of the spare-bedroom freelance writer as it was about Dad's age. Younger comedians were now also writing their own material.

Kenny Everett with Dad in one of his frequent guest appearances on The Kenny Everett Television Show, *1982. 'Off with his head!'*

As he neared sixty, he'd started to realise (courtesy of Willie Rushton, as we'll see in the next chapter) that performing rather than writing might have to feature more prominently in his life again. It was a thought that didn't need too much encouragement, given he'd been performing regularly on *Clue*, in panto, at after dinners and on shows like *The Steam Video Company*. This shift was a little different, though, as it would require him to move away from the context of a format or a panel game and begin reminiscing about his career. He'd have to do the unthinkable, get off whatever rung Ronnie Corbett had thought he was on and appear fully as 'Barry Cryer' once again. It was a time to reset his career.

In 1995 an invitation to host a new programme on the BBC featuring the best in live comedy called *The Stand Up Show* (think *Live at the Apollo* but without the Apollo) put Dad firmly back in the public eye. He'd begun attending the Edinburgh Festival in the late 1980s and early 1990s with Willie and his stints there had convinced producers that he understood the current generation. As an emcee, his nurturing manner made him the perfect blend of empathy and experience to set the tone for the acts. To him, confidence-wise, it was the change he needed and reminded him once again of those nervous few months as a young writer-performer in Leeds navigating the Empire and the City Varieties before going to London and climbing the Windmill to make his name. Now that he was beginning to think about starting his own stand-up career (all over again), where should he go?

Miss Barnett who lived two doors down from us had a dog called Bobby. She always put him out last thing at night for a pee. One night, she'd been in town with some friends and got back late. She came back, popped Bobby out in the garden and promptly fell asleep on the sofa. When she woke up, she found he hadn't returned. So, Miss Barnett went out into the garden and there he was, to put it delicately, making love to another local dog. She tried to stop him with a bucket of water, and then with a broom. All to no avail. She rang up the vet in a bit of a panic, forgetting it was still the middle of the night. She told him all that had happened.

The vet said, snappily, 'Bring Bobby to the phone.'

'Will that stop him?' Miss Barnett asked.

'Well, it's just stopped me!'

14

It all started with a charity gig at the City Varieties Music Hall, the venue where it began for Dad thirty years before. In 1988, Dad and Willie Rushton were metaphorically comparing their scars and war wounds from long careers and lamented the downturn in their professional fortunes. The fact that they were in the dressing room of a BBC1 daytime quiz called *Music Match* may not have helped. Dad was the host and Willie was a team captain (Liza Goddard was the other, for those of you who weren't asking). Dad was also hosting another daytime quiz at the time called *Crosswits* and it looked like the well-trodden path from comedy icon to gameshow host was tapering off into the middle distance.

It's safe to say that *Music Match* wasn't exactly pushing either man to the limit of their talents and they were wondering how the show business carousel had spat them out in a format which had rounds called 'Misfits' and 'Think the Link'. Ever the optimist, Dad was just happy to be working, but Willie suggested they take matters into their own hands. They'd both been asked to appear at a charity event by Dad's beloved City Varieties in aid of the Spinal Injuries Association. Rather than just do separate spots, Willie suggested they craft an evening that they could turn into a viable stage show for the future. They could sell out medium-sized venues on their own, but together they could aim for bigger ones.

Dad and Willie Rushton had been circling each other since the 1960s when they both made their big TV breaks under the aegis of David Frost. Ostensibly they were both part of what became known as the satire boom, but because of Willie's involvement in the launching of *Private Eye* and *That Was The Week That Was*, history has given him the rather restrictive moniker 'satirist', masking an incredible versatility. He probably hated the term polymath, but he had more claim to it than most as he was an actor, cartoonist, editor, journalist and author, whose work ranged from novels and poetry to journalism and children's television. He was as comfortable in a voice-over booth and a TV studio as he was at the MCC or the *Literary Review*. In short, he was a brilliant intellect whose talents as a cartoonist most obviously focused his comic and political outlook. He was most skilled at skewering his targets in short, succinct, often devastating bursts.

Willie was underrated as an actor; he was in *Up Pompeii* with Frankie Howerd in the 1970s and featured in Bernard Miles's *Treasure Island* at the Mermaid Theatre in the 1960s alongside Spike Milligan. Rushton, playing Squire Trelawney, tells Eric Flynn's Dr Livesey about Long John Silver, but he forgot the cue line about him only having one leg. Flynn tried to rescue the situation later in the scene and said: 'And, er, how many legs has he got?' Rushton could easily have played along and confirmed the amount, but instead, he replied: 'Well, you as a medical man should know.'

In 1968, Eric Idle and Dad had been asked to write for Tony Hancock at a point in a career that, to put it mildly, needed some rehabilitation. He'd gone to Australia to make a television series about an English immigrant who was unimpressed by Australian culture. Unfortunately, Tony never completed the series because he died in June of that year. His brother, Roger Hancock (who was also Dad's agent) asked Willie, who was visiting family with his Australian wife, to bring back Tony's ashes. Willie was walking through customs at Heathrow Airport when one of the officers stopped to ask him what he had in his Air France carry-on bag. Willie replied: 'Tony Hancock.'

Dad's relationship with Willie, although not as overtly affectionate as with either Kenny Everett or Graham Chapman, was no less important to him, especially during the period we're about to look at. Dad once described Willie as 'a warm sentimental man who took great pains to conceal it'.

I'm Sorry I Haven't A Clue was clearly more of a melting pot of their collective talents and its cross-generational appeal meant that finding an audience for their stage show was a much easier task. They invited Colin Sell and Graeme Garden to join them (Tim was never really a 'turn' in this context and was usually busy as a comic actor elsewhere), augmenting *Clue*'s presence and giving its audience another opportunity to celebrate its spirit. Now both in their fifties, it says something about their mindset too, that Dad and Willie decided to call the show *Two Old Farts in the Night* ('We can't get done under the Trades Descriptions Act,' Willie said). It was (loosely) a show about growing older with music to suit, and they put together some tour dates reflected the demographic. Willie also thought the title guaranteed some of their target audience might giggle with embarrassment when asking for tickets.

Dad and Willie arrived at one venue to be met by a piano tuner. He was blind, as many tuners are, with compensatory acute hearing, and he was accompanied by his guide dog. The man began chatting and was pleasant enough, but it soon became obvious that he was going to hang around. As they began to set up for their show, after he'd finished tuning, he settled down in their dressing room, still chatting away. Out of the blue, perhaps at Willie's increasingly blunt prompting, the man picked up his dog's lead and said: 'Well, I hope you have a good show tonight, gentlemen.' As he walked out of the door, Willie said, 'How cruel of them to give you a cat.'

As part of their 'Old Farts' tour, Willie and Dad were staying at the Europa Hotel in Belfast. Between 1970 and 1994, the Europa was bombed an extraordinary thirty-three times, gaining it the unenviable reputation of being 'the most bombed hotel in the world'. On the check-in form, it said, 'How did you hear about this hotel?' Willie put '*News At Ten*'.

The original show was more of a variety bill that included a supporting cast of friends. Alongside Graeme Garden (who worked some physical prop comedy with a bat that came out of a box and attached itself to his face) and Colin Sell on piano was a singer called Christine Pilgrim, who'd worked with Dad in old-time music hall. When Christine had to suddenly leave the tour to go and look after her mother in Canada, Dad recruited my sister, Jack, to replace her. Jack had been a professional singer for around five years by this point, having performed in West End musicals and spent some time as a session singer. It marked the first time in nearly thirty years (since Mum at Danny's club) that two Cryers had shared a stage together.

He was sometimes too keen not to come across as nepotistic, so he introduced her as 'Jacqui Cryer. No relation'. Jack was there on merit and took it with good grace (he did follow it by saying 'she gives lessons to tuning forks'), concentrating instead on delivering the opening number – a parody of Edith Piaf's 'No Regrets'. It was restyled as 'No Cigarettes', where she sang about giving up smoking just as the stage filled up with smoke. Dad was often back in the dressing room having a crafty fag and, on one occasion, nearly setting the wastepaper bin on fire.

There was a comedian on the bill of those early shows called Pierre Hollins, a fantastically frenetic and funny man who, aside from playing the guitar, used to jump through newspapers shouting 'Danger is my business!' in a French accent. When we were putting together the list of guests for Dad's memorial, it was great to be able to include Pierre in the line-up. It was thirty years since I'd last seen him and while he'd calmed down a bit, the wildness that Dad loved so much was still there. It also reunited him with my sister and watching them reminisce during the show was a lovely reminder of those days and a testament to Dad's enduring spirit.

As the tour continued, the bill was streamlined to just Dad, Willie, Colin and Jack. Nominally, Dad and Willie were billed as a double act, but they didn't share a stage except to greet the audience and take part in a medley of songs at the end. Willie's act was as the rambling, discursive raconteur and Dad's half was originally just jokes, which is just how he was at the Windmill in 1957. This is not to say that Willie didn't tell jokes, but they were always the more absurdly observational. Dad's favourite joke in Willie's 'Old Farts' routine was: 'What is the difference between erotic and kinky? Erotic is taking a feather and doing something lingering, sensual and beautiful to your partner. Kinky is using the whole chicken.' The centrepiece of his act was singing the Irving Berlin song 'Top Hat, White Tie and Tails', which details the putting on of a high-society gentleman's formalwear for a party. Willie would act out the lyrics to the letter, but soon realises Irving Berlin makes no mention of trousers in the song. He is left fully dressed but with bare legs.

The show toured for a couple of years before it took a surprising turn to a place that would define the last third of Dad's life. In 1990, Willie's son Toby was preparing to direct *The Duchess of Malfi* at the Edinburgh Fringe when Willie rang up to ask Toby's venue if they had any slots left for other shows. A few weeks later, Dad and Willie were debuting their show at the Fringe. Although Dad was only fifty-five and Willie nearly fifty-three, which to most people would be considered no age at all, a combination of the title of the show, Willie's fusty image and Dad's white hair made their seniority enough of a talking point.

Their stage show started out by emphasising the differences between the two men, but as it progressed it began to highlight their similarities. They were both very specific wordsmiths but neither of them brooked pretension of any kind, least of all in politicians. The show was a great success and, alongside *Clue* of course, they continued to tour with each other until Willie's untimely death in 1996. Apparently, his last words about my dad were 'Tell Bazza he's too old to do pantomime'. In a final twist that Willie would've enjoyed, Dad was given this news when he was halfway through rehearsals for *Dick Whittington* in Cambridge. Willie's ashes were buried by the boundary at The Oval, which denied him the gravestone inscription 'Discontinued' that he'd always wanted.

The programme from their original charity show 'Taylor-Made Evening With Friends' gives us a reminder of the fun they had together:

Barry Cryer by Willie Rushton

Barry Cryer is truly a Renaissance Man. Born at the height
of the Renaissance to a family of unimaginative weavers in
downtown Turin. For many centuries, the family firm knitted
white flags for the Italian army. Bending to market forces, the
firm expanded into manufacturing white vests and socks for
Popes. Flushed with new-found prosperity, the family moved to
Leeds to get a better view of the industrial revolution…

He is, of course, today a show business legend with over
a hundred appearances in the Appendices of Kiss-and-Tell
memoirs as varied as those of Dame Nellie Melba, Madge
Brindley and the divine Miss Sarah (a legend in her own
lifetime) Bernhardt. To this day he never appears without a taxi
at the stage door, engine running. He lives in Hatch End with
his extensive collection of manhole covers. Barry Cryer is 93.

Willie Rushton by Barry Cryer

Willie Rushton was born in Kuala Lumpur in 1907, where his
mother happened to be at the time. His father was not present
at the birth, nor indeed at the conception, as a local rumour
would have it. Educated at Shrewsbury, he is an old Salopian.
(OED: 'One born on a slope with consequent leanings.') His
first TV appearance was on 'That Was the Coronation That
Was' in which he played the lead and David Frost played the
dog. Ever since he has been engaged.

Mr Rushton's paintings have been exhibited throughout the
country in galleries, museums and police stations, where his 'Lord
Lucan, front and side face' has proved a lasting favourite. His
hobbies are lycanthropy, shouting at traffic and taking his beard for
a walk. He is delighted to be appearing here tonight as it's cold out.

Dad spoke at Willie's memorial service. It was held, like those of
so many actors, writers and comedians before, at St Paul's Church,
Covent Garden. Memorials have a slightly different tone from

funerals in that they are often seen as more of a celebration of someone's life. It's entirely dependent on the person being honoured, but you still need to know where the line is, especially if the family are present. However, because it was Willie, Dad felt it best to follow John Cleese's example at Graham Chapman's memorial service in 1989 (where Dad was the emcee):

> I guess that we're all thinking how sad it is that a man of such talent, such capability and kindness, of such intelligence, should now be so suddenly spirited away at the age of only forty-eight before he'd achieved many of the things of which he was capable, and before he'd had enough fun. Well, I feel that I should say, 'Nonsense. Good riddance to him, the freeloading bastard! I hope he fries ... Anything for him but mindless good taste.'

Although he'd written a speech for Willie's memorial, Dad took a stroll outside to smoke (he always called it taking 'a breath of fresh air') to work out something to open with. The news had recently featured a story about how controversial music presenter Paula Yates had taken a DNA test and confirmed that she was the daughter of controversial music presenter Hughie Green, whom she loathed. When Dad got up to speak, he announced that it had recently been discovered that Willie was the real father of DJ Chris Evans.

The show with Willie wasn't the only time Dad stepped into a theatre in the 1990s; his lack of writing contracts meant that he was tempted to accept more and more acting roles. Every January and August (which are the quiet months for the profession) during this period, Dad would dramatically announce that he was never going to work again. It taught me that the greatest virtue you can possess in the business is patience. He had always acted at various points, but he was never comfortable being described as an actor. He suffered from terrible imposter syndrome, and I think it was useful for him to have an escape clause for any role he was assuming. If someone called him a comedian, he'd say he was an entertainer. If anyone talked about his writing for performers, he'd always point out he wrote in a partnership. If they called him a writer, he'd say he was a hack. The only thing he admitted to without qualification was being a singer. Be careful what you wish for…

Singing had always been part of Dad's life and he was never shy to air his tonsils (as any *I'm Sorry I Haven't A Clue* fan will testify), but save for pantomime and old-time musicals he hadn't been in a fully fledged musical since *Expresso Bongo* in 1958. In 1993, his old friend Dick Vosburgh suggested Dad to Ian Marshall Fisher, artistic director of the 'Lost Musicals' project. Ian was looking for a comic actor to recreate the role of Louis Blore, made famous by cowardly lion himself, Bert Lahr, in a concert version of Cole Porter's 1939 *DuBarry Was A Lady*. It left Dad hankering for a full-blown tilt at a production once again; however, nothing could've prepared him for the next turn in his musical theatre career.

Just as with Dick Vosburgh, it was another *Two Ronnies* writer, Colin Bostock-Smith, that connected Dad to a musical later that same year. Decades before *Succession* ruthlessly eviscerated media moguls, *Maxwell the Musical* was an attempt by a former trade show promoter called Evan Steadman to do the same thing to Robert Maxwell. I don't know how much Colin had to do with Dad's selection, but no one was more surprised than Dad himself (not to mention his family) that he was offered the gig as a Czech émigré turned newspaper baron. Despite not looking or sounding like him, a fat suit, some hair dye and his best gravelly generic Slav impression all came together to find Dad sitting behind a big desk with a cigar in a rehearsal studio in Bloomsbury, ready to wow investors.

By all accounts, he acquitted himself well, but Dad's greatest skill was always improvisation, not transformation. Without a room to play to, he was shorn of the thing he needed to be truly comfortable. It wasn't a huge disappointment when Dad was told that the production would cast again for the run, but the way they let him know was. A press release talked about a big name carrying too much baggage for the show and that a less well-known actor was now being sought. Dad was also asked by Steadman to help

Two Old Farts In The Night *at the Palace Theatre, Newark, in 1995. Willie Rushton said the title was chosen so they couldn't be sued under the Trade Descriptions Act.*

host a charity auction to raise further funds for the show, as well as invest his own money. It was quite the turnaround and not one that Dad was enamoured with.

I remember Dad feeling a mixture of anger and embarrassment at this turn of events, but true to form, he didn't let it last long. Instead, Dad started to tell his friends soon afterwards about this ridiculous adventure he'd been on. However, the story took one last strange twist as the prospect of having a major West End musical satirising their father suddenly didn't seem so appetising to Robert Maxwell's sons, Ian and Kevin, especially as they felt it might prejudice their forthcoming fraud trial at the Old Bailey. An injunction was granted to stop the show, and months of money and hard work, not to mention no small amount of goodwill, went down the drain.

Dad had to wait until 1998 for another proper run in the theatre when his friend Ian Liston, of the music hall and pantomime company Hiss and Boo, took Alan Ayckbourn's *Season's Greetings* on tour to the Redgrave Theatre in Farnham, the Everyman in Cheltenham and the Theatre Royal in Bury St Edmund's. Dad was offered the role of Harvey, the delightfully dark and deranged ex-security man who spends most of the play permanently sitting in front of the TV at a family Christmas (I won't comment on which element of the casting brief fitted Dad best). It was a real departure for Dad as Harvey is a distinctly unlikeable character who hates everyone, spits insults everywhere and is obsessed with violence. In short, it wasn't the usual cuddly 'Uncle Baz' people were used to.

I'd just finished drama school the year before and was beginning to start work as an actor, so I was thrilled when Dad got this job. It would also give us, as father and son, a chance to bond and share a common language. While he got really good reviews and the public got to see a reverse of his affable persona, he was strangely uncomfortable during the run. He'd really struggled with the lines in the build-up and for a long time even had bits of his script taped to the inside of the prop *Radio Times* that sat by his armchair onstage. I think he still felt like a fraud, falling back once again on that long-held belief that these kinds of performances were for other people with rarer gifts than his.

It was a shame he felt that way as I thought director Kit Thacker got a great response from him and Dad was on to something with this performance. However, like many times in the past, any evolution that Dad undertook as an older man was usually a more gradual one (the idea of revolution scared him) and there was one role waiting for him the following year that fitted him better – like an old, battered straw boater.

Dick Vosburgh was the provider once again. Dick, as we've seen previously, was a benevolently recurring figure in Dad's life and a joyfully willing partner in his lifelong quest for silliness. His heavy eyelids and pointed beard made him a kind of comedy Santa Claus, if Santa had an encyclopedic knowledge of the movies of Virginia O'Brien or the lyrics of Betty Comden. Born in New Jersey, he lived and loved in Britain (marrying actor, photographer and fellow RADA graduate Beryl Roques and having six children) but never lost his accent (delivered in a measured bass-baritone burr) or his distinctively American worldview.

Dad and Dick first met in the early 1960s when they worked together on the Ray Martine show *Stars and Garters* (the variety show set in a pub). There's a story that Dad regularly told about Vosburgh that (surprise, surprise) took place in a gents' toilet. This one was at Thames Television. As is inevitable sometimes, writers can use these venues to sound off about elements of a show that they find frustrating, usually the producer. Dad noticed there was an 'engaged' sign on one of the cubicles behind them. He tried to nod his head silently in the direction of the doors to warn Dick of the potential embarrassment. Without missing a beat, Dick zipped up his fly and said, '... and those are my sentiments, as sure as my name is Barry Cryer.' You'd need to hear his New Jersey accent for the full effect, but you get the idea.

Although a talented performer, Dick's love of classical Hollywood stars like Cary Grant, Rita Hayworth and the Marx Brothers, as we've already discovered, was matched only by his love of words and lyrics. He particularly adored Cole Porter, Irving Berlin and Oscar Hammerstein. Dick was once working with Ronnie Corbett on an old Cole Porter song and Ronnie expressed sadness that there were only three verses. Dick went away and wrote a fourth verse. Ronnie said you couldn't tell the difference. Dick also adapted a Chekhov play into the Tony-Award-winning *A Day in Hollywood/A Night in the Ukraine*, and he was now looking to do a similar thing by changing a Molière play into an MGM-style musical, with Dad playing a boozy, wise-cracking old grump in *A Saint She Ain't*.

Most of Dad's scenes were with the charismatic Pauline Daniels, who played the Mae West role, and the two became fast friends. Pauline had a background in cabaret in Liverpool, which meant Dad could relax in the company of a fellow improviser who also loved tilting the show up on two wheels. It took the pressure off him having to remember lines and he often had fun with Pauline riffing in the style of West and Fields. However, Dad's hang-ups about line learning could only be temporarily shelved as his other scenes occasionally proved. On more than one occasion, he had other co-stars lock themselves in a blank stare as he forgot a cue or dropped a line.

A Saint She Ain't *by Dick Vosburgh and Denis King at the Apollo Theatre,*
1999 with Pauline Daniels (as Mae West and W. C. Fields 'types').

The show gained fantastic reviews for its initial run at the King's
Head, and it earned another West End transfer for Dick and Denis.
The show at the Apollo didn't fare as well, with critics noting that
the production seemed a little swamped in the bigger space, now
sheared of its previous charming intimacy. Individual performances
were applauded but Dad was singled out as 'flat' and 'leaden'. Sadly,
that show was to be the last thing Dick worked on. Dad remembers
him looking drawn at the final performances, but he still had his
wit intact in his final years. When Dick was in hospital in 2007
a nurse passed his door and stopped to ask if he was okay. 'Is it a
boy?' he said.

From a family point of view, we'd become concerned that the
fluffed lines and moments of panic onstage were actually masking a
deeper problem. By the time the show transferred to the West End,
he was approaching sixty-five and while he was still very active,
he'd started feeling a little more tired as the run wore on. I talked

*Dad in armchair: his favourite spot with his favourite things. His family, a telephone,
a newspaper, cigarettes and champagne (usually in that order).*

to Denis King about the show and his recollection left little doubt
as to where he thought the issues began:

> I knew your Dad for more than sixty years and shared a lot
> of moments with him – mostly funny – although there were
> the odd times when it wasn't that funny. I was working with
> him in the West End (*A Saint She Ain't*) when Baz missed
> his entrance due to a slight overindulgence of a certain brew
> between the matinee and the evening performance, leaving the
> young leading man on stage wondering what to do. As I was
> accompanying the show along with another pianist [Chris
> Walker] between us we doodled on the keys for quite a while
> until the stage manager pushed Baz on stage.

While it had become obvious to us that Dad had been drinking
more than usual during the run, what was more concerning was
the fact that he'd shifted his allegiance to wine in the evenings.
For most of his life, Dad was a beer drinker and, as we saw even
during his time with Graham Chapman, he'd never found solace in
spirits. He was also not the kind of pub drinker who was chewing
the landlord's ear off at last orders. His sociability meant the beer
drinking was in the middle of the day and largely dictated by years
of writing in pubs in partnerships.

Having a pint before a gig wasn't unheard of, but Willie
Rushton once slapped Dad's wrist (metaphorically, I think) over
a third pint that had left him a little shaky on the lyrics of the
opening number. On a separate occasion, after the show, Dad
was wondering why the audience wasn't laughing as much at one
of his new gags. Willie suggested that it might be because they'd
loved it more the first time he told it. In the first half. The wine,
however, was starting to turn a very amiable, relaxed and pleasant
man with a reputation for being generous with his time, into a bit
of a grumpy old man. He was by no means elderly, but the answer
for his erratic behaviour didn't lie in a bottle. That was merely a
symptom. The answer lay a little closer to home. Our mum was
suddenly taken ill.

My mother had suffered on and off with anxiety and depression for most of her life, but it had never been debilitating. Until now. As seen in the chapter about her and Dad's first meeting, much of what Mum carried around with her was inherited either genetically from her mother, who suffered from panic attacks, or behaviourally from her father, who'd dealt with the burden of shell shock. It was while Dad was performing in *A Saint She Ain't* that Mum started to suffer some episodes that meant she had to spend some time in hospital.

It rocked Dad severely, as you can imagine. As with many couples, Mum seemed to reserve a special kind of playful silliness and good humour just for him, which is easy to take for granted over a long marriage. Normally, this kind of subtle secret code, when played out, means everything is going to be all right. That gentle reminder of stability was now temporarily but abruptly missing. It was like a light going out for him and the effect caused Dad to panic. It's often when this intimate language is absent, that we understand its effects most clearly. Nearly every night that he was away from home, from very early on in their marriage, he'd ring Mum to either let her know he'd arrived or what time he thought he would be home. That now wasn't possible.

Without making excuses for Dad at this stage in his life, it was a tough time, but he needed to take some responsibility for himself and acknowledge his self-medication. I knew he felt bad about it, because he started the process of giving up wine shortly afterwards. Initially, I think his habit of having an extra glass between shows or at lunchtime was a reaction to feeling the pressure of being the most high-profile name in a West End show. Also, some of the criticisms of his performance in *A Saint She Ain't* were quite harsh and he was feeling sensitive. When you consider that his support system, Mum, had been taken away, I can begin to see the context a little clearer. When I went to see the show in its first week, I was greeted by an ashen-faced father afterwards. I'd never seen him so vulnerable. I'm not sure exactly how many people in the cast knew about what was happening with Mum, because Dad kept it quiet, but they'd begun to rally round. The concept of a theatre cast being like a family is a very real one during times of need and they instinctively responded.

This period, around the turn of the millennium, was one of huge upheaval for the family generally, but also an instructive one. Two of my siblings had young children by this point, making grandparents of Mum and Dad, who were thrilled with their new titles. And while his work, wobbles on *A Saint She Ain't* aside, was going as well as ever, the most important measure of his success at any stage of his life was Mum's health and once she was back home, they began to assess how they might manage their newest challenge: getting old. It was a period that proved beyond all doubt that whatever Dad had achieved in his life, nothing would have been possible without Mum's strength, support and resilience. The secure platform she created for not just him but all of us throughout our lives was created with love and care.

Dad, meanwhile, without Willie by his side and with little intention of going back into narrative theatre, decided to venture out on tour with Colin Sell. Left with just his own material to re-evaluate, it became clearer to him that he wanted more music to be at the heart of his performances in the future, just as it had been on the steps of Leeds Town Hall half a century earlier.

It was a decision that took him back to Edinburgh, where an unlikely double act formed.

A rather shy, timid man was at a party once without his wife and played a game where you had to draw subjects out of a hat and talk for five minutes. When it was his turn, he had to talk about sex. So, he started talking and ended up making everyone laugh.

The next day, his wife asked him about the party and he told her about the game. She then asked what his subject was and he panicked and said 'Yachting'.

Later that afternoon, she was out shopping and bumped into a friend who was at the party. 'Your husband was very funny in our game last night talking about his subject.'

'Well, I don't understand,' said the man's wife. 'He's only done it twice… The first time he was sick and the second time his hat blew off. And he had to be winched off by helicopter.'

15

Hope was born in a blizzard. Well, she nearly was. We returned
with our friends Hil and Drew from St Michael's Hospital in
downtown Toronto because Hope wasn't quite ready to arrive.
I called my parents and told them about the false alarm with their
latest grandchild. I'd got into the habit of keeping Mum and Dad
regularly updated on my wife's pregnancy, partly through the
guilt of voluntarily being nearly 6,000 kilometres away and partly
because there was no chance of them visiting.

'We want to come and see the baby,' said Mum.

I was surprised. Mum hated flying and Dad wasn't too keen on
it either. He'd once been flown to Houston (not Euston as he'd
first thought) for forty-eight hours to do an after-dinner speech
for the British-American Business Association. They even threw in
a helicopter ride while he was there. He thought it might work as
aversion therapy, but it only made it worse.

It was February. Average temperatures in Toronto were always
below zero, but that year was particularly cold, regularly reaching
minus 20. Dad ignored my advice about wearing jeans (they were
his perpetual attire in those days) but did arrive in his John Motson
coat, Russian hat and plastic Elvis sunglasses. Mum, who dressed
like a normal person, didn't enjoy the flight so much as tolerate it.
The last time she was on a plane going to North America (to go to

Disneyworld in 1982), Mum had spent most of the holiday worrying about flying back. She didn't fly again after that. Until now.

That was a trip where Dad and Jack stumbled on a talent show at a nearby restaurant and readily coughed up $50 to sing 'Delta Dawn' to a room full of Mickey Mouse ears. I remember being desperate to join in (I was nine and desperate to do anything) and after much pleading (a tantrum), I was allowed to come on stage with them. 'Desperate' probably summed up my voice at the time too, so the compromise was that my mic was turned off – they weren't mad. I was just there to elicit sympathy from the assembled tourists, who were more interested in acts with kids than great songs. I flaunted it for everything it was worth. Dad and Jack sang like a dream, and I even mimed out of tune, but ultimately, we came second to a woman who sang Dolly Parton while clutching a baby. Dad was livid, Jack had cherry Coke and I felt bad for not being young enough. Fifty dollars was a lot in those days.

Back in Toronto in 2002, we found them one of the serviced apartments near Lawrence Park, which was the most affordable local place for Mum and Dad to stay that had a kitchen. With a new baby, our apartment was off-limits for guests, plus I thought Mum and Dad would settle more quickly in self-catering. It smelled of moths with top notes of raccoon, but it was near the subway and we were five minutes away by car. Mum was excited to wake up with fresh snow on the ground. Three days after the blizzard, my Canadian mother-in-law Nancy came over from London just in time for Hope to be born. Her sisters Lorna and Mary, who lived in Toronto, took Mum and Dad under their wing and my parents were treated to a series of dinners and lunches while we showed Hope off to half the province.

It was fascinating to see Dad out of his comfort zone in Canada. Nobody knew who he was there or wanted to know what Tommy Cooper was *really* like. No one expected him to crack a joke or talk about what Noël Coward got up to with Binkie Beaumont (apart from me). The prime expectations for him were to be a grandfather or a visitor from the Old Country. Obviously, I'd given my wife's relatives a heads-up on what he did for a living and some of the older generation maybe knew a little bit about Morecambe and

Dad and Ronnie Golden in Rock of Ages *at the Gilded Balloon in 2002. This was the show that began his love affair with the Edinburgh Festival.*

Wise. Had Dad worked with Benny Hill or appeared on *Are You Being Served?*, then he might have had more questions fired his way. He was more relaxed and unburdened than I'd seen him for a while (and I hadn't seen him for a while), just curious to hear about these other lives unfolding on the other side of the Atlantic, although he still made notes on his fag packet if heard something he could work into a gag.

I went to check on my parents a few days into their stay. I thought I'd take them for a drink to wet the baby's head. Mum was having a nap in the apartment. 'Where's Dad?' I said. 'He's with his new friends.' It turned out there was a sports bar around the back of the apartment block where Mum and Dad were staying. Not exactly the full Wetherspoon experience that he was used to, but it was as close to a local pub as you might find in walking distance. There are pubs in Toronto, of course, lots of them, and most follow the British model (except with North American flourishes like table service and smiling). *Coronation Street* watch-along Sunday roast parties were a thing for a while when I lived there. Even though my three scenes as an inspector on the Toyah Battersby missing persons case were still fresh in the memory, I could walk the streets unmolested.

The ice hockey, ribs and wings on offer at the sports bar didn't strike me as reasons for Dad braving the cold, but when I got there it soon became obvious why he did. He was holding court, telling jokes and introducing me to the locals. Having had a break from being 'Barry Cryer' for a few days, he'd needed an audience again, whether they knew who he was or not. Living proof that given the right material, comedy was a universal language. People were laughing because of the way he told a joke, not because of who he was. On his trip to Houston, before his speech, he was taken to a British pub and an English woman at the bar came over to ask for his autograph: 'I'm such a big fan, Mr Took.' He flew a long way for that one.

We were sitting with Mum and Dad in Fran's Diner downtown the next day with Hope in a car seat wrapped up in a blue snowsuit. It was fit for a child twice her size and the way she was growing it was just as well. We told Mum and Dad the good news that we'd decided to return home to the UK and had made plans to pack up our apartment in May. Being closer to family was much more important now and we wanted our daughter to grow up knowing her grandparents and immediate British family. The childcare helped too I suppose. I asked Dad what he would be up to in the summer when we got back. He too had a new family: the Edinburgh Fringe.

He'd spent the years after Willie's death taking the leap into one-man show business with his *First Farewell Tour*. Dad always felt the need to support his collaborators and hated the description 'one-man shows' as Colin Sell always accompanied him. Col also sang a song at the start of each half. The combination of so many years as a line writer, sitcom creator, sketch crafter, after-dinner speaker and warm-up man meant that he probably had enough material for three shows. One of the most intriguing aspects of taking the show on the road was therefore not *how* the audience would react but *what* they would react to. Increasingly, because of the longevity of his career and the sheer diversity of the people he'd worked with and written for, audiences now wanted to hear anecdotes as well. Who was he to deny them the pleasure? Dad was a natural raconteur, but he didn't quite know it yet.

Colin Sell said that one of Dad's most important qualities as a writer was his ability as a collaborator. As we've seen throughout his life, including working with Colin, Dad was always at pains to acknowledge other people's contributions. He was just as generous on stage with audiences too, bringing them in from the outset. He wasn't just rattling off material and collecting laughs, he was starting a conversation. He even developed 'Barry's Bucket', so people could write questions for him at the interval for him to answer in the second half. It kept him fresh and challenged his memory in a way that was both unexpected and impressive. The odd question from Dad himself might creep into the bucket, lest the evening go a little off track. The best comments came from members of the audience. 'Thank you for the free pen' being one of Colin's favourites.

Dad soon realised that unless he was to become the new Ken Dodd (as if there could be another), whose shows regularly exceeded four hours, he'd need to keep an eye on his running order. A man once called out: 'Doddy, the last train's at midnight!' Ken Dodd replied, 'You're leaving at the interval?' I bought him a small lectern to keep his notes on and there was always Colin to guide him back (to which Dad would often say 'I'm working him with my foot'). The only time the lectern backfired was when he did a show in Brighton with Joan Littlewood, the legendary theatre director, in the audience. She came round to his dressing room afterwards and said: 'What's that book for? I always thought you were a fucking amateur.' It was one of the best compliments he ever received.

Dad had always wanted to do a good, old-fashioned rock 'n' roll show. Generationally, he was in his twenties in the late 1950s, so if anything by Bill Haley, Elvis, Little Richard or Chuck Berry came on the radio, he'd groove away as much as anybody. He was also partial to a bit of gospel and soul too, favouring people like Mahalia Jackson, James Brown and Ray Charles. One of his great pleasures later in life was hanging out backstage with Jools Holland and his band when they were on tour. Another joy was reuniting him for our podcast with the great guitarist, singer and raconteur Joe Brown, who was to music what Dad was to comedy. They matched each other blow for blow, the rhythm of the exchanges feeling more like a jam session than a conversation. Music was everywhere. He was also married to a singer and the father of a singer as well as having a grandchild that blows the trumpet like an angel (that plays trumpets).

In 2002, Dad was having a drink at the Hackney Empire with Arthur Smith when he was introduced to a man called Tony De Meur. Dad asked him what his real name was, but it turned out that it really was Tony De Meur. His stage persona was 'Ronnie Golden' (but Dad still thought Tony De Meur a better name). In his solo career, Tony opened for the likes of Engelbert Humperdinck, Tom Jones and Scott Walker, before forming the new wave outfit Fabulous Poodles, who made a dent in the US in the late 1970s. He'd also worked as a stand-up in the early 'alternative' days of the Comedy Store. Tony was currently the frontman for a band called Ronnie and The Rex, the late-night house band at the Edinburgh

Fringe's Gilded Balloon. Like a lot of musician-comedians, he started by just playing music but the links got longer. Dad, by contrast, had started as a comic and then brought more and more music into his act. They met somewhere in the middle. It's safe to say the answer to Dad's opportunity to do a good, old-fashioned rock 'n' roll show was staring him in the face and not just because it was his round. They met up again at the King's Head in Crouch End, where Dad told a few jokes and Tony played a few songs. Afterwards, Dad asked him if he was interested in putting a more formal show together for the Fringe.

Crucial to making anything happen was Steve Ullathorne, part promoter, part photographer and all Edinburgh legend. He'd been 'court photographer' to most of the UK's top stand-up acts for the last thirty years and his exhibitions and posters are a big part of the fabric of the Fringe. When Dad first went to Edinburgh, it was just another stop on an existing tour show but by the end he'd become part of the furniture (probably an Ottoman, if he got to choose). If there was one person I would credit most with helping Dad transform himself and his show into Edinburgh favourites, it would be Steve. Dad, Tony and Steve got together for lunch one day and struck up an immediate rapport. Steve suggested they try some material out at a loose, anarchic comedy night he ran at the 100 Club in Oxford Street. Comedians would regularly come down and sing with a band, and it was as close to an Edinburgh-style night as could be found in London. Steve said that it only took the horn section to pipe up and he was hooked.

They talked afterwards about Edinburgh and Steve said that he had stand-up and poet John Dowie and legendary comic songsmith Neil Innes booked in for a studio slot at the Traverse Theatre at the Fringe. Dowie had told him the Traverse needed a main house act after an American comic had pulled out. Dad and Tony were seen as the ideal replacement. Dowie then came on board to co-write and direct (claiming later it was a 'career high') and the Edinburgh adventure was up and running.

Dad was often asked at this time why he continued to work, given he was past retirement age and had little to prove. The short answer was that he didn't seem to know any better. He didn't have many hobbies, nor did his fear of flying allow a huge desire to travel. His health at this point was stable although there were some scares later, culminating in the development of lung cancer, which he managed to keep at bay for the last eight years of his life. His desire to perform was undimmed throughout. Even into his eighties, when he'd slowed down considerably and succumbed to the occasional fall, he was always on the lookout for another opportunity. Being a 'people-a-holic' best describes his motivation for continuing to work.

The first run of *Rock of Ages* at the Traverse was partly critical success, partly organised chaos, but wholly a financial folly. Hiring a full band meant there was very little left in the coffers for the following year. Dowie stayed on to direct the next, *Unplugged*, but, as the name suggests, the band was gone, and Dad and Tony committed themselves to developing a more economical and intimate show. The material remained largely intact but a cunning change in the running order put the critics off the scent for a while. As the two men got more and more used to each other, the tone of the show changed from watching a gig to eavesdropping on a conversation.

Dad's image began to change too. Steve's early publicity shots contrasted Dad's white hair with a black shirt and a black background. Dad started wearing a black shirt on stage, echoing the original 'Man in Black', Johnny Cash, and it helped that Dad's register could reach his vocal depths too. Tony even penned a Springsteen pastiche that included a Cash impression. Steve encouraged Dad to ditch the glasses too (as we've seen, he didn't need them) and he'd gone from blazer-wearing BBC stalwart to comedy rock Fringe icon in a matter of a couple of years.

There was also to be a change in venue. While the Traverse has a fantastic reputation for new theatre writing, it contrasted too strongly with Dad and Tony's style. The Gilded Balloon, which Steve and Tony knew well, is more of a multi-venue social hub. Karen Koren, who ran the Gilded Balloon, had an afternoon slot in their Teviot venue, which was right at the heart of the action.

This could support Dad's sociability and mean that he could arrive at lunch, and chat with jugglers, magicians and poets in the early slots before doing his own show. Afterwards, he could relax in the famous Loft Bar and talk to headline comics, critics and promoters. The audience was much more diverse, too.

He gained a reputation later in life for phoning an increasingly eclectic list to wish them a happy birthday, many of whom he met during this period. A good example is Stewart Lee, who Dad met in the Loft in 2005, when Stewart was doing his *90s Comedian* show down the road at the Underbelly. Although critically lauded, the show was, in Lee's words, 'an insane overreaction to religious censorship' (he'd wrangled with far-right Christian groups over his musical, *Jerry Springer: The Opera*). One bit of his act ends with an incident at his mother's house where a drunk and ill Lee 'vomits into the gaping anus of Christ'. Stewart had never met my father before but he saw Dad in the Loft Bar looking at him sternly. Lee, by his own admission, was 'a tiny bit drunk' and went over to confront Dad:

'What's the matter?' said Lee.

'I'm pissed off with you,' said Dad.

'What have I done to upset *you*?'

'You've nicked my act.'

'How have *I* nicked your act?'

'You've stolen my bit about vomiting into the gaping anus of Christ.'

I'm delighted to say that it's a story Stewart told at Dad's memorial in 2022, adding the detail: 'How was I supposed to know that he'd written an almost identical routine for Morecambe and Wise almost thirty years earlier?'

The success of Dad's Edinburgh adventure was also down to his chemistry with Gilded Balloon Artistic Director Karen Koren. As she did for many Edinburgh favourites, Karen created the perfect environment for Dad and Tony to thrive. They arrived at a crucial time for the Gilded Balloon as the venue was expanding into the old student union building following a fire in their original Cowgate site. The shows with Tony were, although themed, full of separate satirical or topical songs (like 'Big Fat John', 'Shoe Bomb' and 'Bono') or meditations on growing old (like 'Freedom Pass', 'Zimmer Frame Blues', 'Stannah Stairlift' and 'Unplugged!'). In many ways, Dad was back to his writing origins in the West End revues of the 1960s, except with Tony, he had a multi-instrumentalist who could play in different genres. Their combined talent was a compelling blend. If Dad needed a kickstart for a parody, Tony would find the melody or the guitar riff, or if Tony was stuck on a lyric, Dad would fashion the neatest rhyme or the perfect word. Dad also began to feel a little more at home making jokes about his upbringing. Once a moot subject, by the early 2000s he was doing jokes like:

'My Dad was an Elvis impersonator, but the trouble is there wasn't much call for that in 1938.'

In 2010, seven years after Dad first started at the Gilded Balloon and following shows with Tony called variously *Men In Beige*, *At Their Pique!*, *Little Richard III* and *A Century Of Songs*, he returned to do a show called *Butterfly Brain* (loosely based on his book of memoirs but styled as 'sit down comedy'). This time Mum decided to join him, not just as a companion, but as a performer in her own show. In a fantastically inspiring move, after nearly forty years of only singing together at birthdays and reunions, my mum and Jackie Hockridge had decided to reunite the Taylormaids. Jackie had carried on touring (with her family) since the mid-eighties, but when Ted died in 2009, she considered stopping. Mum suggested they get the act together again, as it would help Jackie get through what was going to be a tough time.

The Gilded Balloon gave them space for a few days and Colin Sell helped them collect a mix of stories and musical numbers from their career. They played a couple of warm-up gigs and promoted the week-long show before travelling up with Dad. They were in good spirits as the first show promised to be a good house, but Jackie noticed Mum being particularly chatty at the start. Occasionally

Mum would then drop a line or a word, but she'd smile and carry on with the air of someone just enjoying herself. Mum had always been a very disciplined performer and while her relaxed manner was welcome, it seemed out of character. They came offstage, Mum sat down and then went white as a sheet. She felt dizzy and couldn't remember a thing about the performance. Mum had got nervous with shows in the past but this seemed different. We all worried that she was experiencing similar symptoms to a decade earlier but soon realised that this felt closer to some kind of amnesia. Dad was called to the dressing room by Karen Koren and they all had a heart-to-heart.

The experience had shaken Mum. She went back to the flat, slept through the night and when she woke, decided that she wanted to go home. However, she felt so guilty over having to cancel that she offered to pay Karen for the rest of the run. Karen refused and even gave Dad a few days too. He returned to the Gilded Balloon later that week. Karen could not have done enough for Mum and Dad during this period and my family owes her quite the debt.

Happily, the dizzy spells didn't return, and the experience did not deter Mum and Jackie from reuniting the following year. While they didn't return to Edinburgh, they agreed to take up an offer to perform together again at Queen Elizabeth Hall on the South Bank. Hearing them both on *Woman's Hour*, chatting happily, promoting their show as part of the Women of the World Festival, was a proud moment for all of us and evidence that Mum's recovery was, if not complete, a process of steady, increasing strength in the right direction. Incredibly, the booking for the South Bank came from a woman who had seen their show in Edinburgh.

Age was starting to catch up with Dad, too. He'd had a couple of visits to the hospital, including a leg break after a couple of falls and gradually the length of each visit to the Fringe got shorter. *Barry Cryer and Ronnie Golden: Historical Objects* in 2018 was eventually just a two-day stint. Dad, now in his early eighties, was wondering if his body would allow him to keep performing. Steve, Karen and I organised a Roast for his eightieth birthday during his and Tony's *Old Masters* show in 2015. Old friends like Arthur Smith, Kevin Day, David Benson, Phill Jupitus, Stephen K. Amos and John Lloyd filed out like medieval courtiers in front of a king. We even had Dad placed on a golden throne. Dara Ó Briain, Ed Byrne, Stephen Frost, Eddie Izzard and Colin Sell joined him on the stage at the end.

Roasts were rare things in this country back then and we had difficulty getting the tone right. In the States, there is more of an established tradition of ruining the reputation of your friends and peers in front of an audience before embracing them afterwards. In the UK, we seem to prefer a year-round general spirit of piss-taking of each other that doesn't require the formality of a stage. Or the hug afterwards. Dad loved having the mickey taken out of him and really enjoyed the evening. However, the audience seemed a little confused as to why cuddly, affable 'Uncle Baz' was being torn to shreds. Stephen K. Amos even had to stop halfway through to say 'I can't do this. You're too nice'. It was a tribute to how strong Dad's friendly persona had remained over the years. Just like jokes, some roasts work better in a dressing room rather than on a stage.

Much more straightforward in tone was Dad's eightieth birthday celebration that we held at the Palace Theatre, Shaftesbury Avenue in October later that year. That evening was a surprise too as Dad had thought we were going to a family dinner in Soho. Instead, we detoured to the theatre and Jo Brand, Count Arthur Strong, Michael Palin, Andy Hamilton and John Moloney all delivered stories and memories in front of Dad, once again sitting regally with Mum, this time up in the Royal Box. He was miked up for the whole evening, which was rather dangerous, but he behaved himself well enough to leave most of the talking to the guests. My sister Jack and Jenna Russell completed the line-up for the first half. There was a reduced *I'm Sorry I Haven't A Clue* hosted by David Mitchell, which Dad took part in, and this gave way to spots by Ronnie Golden, Neil Innes, Sheila Steafal (with Denis King), Milton Jones, Robin Ince, Peter Serafinowicz and Arthur Smith. I'm sure they wouldn't mind me pointing out that the proudest moment for Dad was getting to sing 'Doctor Jazz' on stage with Humphrey Lyttelton's band, featuring his grandson Evan on trumpet.

As an older performer, Dad grew increasingly frustrated at how TV treated his generation. It's one of the reasons why he became such a supporter of the *Oldie* magazine, regularly speaking at their lunches and happily giving his time at their charity events. He never felt old inside and believed his mindset was probably shared by most of their readers. He wanted to celebrate his age and I know that the magazine loved having him as one of their champions. Besides, I always knew where to find him on the first Tuesday of every month. At one of their lunches.

Dad also grew to love the Fringe Festival and the Fringe Festival loved him in return. The ability for Dad to meet new talent and renew friendships with old colleagues also meant that his reputation for being a cross-generational comedian was cemented there. He seemingly never had a bad word to say about anyone but this is not to say he wasn't capable of insulting someone, he'd just do it gracefully. If someone was threatening to spoil an atmosphere, he'd say 'Kill them with kindness'. If a particularly obnoxious person was around, he'd say: 'He's very difficult to ignore but I'm told it's worth the effort.' Even this would let the person down gently without humiliating them. He hated public displays of dissent and would invariably use humour to quell them. Lines like 'he thinks charisma is the 25th of December' and 'they could light up a room just by standing away from the window' were graceful ways of taking the sting out of bullies.

It's how he learned to survive in an industry notorious for being fractious and, for that lesson, I will always thank him. Karen Koren agreed that this attitude to the business is incredibly refreshing. In a business that has a culture renowned for being cut-throat, she thinks Dad's generosity was one of the main reasons why he stuck out: 'What is brilliant about Barry was that when he came, he loved the young, new comics. He just was interested. And not many of his generation were. He knew their jokes. He knew their material and he was really interested. And I absolutely loved that. And the fact that he wanted to come back year after year after year, it was incredible.' As Dad himself said: 'I may talk about the past but I don't want to live there.'

The lasting image I have of my father as a performer was not during his last performance or even at Edinburgh but before a show he did, near where I lived, in the middle of his last tour. He was dressed in a white tuxedo jacket with a red carnation in the lapel and a colourful waistcoat underneath, complete with a watch chain. Once he'd found somewhere to light up 'a breath of fresh air' and phoned Mum to say that he'd arrived safely, he sat down in his dressing room to rifle through his old battered white plastic shopping bag he always brought with him. It had 'Gucci' written in black marker on the side. It contained most of his worldly possessions, including indigestion tablets, a bent metal comb, liquorice allsorts and about six different colours of biro. He was like a cross between Mary Poppins and a vagrant.

He located a crumpled postcard with that evening's topical jokes written in his blocky bullet-pointed shorthand and slumped in his chair. He was bent over, breathing heavily and uttering occasional sighs that forced him to say 'Oh boy' at the end. He was shattered. Knocked out by travelling and sixty years of performing. How was this frail little old man going to be capable of standing on a stage for two and a half hours, singing, joking and entertaining an audience? The call to the stage came over the tannoy and Colin rushed past in the corridor, wishing Dad a good show. Dad wished back. Tour manager Paul Harvey asked him which sandwiches he wanted at the interval.

Dad rose from his chair and shuffled backstage following the arrows. He was still hunched over as he reached the wings. Colin was in full voice, hands rocketing up and down the keyboard, warming up the audience. As he got to the end of the opening number, Dad bent down, took his slippers off and put his shiny patent-leather loafers on. He winced slightly as a nerve jangled in his back but then a most extraordinary thing happened. As the audience applauded Colin's opening song and Colin turned to the wings to acknowledge 'Mr Barry Cryer!', my father rose a full half foot in height and strode purposely onto the stage, eyes twinkling, greeting Colin and the audience with a youthful 'Good evening!' They were straight into the first number.

I'll never forget the slippers.

A man and his wife are walking one day when they spot a bloke sitting alone in a bus shelter on the other side of the road.

'That looks like the Archbishop of Canterbury,' says the woman. 'Go and ask him if he is.'

The husband crosses the road and asks the man if he is the Archbishop of Canterbury. 'Fuck off,' says the man.

The husband crosses back to his wife, who asks: 'What did he say? Is he the Archbishop of Canterbury?'

'He told me to fuck off,' says the husband.

'Oh no,' says the wife. 'Now we'll never know.'

Epilogue

That was the last joke Dad ever told. It was to a nurse at Northwick Park Hospital in north-west London the day before he died. He looked at me later that day and said, 'This is serious.'

On 25 January 2022, despite the compassion, dedication, skill and respect of doctors, nurses and consultants at the hospital, he died. We had expected our conversations with Macmillan Cancer Support to feature more heavily, but Dad had decided it was time to go. Timing was always his forte. However, thanks to Dr Denton's comforting words and guidance, and the nurses Liam and Nisan, we were well prepared for an encore, but the curtain remained closed. Managing an archbishop joke hinted at a spirit of closure, but making strangers feel welcome with a smile and a laugh is as fine a way to go as you can imagine. We'd imagined plenty of worse ways to go that week.

A small gathering of family and friends at a crematorium in west London followed about a month later. Mum found the courage to tell the jokes Dad fashioned over the years about their history together, Michael Palin spoke on behalf of Dad's friends, and David, Jack and I said a few words about various aspects of Dad's life. Colin Sell played 'Show Me the Way to Go Home' and my nephew Evan once again accompanied on trumpet.

Growing older, it's inevitable that funerals and memorials become more commonplace, and Dad had more than his fair share to attend. Naturally, he was invited to speak at many of them. He knew better than most how much the role of the speaker was a divided responsibility. You need to respect the wishes of the person you are honouring by not being too solemn or reverent (depends on the person, of course, but their friends will soon let you know) while at the same time remembering that it can be a very sensitive time for the family (and they may not have the same brutal sense of humour as your subject did). I reflected on the day that the one person most qualified to speak wasn't available, but evidently, his spirit was still with us. An old friend told me that it was the most fun they'd had at a funeral in a long time. We discussed taking it on tour but felt that once was enough.

I don't know how long I've got left – I don't even buy green bananas any more.

Barry Cryer

We've heard about funerals and memorials Dad attended in the book already. Still, it's worth mentioning a couple of others that Dad used to cite as particularly noteworthy. For instance, when my Uncle John (Dad's brother) died, his funeral took place on what Dad described in his memoirs as a typical funeral day, full of wind and rain. A young local vicar took the service, and although he hardly knew my uncle, Dad said that he gave a wonderful eulogy, which especially pleased John's widow, Mary, and her son, Andrew. However, when the young vicar launched into the Lord's Prayer, you could hear that he had a tickle in his throat. He could've taken the opportunity to clear it properly, but chose not to, meaning that when he got to 'in the name of the Father, the Son,' the tickle returned, and he ended up saying '… and the Ho-ho-holy Ghost'. My mother's elbow had never dug so deeply into my father's side. Once again, Dad revelled in things benevolently coming apart at the seams.

Marty Feldman once filmed a funeral sketch at a church for one of his shows. Marty was dressed as a priest when he came around the corner to be confronted by a group of people dressed in black. He assumed they were extras for the sketch, so he lifted his cassock and shouted, 'Good morning, girls!' They were real mourners.

> *We had the family round one night, and we got onto the rather strange subject of what we would have on our gravestones. What I want is: 'The goose is dead.'*
>
> Barry Cryer, 'A Life In The Day Of', *Sunday Times Magazine*, 21 March 1999

Dad always wanted his memorial to combine a New Orleans funeral parade with an Irish wake. Hands up those of you who had that on your bingo card? He didn't want anything that included a formal reading or sounded like a formal service, ultimately wanting people to talk among themselves and trade stories about him. He wanted to have one last party and, to honour that, we sought out somewhere where he would be most at home: in a theatre, in front of an audience, surrounded by family and friends making people laugh.

I'd been given permission by Laurence Miller at Nimax Theatres to use the Palace Theatre, Shaftesbury Avenue, for Dad's eightieth birthday celebrations in 2015, so it seemed like he would be the best person to talk to for a memorial. Also, as Dad began his London career at the Windmill Theatre in Soho, I decided that part of Soho would be a good place to hold a proper West End show in his honour. The theatre next door to the old Windmill was the Lyric, which also happened to be a Nimax venue. It was the perfect place. The date was fixed for June, and a bill was invited. I'm happy to report that a memorial for Barry Cryer is one of the easier producing gigs (most people said 'yes') but as Dad said, life can be badly written and touring schedules deprived us of Rob Brydon, Lee Mack and David Mitchell appearing in person. *I'm Sorry I Haven't A Clue* was also performing their live show that night, not just robbing us of contributions from Colin Sell, Jon Naismith and Graeme Garden but also providing *Clue* fans with a tough decision.

Mum, my siblings and I had all begun to fray around the edges by this point in the summer and were it not for Harry Hill, Ed Smith and Giles Wakeley at Phil McIntyre Entertainments, I'm not sure I would have got the show over the line by myself. Celebrating Dad's life was the lift the family needed but doing so in public seemed like a tougher proposition. However, if the funeral was about what we lost, the memorial would celebrate what we had. The best way to keep people's memories alive is by telling stories about them.

Dad would have to make an appearance, of course (several). He'd originally wanted to make a short video for people to watch, where he would pop up, in his words 'like Kenny Everett', and say, 'Hello. I know you're all having a good time in the pub right now, but I don't care because I'm going for a drink with Eric Morecambe.' While we couldn't provide that for the audience, we had a suitable replacement. As I have mentioned, Dad would often be called upon to pay tribute on radio or television to colleagues who died. His great friend Paddy O'Connell once encouraged Dad to do the same on Radio 4's *Broadcasting House* about himself. Dad talked of being 'stitched at the hip' with Barry Cryer and how they were 'very similar'. Barry was 'a joy to be with' and they were 'like one person'. It was a wonderfully dry and mischievous turn by Dad and Paddy and we played the clip at the memorial. It set the tone beautifully.

The *Broadcasting House* clip was followed by a video from Stephen Fry that established a common thought for the evening, Dad's generosity towards other comedians, be they old or young:

> The wonderful Barry Cryer. He had so many qualities. The most extraordinary one, perhaps (because it's so rare among comedians), is that he was always welcoming of new talent in comedy. Always. He never succumbed to envy and bitterness. He saw all comedy as one. Comics are, to a large extent, awful. Resentful, bitter and sharp-elbowed. So, his loss is keenly felt every day. Not just by his friends, but by millions around the world.

After such a moment of tenderness, he told a football-themed parrot joke, just the kind of palate cleanser Dad would have approved of, and introduced a blast of 'The Purple People Eater'.

Then came the saga of 'the woman reading the Bible on a train': Rebecca Front, in conversation on stage with Paddy O'Connell, having confessed to not being comfortable telling jokes, was then asked by Paddy to do just that. The joke, for reference, at least when Dad told it, went something like this:

> A man sits down on a train opposite a little old lady [in Rebecca's version, it was a nun on the Tube – please refer to previous notes on adapting jokes to your own voice]. Once the train starts moving, the old woman takes a Bible out of her bag and reads. The young man notices that she immediately puts the Bible away when the train gets to the next station. When the train gets going, she brings the Bible out and starts reading it again. She repeats this between every station until, eventually, the man can't bear it any more:
>
> 'Excuse me, I've noticed that whenever the train is in a station, you put your Bible away, but once the train starts up again, you bring the Bible back out and start reading again. Can I ask why you do this?'
>
> The old woman replies, 'Why don't you just fuck off?'

Despite her protestations about her own joke telling, Rebecca neatly landed the punchline, and as far as the audience was concerned, that was the last time they'd hear that joke. That was until a very knowing Barry Humphries came onto the stage in the second half to beautifully deconstruct the joke as a short farce set in J. Sheekey's restaurant. 'I wonder if there is anyone here who knows this story…' he said, dryly. This unfortunately cast Stephen Merchant in the role of sitting duck, as his tribute (later and on video) ended with that same old woman's unmistakable punchline chiming out for a third time. The joke had taken on whole new forms, as a mantra of comic universality or even a meditation on the cyclical nature of memory in old age, or perhaps it was just an excuse to shout 'fuck' in the West End, like all those angry young men in the 1950s.

The great Wirral stand-up, singer and Dad's co-star in *A Saint She Ain't*, Pauline Daniels, a veteran of Liverpool theatre and working men's clubs, reprised Dick Vosburgh and Denis King's double entendre-laden song from that musical, 'The Banana In My Pie'. Bernie Clifton, Joe Brown and Jools Holland appeared separately on the screen to celebrate Dad's good nature, loyalty and generosity, but another theme was beginning to emerge. Dad had called each of them on their birthdays but guitar-toting comedian Pierre Hollins, who had appeared with Dad and Jack on the Willie Rushton *Two Old Farts* tour, claimed never to have been called up on his birthday by Dad. He conceded that might be because he was 'the angriest unicyclist in their price range'.

Milton Jones chose to celebrate with a series of grandfather gags before pointing out Dad's distinctive standing among comedians as someone who 'laughed at jokes he didn't even write. I wish he was here now.' John Moloney then reprised a routine about his cat at the vet that Dad himself had requested at his eightieth birthday show in 2015. Tony De Meur, as Ronnie Golden (complete with his band The Rex), opened and closed the first half, with songs from his Edinburgh shows with Dad.

Sandi Toksvig, also unfortunately on tour, left a heartfelt video message that fondly remembered Dad's machine-gun gag-telling during train journeys to and from recordings of *I'm Sorry I Haven't A Clue*. 'I learned more about timing on one train journey with Barry than from any other comic.' She was close to tears at the end, as was Miriam Margolyes in her piece to camera, with both women lamenting being unable to speak to him again. Finally, Dame Judi Dench's video said that his death felt as if 'a large piece of Yorkshire had fallen into the sea'. One of the most gratifying aspects of the evening was the level of personalised material created in tributes. Emma Thompson and Greg Wise's video reimagined *All That Jazz* as *All That Baz*, while a Stateside Eric Idle said Dad, 'his dear friend', had guided and mentored him in his early years before echoing the story Michael Palin told at the funeral, of how Dad used to do the studio warm-ups for Monty Python and made the audience double over in laughter. The same audience then 'fell silent as we performed our sketches'.

Stewart Lee picked up the birthday phone calls theme, instead offering that they were, in fact, a tedious chore for Dad, saddling him with hours upon hours of calling up people he neither knew nor respected. To cap it all, Dad's decades-long dispute with Gyles Brandreth over some hedge trimmers saw no sign of abating.

Despite being on stage in Buxton, Colin Sell and Jack Dee's videos were able to represent *I'm Sorry I Haven't A Clue* on the night, with Jack Dee being another who chose to tell a joke in Dad's memory. This was one of Dad's favourites from his after-dinner years:

> A man shoots a golden eagle, a protected species, and ends up before a judge. 'I'm so sorry,' says the man. 'I didn't mean to shoot it but it flew into my sights, and I shot it by instinct.'
>
> 'Well, that seems perfectly reasonable. Do you mind me asking what you did with it afterwards?' asked the judge.
>
> 'I ate it,' the man said. 'It seemed like the only way to honour such a majestic animal.'
>
> 'You ate it?' said the judge. 'What did it taste like?'
>
> 'Rather like swan.'

Count Arthur Strong and Eddie Izzard both appeared on screen to salute Dad's enduring support of younger comedians, with Eddie then appearing on stage to watch her own tribute. 'One life. Live it well. You lived it well,' she concluded. Arthur Smith continued, 'What can you say about Barry that hasn't been said before? He was just a quiet bloke, was not very funny, was a brilliant ballerina and everyone hated him.' He then quoted John Dryden's *Happy the Man*:

> Happy the man, and happy he alone,
> He who can call today his own:
> He who, secure within, can say,
> Tomorrow do thy worst, for I have lived today.

However, Arthur wasn't the last to quote poetry (something close to Dad's heart) as Gyles Brandreth offered *Flowers* by David Walser. He then comically reworked *Christmas Day in the Workhouse*, the ballad written by his ancestor George R. Sims. However, in a moment that spoke volumes for Dad's ability to connect people from disparate parts of the comedy sphere, Gyles began his bit with a call back to Stewart Lee's joke about the hedge trimmers. Rob Brydon, Lee Mack and David Mitchell recorded their tribute naked and lined up in bed together, with Mack having to explain to Mitchell that they weren't there to make a reference to Morecambe and Wise. Instead they were there to make sweet love to each other in honour of my father's memory.

Matthew Sweet brought Barry Humphries to the stage and before he provided his meta-theatrical take on the 'Old Lady on the Train', he generously gifted back to us a line Dad had uttered when told about the time Humphries met Mick Jagger. When Humphries pointed out the crow's feet on the Rolling Stone's face, Jagger had insisted: 'They're not crow's feet; they're laugh lines.' Dad replied to Barry: 'Nothing's that funny.'

Back on the screen, Ross Noble was in a reflexive mood. 'With Barry, it wasn't ego, it was all about the passing on of the joke. I never heard him say a bad word about anyone, and I never heard anyone say a bad word about him.'

My sister Jack read a specially written poetic eulogy by comic John Dowie (who'd directed the very first Edinburgh show for Dad and Tony De Meur). Jack was then flanked by her husband, Matt, and their great friend Mark Allen to play a couple of songs as their band, the Kites. As a trio, they'd provided me and Dad with the theme tune to our podcast *Now Where Were We?* It marked an extra personal angle to what was Dad's last professional job. Jack then mentioned that the Kites were also present at Dad's last live gig (one that I joined them for the previous October), where we sang 'Tonight You Belong to Me' (a song Jack and Dad sang regularly at home and on stage). The Kites reprised that song for the memorial as a tribute.

With Matt, wearing one of Dad's old suits, at her side, Jack added, 'For a man with such short arms, he [Dad] had an incredibly long reach' before turning the spotlight on Mum to take the applause.

'If it weren't for Mum, we'd have been weaned on the BBC bar and raised on the set of *Blankety Blank*.' She paid tribute to Dad for sharing his love of music with her. It was a love, she said, that informed her decision to become a singer. If you've ever heard her sing, that is quite the legacy.

Harry Hill closed the show with a blisteringly irreverent quick-fire routine about generational differences while heralding the silliness of 1970s TV comedy shows like *Jokers Wild* and *Hello Cheeky*, which inspired Harry to get involved in comedy in the first place. Ronnie Golden joined Harry on stage to sing 'Peace and Quiet', the Edinburgh favourite Dad and Ronnie used to close their shows at the Festival. The message of the song is simple: as the name suggests, it's a hymn to tranquillity and silence that laments the chaos and turbulence of modern life and, in doing, steadily gets louder and louder before slowly reaching a deafening crescendo of screeching and wailing. It demands you adopt a respectable, dignified persona with a deadpan face while simultaneously allowing the occasion's formality to crumble and the wheels to come off the show. In other words, Dad to a fault.

When it came to writing his autobiography, *You Won't Believe This, But...* in 1998, Dad's agent at the time Emma Darrell called to give her thoughts. 'This is terrific stuff, Barry,' she said. 'Lots of great stories and anecdotes. But they're all about other people. You aren't in this.' Perhaps it was the combination of a Yorkshire 'don't get too big for your boots' upbringing and an instinct for modesty (mainly honed by his mother's example), but Dad often felt embarrassed talking about himself. I hope this biography has gone some way to correcting that particular imbalance.

Willie Rushton once said that Dad would drop dead in the middle of a gag. Willy was right about so many things, but not this one. If Dad really thought his life was a joke, it was well crafted, beautifully timed and expertly delivered. He also managed to get to the punchline. In the last few weeks of his life, Dad uttered an extraordinary statement. After a challenging and confusing episode in the hospital, he said, 'I can't phrase.' The supreme technician, economical and pertinent to the end, found precisely the right words to say when he thought he couldn't.

I went to the hospital to see Dad after he had been admitted with pneumonia and I remembered an aspect of the story of his visit to Humphrey Lyttelton. He'd read somewhere that hearing is the last thing to go and that's why he kept talking even if there wasn't a reaction. I shared Dad's sense of discomfort when I saw him, old and emaciated. I didn't recognise him either, but there was a twinkle, I could be sure of it. I scrolled through all the things I wanted to say, we all did. We told him we loved him; my brothers talked him through what was happening and Mum and my sister sang with him. Yet, the Humph story still rattled around in my head. I had a moment with him alone that I felt might be the last. I played him a Goon Show clip on my phone, talked about Vincent Price (for some reason) and then, just as I was about to leave, I leaned over the bed and thought about being glib. I couldn't.

> I don't know you, and I didn't know your Dad, but I once
> shared a tube journey with him from Rayner's Lane to
> Uxbridge. It was one of the funniest twenty minutes of my life.
> *Anonymous on Twitter* (two days after he died)

Dad scattered his mother Jenny's ashes in Yorkshire. It was a return home for her, but Dad said he found it a challenging experience. He hadn't realised what ashes looked like, and while still in shock, he turned the urn upside down, and they blew straight into a cow's face. Dad always said his idea of heaven was a boisterous, colourful place with much shouting and laughing. A bit like Edinburgh during the Festival. For his mother, he imagined heaven would be a quiet, tranquil place full of pursed lips and disapproving looks. A bit like Edinburgh the rest of the time.

When it came to our discussion as a family about where Dad should be laid to rest, it was less clear-cut. He'd spent so much time living down south that there were so many London buildings and places we felt deserving of holding a resonance for him and, in time, for us. We initially wanted to scatter his ashes close by one of these places. However, Mum, Tony, David, Jack and I felt that there was such a solid pull to Yorkshire that it was time he went home, too.

For a start, Jenny was probably wondering where he'd got to. Mum, struggling to walk long distances and having problems travelling, chose not to join us. She endorsed the trip, knowing that wherever we took him, his place was always with her in the memories of the life they created and nurtured for sixty years.

The early chapters of this book will tell you that Airedale in Yorkshire is where the majority of Cryers on my father's side come from, and that is where we met to say goodbye – Tony, Dave, Jack and me. I won't say precisely where, but the river, with its calming energy, constantly moving and bending to the will of the landscape, seemed the most fitting place to leave him.

As his ashes travelled down the Aire, I imagined him passing relatives, his Mount Pleasant home offset in the distance, while his grammar school and university looked on, before passing the site of the old Empire Theatre and the current City Varieties and finally connecting with the River Ouse and out into the Humber. As he went, he would collect his goodbyes, hovering before the North Sea carried him off into the night and offering a final promise of 'Just the one' northwards to Edinburgh and southwards to London. It's comforting to think of him diffusing himself slowly into the waters around us, wrapping himself around the shores and coastlines of the British Isles, where he was celebrated and loved.

He always gave good hugs.

I want my epitaph to say, 'Hello' as though I were greeting a passerby. I intend to seize every day I have left of my life. The journalist John Diamond once said that happiness was now, this minute. I thought that was the most moving and powerful thing I'd ever heard.

Barry Cryer, *Mail on Sunday*, 30 November 2003

Dad, having written with you on several occasions and enjoyed your company, wisdom and affability, I was dreading writing this book alone, but you were there all along, guiding my hand.

I knew you wouldn't let me down.

Same time tomorrow?

Dad's eldest granddaughter, Ruby (daughter of Jack and actor Garry Cooper), turns 18 and gives Th[e] Cryers another chance to have an 'Inlaws & Outlaws' party.

Back Row: (l-r) David Hodgson, Matt Hodgson (husband of Jack), Jayne Jenkins, Tony Cryer, Harriet Vyner, Jenna Russell, Ray Coulthard (with their daughter Betsy), the author, David Cryer. Middle Row (l-r): Tom Hodgson, Terry Cryer, Jack Cryer, Ruby Jack Cooper, Garry Cooper, Barry Cryer, Nora Cooper, Suzannah Cryer (with Connie Cryer). Front Row (l-r) Archie Cryer, Evan Cryer-Jenkins, Hope Cryer, Martha Cryer, Gracie Cryer (RIP). Picture taken by Jane Hodgson.

Index

A Note on the Author

Bob Cryer is an actor and writer best known for *Coronation Street* and *Hollyoaks*. He is the youngest child of Barry Cryer. He collaborated with his father on Barry's book of anecdotes, *Butterfly Brain*, in 2010. Shortly after, they created the book series *Mrs Hudson's Diaries*, which was adapted into a play for Wilton's Music Hall. *Mrs Hudson's Radio Show* soon followed for Radio 4 in 2018. Their joint podcast, *Now Where Were We?*, launched just before Barry's death in January 2022

www.bobcryer.com | @bobbicee

DRY GIN

GOOD SHOW
THEY'VE GOT
OLD ALES
At the bar
SOUTH LONDON BREWE...

93, Westbourne Terr...
London W.2
15. 6. 61.

Dear Barry,
Will save the
next dance for you!
Do hope you are
feeling much better.
Let's know how y
are getting on?
Love Fred!
P.T.O.

TAKE-OFF 1·15am.

Just a little note!

12, Mount Pleasant Avenue,
Leeds.8.
Yorks.

June 27th, 1961.

Dear Terry - that Fred jazz has had it as far
as I'm concerned,
             How are you, love? That last en-
      s Northern, rather than theatrical,
      - I've been using it for YEARS.
      for writing that last massive missive
      he factory? Regards to your Dad - I'
      him, but what the hell! He sounds g
    i from the Dicks in Italia - really,
    re. I think He's got the Winston's
    Bruce wouldn't pay out in lira. Te
    and the temptation was - well, you
    ced I referred to Ted as He. I kn
    olster his ego, but that's ridicu
    ty of sun, booze (why can't they
    London?), and the other. I thin
    ere in the midst of University
    k and I really made the prover
    lf in every way - ah me, back t
    k. By the way, I return to To
    ve. (2nd) So? She says. Am r
    lark in the club. Thank God.
    HAYES RUN? Please give Danny
    - must come in and catch
    ich I haven't seen yet. As
    ext week don't bother to reply t
    then. I'M KIDDING.
       Must close - the draught is now AGONY,
              Yours (approx) Barry P.T.O.

SCENES

The Deep South Jazz Club
The Tom-Tom Coffee Bar
A Recording Studio
Bongo's Home in Hoxton
The Intime Theatre in Soho
Johnnie's Flat in Soho
A Street in Soho
The Flat in Soho
The Odium Palace Cinema

The Diplomatique Restaurant
Bongo's Dressing-Room
e's Apartment off Bond Street
Outside Claridge's Hotel
The Villa Esperanza, Majorca
A Street in Soho
London Airport

Corporation Ltd.
Settings by Alick Johnstone, Stage
Millicent Martin's, Miss
Elizabeth Curzon. Miss
hes by Josef Roth. Miss
l's and all other costumes
avide. Nylon stockings by
em Co. Lighting equip-
Spectacles by Negretti &
retti Ltd. Telephones by
Ronson. "King Siz
Wardrobe care by Lux.

STANLEY BRIGHTMAN
DONALD ROSS
NAOMI DUNNING
BEN O'HM
Outside CURZON
SUSAN HAMPSHIRE
GEORGE FEARON
FRANK SLEAP
...on: TEM. Bar 4011

and such doors must a...
anxiety free from
t be permitted to stand
the other gangways. If
shall be strictly adhere
howered and raised in
Ambulance Brigade

1935 /
① SILVER JUBILEE
HAILE SELASSIE/MR
② ...TAX/
③ ...T/
④ MUSSOLINI/ABYSSINIA/GERMANY/
...MILL
MAR 23rd /1958/
① MY FAIR LADY/ GER...ART/
② BONGO AUDITION/ SHER... LOVE/
③ ✱ FINLAND No.1/ PALMERSTON/
④ ELVIS/ARMY/ CHEESE/

✱ AWARDS/ ✱SCOFIELD✱
MAGNANI/ GUINNESS/
MUPPETS/ HEPBURN/
HOVE/ MILLINER/DELIBES/

TINNITUS.

FASTEN YOUR SAFETY BELTS FOR A NIGHT OF FUN AND GLAMOUR
WITH A WELCOME RETURN OF
TAKE OFF AT 1.15 a.m.

DANNY LA RUE

Starring in his own production
ANNE HART WITH RONNIE CORBETT
CLOVISSA NEWCOMBE PAULA BELL
STYLIA RUSSELL

BARRY CRYER
TERRY DONOVAN

93, Westbourne Terrace

Dear Barry,
I picked mys...
did a cou...
+ generally f...
with mirth (...
funny she is
had me in
tried writing
thanks

AH - THERE YOU ARE!

B.O.A.C

Music by:
...HAYES AND HIS MUSIC

N...
Ne...
WIN...
...TIPL...
SHARP...
LENIN/ FR...
9'10"/ ...
LAMP POST...
BATMAN/OZ...
BLACKSHIR...
MORE I SEE/ YO...
INTRO T...